Ready-to-Use

ENGLISH WORKSHOP ACTIVITIES

for Grades 6-12

Ready-to-Use

ENGLISH WORKSHOP ACTIVITIES
for Grades 6-12

*180 Daily Lessons Integrating
Literature, Writing & Grammar Skills*

MARY ELLEN LEDBETTER

JOSSEY-BASS
A Wiley Imprint
www.josseybass.com

Published by Jossey-Bass
A Wiley Imprint
989 Market Street, San Francisco, CA 94103-1741   www.josseybass.com

Jossey-Bass books and products are available through most bookstores. To contact Jossey-Bass directly call our Customer Care Department within the U.S. at 800-956-7739, outside the U.S. at 317-572-3986 or fax 317-572-4002.

Jossey-Bass also publishes its books in a variety of electronic formats. Some content that appears in print may not be available in electronic books.

Library of Congress Cataloging-in-Publication Data
Ledbetter, Mary Ellen.
    Ready-to-use English workshop activities for grades 6-12 : 180 daily lessons for
  integrating literature, writing, and grammar / Mary Ellen Ledbetter.
        p. cm.
    ISBN 0-13-041730-0 (spiral)
    ISBN 0-7879-7555-9 (paperback)
      1. Language arts (Secondary) I. Title: English workshop activities for grades 7-12.
    II. Title.

LB1631.L335 2002
428'.0071'2—dc21   2001058299

Printed in the United States of America
FIRST EDITION
PB Printing 10 9 8 7 6 5

Acknowledgments

The author thanks her students, who are always willing to put pen to paper to see where the journey takes them. Their efforts are the subject of this book and prove--as Willa Cather believed--"that most of the basic material a writer works with is acquired before the age of fifteen."

My students have written honestly--with love, with sorrow, and with humor--and have created products worthy of praise and analysis. I will never tire of the beauty they create.

Graphics are from the following sources:
Copyright: Corel Corporation, 1994, Corel Gallery Clipart Catalogue--Version 1.0 (First Printing) and Corel Gallery 2, 1995.
Copyright: 1987-1995, T-Maker Company, Incredible Image Pak and Click Art Studio Series Design Group, Novell, Inc., 1994, Word Perfect, Version 6.1.
Copyright: Corel Corporation, 1997, Corel Printhouse Magic--Version 3.0.

Dedication

For my mother and father,
Louise and A. R. Pettyjohn,
who always
found time to listen

About The Author

Mary Ellen Ledbetter was born in Texas City, Texas; attended Texas Lutheran College; graduated from Western Michigan University with a B.A. in English and speech, and earned an M.A. in English from Michigan State University. She has taught in public schools in Michigan and Texas as well as at San Jacinto College in Pasadena, Texas. Ms. Ledbetter has been an instructor in the Writing Process Workshop for teachers, has been a presenter at TMSA and NCTE, has received Goose Creek CISD's Board of Trustees' Bell Award for Outstanding Teacher in 1995 and 1997, and is currently a presenter/consultant for the Bureau of Education and Research in Bellevue, Washington. She is also the instructor featured on a two-part video produced by the Bureau as well as the author of **Writing Portfolio Activities Kit** and **Writing Research Projects Activities Kit**, both of which were published by the Center for Applied Research in Education.

About This Resource

English Workshop Activities for Grades 6-12 provides 180 **ready-to-use, unique assignments, called "Dailies,"** for **integrating writing, grammar, and literature.** By completing each "Daily," students have the opportunity to read a brief passage; analyze it in terms of its **stylistic devices, grammar and usage, and literary elements**; and respond in a similar **writing mode.**

Philosophy of Daily Integration:

The philosophy behind **English Workshop Activities for Grades 6-12** is that if students are consistently presented with and asked to study language rich in stylistic devices, they will begin to internalize the components of "good writing." Just as in the learning of any skill, learning to write well is based on **modeling, analyzing, and practicing**, all of which are incorporated into the Dailies in this resource. To complete the dailies, students will engage in the following **three-step process:**

● First, **students read a Daily passage that exemplifies writing at its best**. These passages are a combination of published student writings, classroom samples, and teacher models. Motivated by reading quality samples written by their peers, students will become fluent writers. Especially of note are the ways that the authors of the passages have used **"Smiley-Face Tricks."**

● Next, **students answer the questions following each passage**. These questions ask students for an analysis of grammar/usage, literary elements, and writing skills (stylistic devices), **emphasizing for students that these elements cannot be separated.**

The questions highlight **reading skills** such as inference, prediction, and fact/opinion; **literary elements** such as conflict, tone, irony, and characterization; **grammar, usage, and mechanics skills** such as verb tense, pronoun referents, subject/verb agreement, vivid verbs, and comma rules; and **stylistic devices** called **"Smiley-Face Tricks"** such as repetition for effect, Magic 3's, figurative language, expanded moment, and humor.

●Frequently, students are asked to **write their own examples** or entire passages, based on a device inherent in the sample excerpt or on a specific genre. In this way, students practice their own writing.

How To Use the Dailies

The Dailies in English Workshop Activities for Grades 6-12 are organized into groups of five, one for each day of the week, for 36 weeks. Each week's Dailies **focus on a different set of skills** associated with a specific writing mode such as the vignette, character sketch, how-to paragraph, or poem. An **answer key** is provided for each group of Dailies with suggested answers or with the stipulation that answers may vary.

There is no steadfast order or level of skills in the arrangement of Dailies. The lessons can be selected from the beginning, middle, or end of the book, depending on the skills or writing modes that the teacher wishes to cover during a particular week. The teacher may reproduce a packet for each student in the class, a packet for a group (e.g., three or four students who complete an activity together), different packets for pairs of students, or a class set of packets for students to complete independently as a basis for evaluation. You may wish to use the Dailies in a variety of ways including:

1.   Dailies **can be completed orally** as warm-ups for 10-20 minutes at the beginning of each class. **One piece can be used per day**, or--depending on the class time and length of the Dailies assignment--one piece can be **extended to several days' worth of warm-ups.**

2.   A Daily can also be used as the **focus lesson for the day**, especially if it contains skills that need to be learned or practiced.

3.   A Daily can be used as a **cool-down** or as a **review at the end of a class**, as a **homework assignment**, or as a **mini-lesson** to reinforce specific skills as needed by groups, pairs, or individual students.

How To Use the Glossary and Smiley-Face Tricks

Dailies may be **completed orally, in writing, or through a combination of both.** In order to complete the Dailies, students will need to become familiar with the **Glossary** terms and the **"Smiley-Face Tricks."** At the beginning of the year:

1. Students should be given a copy of the **"Glossary of Terms"** and the **"Smiley-Face Tricks"** that follow this section to keep in their binders.

2. **Before beginning the program of Dailies**, review all the tricks and the glossary terms so students have an initial understanding of them.

    ✓An effective learning device is to **require students to write a sample of each definition or trick, using experiences from their own lives.**

    ✓These samples may be **"graded" in class** by having each student read a designated trick per day (e.g., Each student will read his/her Magic 3 today).

    ✓The **class can decide which examples are correct and which ones need revision**. In this manner, the class is exposed to various methods of creating the same literary device.

3. Since many of the Dailies require that students identify Smiley-Face Tricks that writers have used in the passages, they will need to **refer to their copy of the tricks** in order to answer the questions.

4. In addition, if a specific literary term or device is not defined in the Glossary, students may need to **locate a rule for its usage in a classroom resource.**

5. The nature of the Dailies **will lead to class discussion** when students compare their responses. Teachers may allow time for discussion, which can be a beneficial learning experience for all.

How To Grade the Dailies

Completed "Dailies" can be **collected and graded**, or, as an alternative, **oral responses to specific questions may be graded for a few students at a time.**

✓**Not all students need to be called on daily**. Record-keeping for this method is easy in that a student either has a grade or no grade for that assignment "slot." No grade indicates that a student needs to be called on next time.

✓Dailies may be **graded by the day or by the week or by one question at a time.**

✓Students' papers can be **exchanged and graded daily by their classmates**.

✓**Extra credit** can be given to students volunteering responses that show critical thinking and can be supported with evidence from the passage.

More and more English classes today are taking the form of **workshops**, where students work in pairs or groups to read, write, discuss, explore, and analyze various literary genres. **English Workshop Activities for Grades 6-12** helps teachers build enthusiasm and excitement for this type of learning environment, where students learn that good writing involves grammatically correct, stylistically sophisticated sentences that result in literature rich and deep enough to be analyzed and discussed for its literary merit.

Smiley-Face Tricks

1. Magic 3 -- Three items in a series, separated by commas that create a poetic rhythm or add support for a point, especially when the items have their own modifiers.

"In those woods, I would spend hours **listening** to the wind rustle the leaves, **climbing** trees and spying on nesting birds, and **giving** the occasional wild growl to scare away any pink-flowered girls who might be riding their bikes too close to my secret entrance." (Todd, college freshman)

2.   Figurative   Language--Nonliteral comparisons—such as similes, metaphors, and personification—add "spice" to writing and can help paint a more vivid picture for the reader.

"When we first moved into the house on Orchid Street, I didn't like it. My room was hot, cramped, and **stuffy as a train in the middle of the Sahara.** And the **looming skeleton-like gray and white frame** of the place scared me. I dared not imagine living there, but the backyard, oh, the backyard. It was a huge, long mass of plentifully growing trees and blackberries. Goodness, how I loved them." (Teri, grade 7)

3. Specific Details for Effect--Instead of general, vague descriptions, specific sensory details help the reader visualize the person, place, thing, or idea that you are describing.

"It's one of those experiences where you want to **call a radio station** and tell your problems to **some guy who calls himself Dr. Myke**, but who isn't more of a doctor than your pet hamster is, one of those experiences where you want to **read a sappy Harlequin novel** and **listen to Barry Manilow** with a box of bonbons as your best friend, one of those experiences where you wouldn't be surprised if someone came up to you and asked **exactly what time yesterday you were born**. Yeah, one of those." (Ileana)

"Remember the time I worked all day Saturday on an English paper? Sunday I accidentally left the only copy I had at your house. You politely handed it back to me the next day, first period, when it was due. But all over page one you'd drawn **zombies**; page two contained **detailed pictures of yet-to-be-discovered worms**; page three was **visited by various space aliens**; the fourth page **featured scenes from Australia and Florida**; and the last page was **covered with 'Mr. Jenkins is from the Stone Age,' 'English stinks,' and 'Mr. Jenkins is a four-eyed geek.' Maybe that's why he gave me a D-."** (Liz)

4. Repetition for Effect--Writers often repeat specially chosen words or phrases to make a point, to stress certain ideas for the reader.

"The veranda is your only shelter **away from** the sister in bed asleep, **away from** the brother that plays in the treehouse in the field, **away from** your chores that await you." (Leslie)

5. Expanded Moment--Instead of "speeding" past a moment, writers often emphasize it by "expanding" the actions.

"But no, I had to go to school. And as I said before, I had to listen to my math teacher preach about numbers and letters and figures....I was tired of hearing her annoying voice lecture about 'a=b divided by x.' I glared at the small black hands on the clock, silently threatening them to go faster. But they didn't listen, and I caught myself wishing I were on white sand and looking down at almost transparent pale-blue water with Josh at my side....I don't belong in some dumb math class. I belong on the beach, where I can soak my feet in caressing water and let the wind wander its way through my chestnut-colored hair and sip Doctor Pepper all day long. I want to grip a straw all day, not a mechanical pencil that will try unsuccessfully to write the answers to unsolvable questions." (Shelly)

6. Humor--Professional writers know the value of laughter; even subtle humor can help turn a "boring" paper into one that can raise someone's spirits.

"He laughed? I'm nothing. I'm the rear end of nothing, and the devil himself smiled at me." (Andrew)

"And you--yes, you Justin!--were the guilty party who, after I took off my shoes to enjoy the hot pavement in early spring, put a frog in them. Of course, I didn't look at the shoes when I put them back on; it was the **squish** that gave your prank away." (Liz)

7. Hyphenated Modifiers--Sometimes a new way of saying something can make all the difference; hyphenated adjectives often cause the reader to "sit upand take notice."

"She's got this blonde hair, with dark highlights, parted in the middle, down past her shoulders, and straight as a preacher. She's got big green eyes that all guys admire and all girls envy, and this **I'm-so-beautiful-and-I-know-it** body, you know, like every other super model." (Ileana)

8. Full-Circle Ending--Sometimes students need a special ending, one that effectively "wraps up" the piece. One "trick" is to repeat a phrase from the beginning of the piece.
piece.

Beginning:

"Hey, you, with the green and neon-orange striped shoelaces, you who always pulled on my old frazzled white ones in math. Hey, you, who always added your versions of 'art' to my math problems for Mrs. Caton's class so that $9 \times 7 = 64$ turned out to be a train with puffs of smoke and two boxcars and made me get an 83 instead of a 93 since Mrs. C. doesn't count locomotives as correct answers."

Ending:

"Now Justin still sits behind me in math with his neon-green and orange striped shoelaces and pulls on my old white frazzled ones. He still draws zombies on my homework, but he hasn't dumped another pitcher of Kool-Aid on me--not yet at least. Oh, and by the way, in case you're wondering, his first words when he opened his eyes were, 'It was James Kenton who hid your clothes and made you walk around in a chicken suit...I'm not that mean.'" (Liz)

Glossary of Terms

You will need to become familiar with many of the terms listed in this glossary in order to complete the Dailies.

Literature Terms

Adage--a traditional saying or proverb

"The first thing you learn in life is you're a fool. The last thing you learn in life is you're the same fool" (Bradbury 62).

Alliteration--a figure of speech formed by repeating the same initial consonant sound in several words in close succession

"boys, behave" (Bradbury 4)

Allusion--a reference in a story to the proper name of a character, thing, or setting from another literary work or from real life.

It's not as if I were Scarlett O'Hara and you were Rhet Butler.

(The author is referring to the fictional characters in <u>Gone with the Wind</u>.)

Assonance--a figure of speech in which the same accented vowel is repeated through several words in succession

"trunks of junk" (Bradbury 76)

Conflict--a struggle between opposing forces

External--between two characters or forces (e.g., protagonist vs. antagonist; character vs. the elements)

"Suddenly she spun her green, gnarled finger at me. 'You!' she snarled, her eyes wide. 'And your name is?'

'Jabari,' I gasped, still in shock that she had picked me.

"You will read the first two paragraphs and answer the sample question. Aloud!'

"The air became as still as death. The entire room seemed to stare down on me as I began to read." (Jabari)

(The protagonist is being singled out by the "creature teacher"; the conflict is between the teacher and the student.)

✎ Internal--struggle within a character (e.g., a character's coming to terms with the fact that he or she is not "like everyone else")

"And then there's me, my legs twisted around each other, my nails gnawed to a nub, my hands clammy--with forehead and underarms to match--trying unsuccessfully to figure out where I was when God passed out instant recall. There's so much injustice to this system. There's so much I know that I won't be able to express today." (Mary)

(The protagonist is taking a college entrance exam and is worried that she will not be able to answer all the questions correctly; the conflict is between the protagonist and herself, what she perceives to be her weakness--instant recall.)

Hyperbole--an exaggeration for effect

"He hit the rug so hard all the dust of five thousand centuries jumped from the shocked texture" (Bradbury 66).

Imagery--the use of sensory words (sight, sound, smell, taste, feel) to describe an object or person

"And he heard a thousand people in another sunlight, and the faint, tinkling music of an organ grinder playing "La Marimba'--oh, a lovely, dancing tune" (Bradbury 133).

Glossary of Terms

Inference--a conclusion based on a premise

"Douglas moved his right hand stealthily to the ticking, pulled out the watch stem. He set the hands back" (Bradbury 107).

(Readers can infer that Douglas did not want his friend, John Huff, to move so he set the hand of his watch back to avoid facing reality.)

Irony--the opposite of what is expected

"More than once he [the junkman] had delivered babies at four in the morning and only then had people noticed how incredibly clean his hands and fingernails were--the hands of a rich man...." (Bradbury 208).

(It is ironic that Mr. Jonas, the junk man, the man who deals in people's discards and rejects, has "incredibly clean" hands, those of a "rich man.")

Literary Apostrophe--an address to someone not present, or to a personified object or idea

"I don't want to die! Douglas screamed, without a sound. You'll have to anyway, said the voice, you'll have to anyway..." (Bradbury 189).

Metaphor--comparison between two unlike things not using "like" or "as"

✏️ Explicit--a metaphor that uses a "be" verb (i.e., is, am, are, was, were, be, been, being)

"The words were summer on the tongue" (Bradbury 13).

✏️ Implicit--a metaphor that is implied rather than stated, one that does not use a "be" verb

"...a great swelling symphony of lawn mowers..." (Bradbury 48)

Metonymy--a figure of speech in which one word is substituted for another associated with it

We are studying Shakespeare.

(We are not studying "Shakespeare" but, in fact, Shakespeare's works.)

Paradox--a seemingly contradictory statement that, on closer examination, may be true

""Leo Auffman was too busy noticing that the room was falling swiftly upward" (Bradbury 55).

Personification--giving human attributes to something nonhuman

"dead cement" (Bradbury 19)
"...for last year's pair (of tennis shoes) were dead inside" (Bradbury 20).

Simile--a comparison between two unlike things using "like" or "as"

"He made careful stacks of nickels, dimes, and quarters on the counter, like someone playing chess" (Bradbury 22).

Symbol--something that stands for more than just itself

"...you need Old Colonel Freeleigh to shove and say look alive so you remember every second!" (Bradbury 89).

(Colonel Freeleigh is symbolic of the Time Machine because he takes boys back through time by telling them stories of his past.)

Theme--the main idea; the lesson learned

"Time hypnotizes" (Bradbury 75)

Tone (author's attitude toward his/her work); **Mood** (reader's response to the work)

" 'I wish your father was home,' said Mother....The Lonely One's around again. Killing people" (Bradbury 40-41).

(Frightening tone and mood)

Grammar Terms

Coordinate Adjective--Two or more adjectives modifying the same noun require a comma to separate them.

Last night there was a cold, stinging wind.

Interrupter (Parenthetical Phrase)--A group of words that interrupts the "train of thought" requires commas to set it off from the main clause.

My mother, on the other hand, was a prolific reader.

Subjunctive Mood-- A mood of a verb used to express uncertainty, a wish, or an unlikely condition.

If I were rich, I could travel anywhere.

Writing Terms

Hyphenated Modifier--Use a hyphen between words used as a one-thought modifier immediately before a noun

She gave me that go-to-your-room look.

Character Sketch--A brief picture of a character painted with words. The author may choose actions, speech, inner thoughts and feelings, what others say, and/or environment.

"He could jump six-foot orchard walls, swing up branches faster and come down, fat with peaches, quicker than anyone else in the gang. He ran laughing. He sat easy. He was not a bully. He was kind" (Bradbury *102*).

Vignette--A small literary sketch; a slice of life

In <u>Dandelion Wine</u>, when Great-grandma is dying, she calls her family to her death bed and tells them that they are not to worry about her impending death. Her recounting of her life is a perfect example of a vignette or slice of life.

Methods of Sentence Combining

Independent Clause--A sentence having a subject and verb

My knees were shaking. I walked to the principal's office.

Compound Sentence--Two independent clauses separated by a comma and a conjunction

My knees were shaking, and I walked to the principal's office.

Adjective Clause--A dependent clause (one that cannot stand alone) that modifies a noun or pronoun in an independent clause; adjective clauses usually begin with words such as "who," "whom," "which," or "that."

My knees, that had felt like rubber, suddenly stopped shaking when I entered the principal's office.

Adverb Clause--A dependent clause that modifies a verb, adjective, or another adverb in an independent clause; adverb clauses usually begin with words such as "when," "since," "if," "because," "after," etc.

When I walked into the principal's office, my knees started to shake.

✏️**Participial Phrase**--A verb phrase used as an adjective to modify a noun or a pronoun. Participial phrases can be present (using an "-ing") or past (using an "-ed").

Shaking in the knees, I walked into the principal's office.

✏️**Noun Absolute**--a noun that has no grammatical function in the sentence in that it is not the subject, direct or indirect object, predicate nominative, or object of the preposition; a noun absolute is followed by a present or a past participial phrase.

My knees shaking, I walked into the principal's office.

(The noun absolute is "Knees.")

All quoted material is from:

Bradbury, Ray. Dandelion Wine. New York: Bantam, 1990.

Activities & Skills

Ready-to-Use

ENGLISH WORKSHOP ACTIVITIES

for Grades 6-12

Dailies

🕐   As I take a huge spoonful of cereal into the immense, dark, wet cave of my mouth, Angie throws a handful of cereal at me. I look at her with that this-means-war-and-I'm-serious look. To show my gratitude for her gift, I throw a handful of my own cereal. Next thing I know, we've started a war where our only deadly weapons and explosives are bowls full of cereal. Fruit Loops and Crunch Berries fly left and right while we, the two brave warriors, fight to protect our pride, our humankind, our place mats (Davis, A'Rynn, "Sisters").

1. Quote a metaphor and state whether it is explicit or implicit.

     A.   Quote:_____

     B.   Implicit? Explicit?_____

2. Quote a sentence with a comma and explain its rule.

     A.   Quote:_____

     B.   Rule:_____

3. Where can you infer that the passage takes place? Support your answer.

     A.   Inference:_____

     B.   Support:_____

4. What is the rule for the hyphens?_____

5. What is the tone of the passage? Support your answer.

     A.   Tone:_____
     B.   Support:_____

Dailies

🕐 Most preppy, rude girls dyed their hair blonde, but they didn't really need to because they were still blonde with an I.Q. of a dead flashlight battery no matter what they did. (Anderson, Jennifer, "The Preppy Ones").

1. What is the rule for the first comma?_____

2. What can you infer about the narrator of the passage? Support your answer:

   A. Inference:_____

   B. Support:_____

3. What is the rule for the second comma?_____

4. What is the tone of the passage? Support your answer.

   A. Tone:_____

   B. Support:_____

5. Write a stereotypical statement about boys, using the same tone as the author's and including at least one figurative language device.

   _____

   _____

   _____

Dailies

After I had finished all the ten million things I had to do, I decided to go for a bike ride. I straddled the banana seat of my ten-speed blue-and-silver Schwinn and set off. The wind kissed my face and blew back my hair. Halfway to Taryn's house I realized just where I was going: to Taryn's house. I decided to keep going and then I could confront her about Brett. AS I turned the corner, what I saw next was the most terrifying thing that has happened to me (Ponder, Danielle, "Taryn's House").

1. Quote the hyperbole in the passage:_____

2. Quote the personification in the passage and underline the human trait:

   _____

3. Explain the change in tone in the excerpt:

   _____

4. What is the rule for the first comma?_____

5. Quote an example of humor:_____

6. How does the author "hook" the reader?

   _____

7. Why does the author use "had finished" instead of "finished"?
   Explain the difference in tenses and what they imply.

   _____

Name:_____Class:_____Date:_____

Dailies

🕐   Impatient. Worried. Nervous. These feelings strangle her every last breath of air until she places her lips on the rim of the delicate cup that lies on the saucer as she seductively drums her fingertips on the marble-slab table. Gently brushing crumbs off the floor--the same floor that is being tapped on by the heels of this lady's shimmery blue flats--the janitor admires the lady in the orange hat. But it's time to close. What is she waiting for? When will she leave? Hopefully never. The janitor is dancing to the rhythm of his thoughts.

As he glides a little closer to the table with the lady in the orange hat, she listens to the beat of the swoosh-swoosh of his broom. Then she hears it--an interruption of some sort. It is fast, crisp, staccato. She turns her head and moves her eyes all the way around the coffee shop. The thought of not knowing where the mysterious sounds are coming from makes her jump out of her seat.

The janitor quickly grabs at his chest and runs toward the closet at the back of the shop. The lady in the orange hat, confused, sits back down, letting her legs cross slowly. How did she hear my heartbeat? The janitor takes his index fingers and places them on his temples as he heavily thinks about organizing his feelings for this stranger, this lady, this lady in the orange hat (Martinez, Sophia, "The Lady in the Orange Hat").

1.   In what verb tense is the excerpt written?_____

    ✓List five verbs to prove your answer:_____,_____,_____

    _____,_____

2.   Explain what is happening in the excerpt:_____

_____

3.   Quote a "smiley-face" passage and explain what type it is:

    A.   Quote:_____

    B.   Type:_____

4.   What is the comma rule for the first sentence in the second paragraph?

    _____

5.   What is the tone of the passage? Give support for your answer:

    A.   Tone:_____

    B.   Support:_____

6.   This excerpt was created by the author's viewing of the picture <u>The Automat</u> by Edward Hopper. One person alone is in the picture--the lady in the orange hat. The author has imagined another character and "paints" him in with her words, bringing both characters to life. Write a descriptive vignette of a picture your teacher provides or a picture that you know, where you bring life to the static characters.

_____

_____

_____

_____

_____

_____

_____

_____

_____

Dailies

🕐 " `Hey, Brandon, there is a spider on your leg!'
      My blood was a block of ice, my heart was a generator without a cord, and my brain shut off as quickly as a deer when a shot goes off. Slowly I looked at my leg. It was a large *Latrodectus mactans,* or black widow" (Rosenbaun, Brandon. **"The Camping Trip"**).

1.   Why are the single quotation marks used?_____
      _____

2.   Quote the magic three:_____
      _____

3.   Quote a metaphor and explain whether it is implicit or explicit:

      A.   Quote:_____

      B.   Type:_____

4.   Quote a simile:_____

5.   What is the rule for the first two commas?_____

6.   Why are the italics used for *Latrodectus mactans*?
      _____

7.   Write a short passage with the same tone, using at least one metaphor, about something that has happened to you.

      _____

      _____

Answer Key

*Accept other answers if supported.
*Answers for writing questions will vary.

"Sisters"

1. A.   "Immense, dark, wet cave of my mouth"
    B.   Implicit
2. A.   "To show my gratitude for her gift, I throw a handful of my own cereal."
    B.   Introductory phrase
3. A.   Kitchen/dining room
    B.   "cereal" and "place mats"
4. Hyphenated modifier
5. A.   Humor/parody
    B.   "I look at her with that this-means-war-and-I'm-serious look," "deadly weapons," and "protect our pride, our humankind, our place mats"

"The Preppy Ones"

1. Coordinate adjective
2. A.   Readers can infer that the narrator is not a "preppy" girl.
    B.   The narrator makes a distinction between herself and the "preppy" ones, as opposed to including herself in their category. Besides that, she makes fun of them, referring to them as "rude" and "blonde(s) with an I.Q. of a dead flashlight battery."
3. Compound Sentence
4. A.   Humor
    B.   "still blonde with an I.Q. of a dead flashlight battery"
5. Answers will vary.

"Taryn's House"

1. "all the ten million things I had to do"
2. "The wind <u>kissed</u> my face"
3. At first, the narrator has a carefree attitude, as evidenced by the "wind kissed my face and blew back my hair."   Later, however, the tone switches to suspense in that we realize that something "terrifying" is about to happen.
4. Introductory adverb clause
5. "Halfway to Taryn's house I realized just where I was going: to Taryn's house."
6. The excerpt ends on a note of suspense. Readers can't help but wonder what the "most terrifying thing" is.

7. "Had finished" is past perfect, whereas "finished" is past. The author uses "had finished" so that the reader realizes that the "ten million things" are done, and now the real story can start--in past tense.

"The Lady in the Orange Hat"

1. Present tense--strangle, places, lies, drums, brushes
2. A janitor in a coffee shop falls in love with a lady in an orange hat.
3. A. "She places her lips on the rim of the delicate cup that lies on the saucer as she seductively drums her fingertips on the marble-slab table."
    B. Specific details for effect
4. Introductory clause (adverb clause)
5. A. Romantic
    B. "The janitor is dancing to the rhythm of his thoughts."
6. Answers will vary.

"The Camping Trip"

1. The passage is already quoted; therefore, the dialogue must be enclosed in single quotation marks.
2. "My blood was a block of ice, my heart was a generator without a cord, and my brain shut off...."
3. A. "My blood was a block of ice"
    B. Explicit--An explicit metaphor has a "be" verb (i.e., "was").
4. "my brain shut off as quickly as a deer when a shot goes off"
5. Direct address
6. Foreign words are put in italics.
7. Answers will vary.

Dailies

No real life, no real plans
I am in school, after all
and my friends aren't
like a colony of ants
and my family isn't
like a pride of lions
It's just plain ol' simple me
me the simple one
just the speck
in your eye (LaRue, Jesse, "Song of Myself").

1. What can you **infer** that the narrator thinks about school? **Support your answer** with a quote from the poem.

   _____

   _____

2. Quote two **similes** and **explain what they have in common:**

   _____

   _____

3. Write another **simile** that could **fit in** with the two above:

   _____

4. Why does the author use an **apostrophe** in "ol'"?

   _____

5.   Quote the **metaphor** and explain whether it is **explicit or implicit**:

_____

6.   How is the excerpt **ironic**?

_____

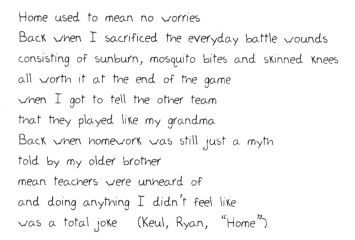

Home used to mean no worries
Back when I sacrificed the everyday battle wounds
consisting of sunburn, mosquito bites and skinned knees
all worth it at the end of the game
when I got to tell the other team
that they played like my grandma
Back when homework was still just a myth
told by my older brother
mean teachers were unheard of
and doing anything I didn't feel like
was a total joke   (Keul, Ryan, "Home").

1.   Quote a **metaphor** from the poem and explain whether it is **explicit or implicit**:

_____

2.   Rewrite the **metaphor** using **literal language**:

_____

3.   Quote a **simile** and explain **why it is effective**:

_____

_____

4.   Quote a **magic three**:_____

_____

5.   What can you **infer** about the narrator? **Support your answer.**

_____

_____

AFTER PASSING THROUGH BRIAR AS THICK AS TANNED COWHIDE, BRAMBLE THORNY AND BARREN, AND BRUSH AS SECRETIVE AS THE MOON HIDING BEHIND THE SUN DURING AN ECLIPSE... (POLIMIS, KIVAN, "SONG").

1.   **In at least 50 words**, write an **ending** to the author's sentence:

_____

_____

_____

2.   What two **adjectives** modify "bramble" and **what is unusual about their placement?**

_____

_____

3.   Quote the two **similes:** _____

_____

4.   What **literary device** is exemplified by the author's use of "briar," "bramble," and "brush"? Define the device and explain how these are indeed examples:

_____

_____

5.   Choose one of the two similes and **rewrite it using a different comparison.**

_____

_____

Tap, tap, tap. I walk down the street of my home town.....In one breath I inhale memories of Sunday picnics, family reunions, and hopscotch afternoons.....I look down at the old brick road and could swear it smiled at me, welcoming me and telling me to remember the sunny days when my friends and I skipped and chanted, the lap of strawberries dazzling our tongues...(Kirch, Amy, "I'm Home").

1.   Quote a **magic three:**

_____

_____

2.   Quote a **repetition for effect** and explain what other **literary device** it could represent:

_____

3.   Quote a **personification:**_____

4.   Quote a **vivid verb** and **replace it with a common one** to illustrate the importance of word choice:

_____

5.   Quote a **metaphor:**_____

6.   What is **particularly effective** about the author's use of the **phrase** "a lap of strawberries"?

_____

Dailies

"But now what happened to the days when tic-tac-toe was your favorite game and the show you could not live without was 'The Teenage Mutant Ninja Turtles'? What happened to when your appearance was the least of your worries because you were too busy deciding which kind of chips you wanted in your lunch box....?" (French, Chloe, "Home").

1. What do the **single quotation marks** around "The Teenage Mutant Ninja Turtles" represent?

    _____

2. Quote two **symbols** in the excerpt and **explain what they symbolize:**

    _____

    _____

3. What do you call the **four periods** at the end of the excerpt and what is their **purpose? Explain why there are four, not three.**

    _____

4. Why is the **question mark** outside the quotes instead of inside?

    _____

5. Using the author's **repetition for effect** ("what happened"), **add at least 50 more words that could fit in the excerpt:**

    _____

    _____

    _____

    _____

Answer Key

*Accept other answers if supported.
*Answers for writing questions will vary.

"Song of Myself"

1. Readers could infer that the narrator believes that being in school is equivalent to having no life. He writes that "no real life / no real plan / I am in school, after all."
2. "my friends aren't / like a colony of ants" and "my family isn't / like a pride of lions" Both similes make a comparison between groups of people and animals.
3. Answers will vary.
4. The apostrophe stands for the "d" in "old" that the narrator omitted.
5. "me the simple one / just the speck / in your eye"--An explicit metaphor uses a "be" verb, whereas an implicit metaphor does not. This metaphor, however, has an elliptical "be" verb, which could make it explicit. A student could, though, make a case for the phrase's being implicit (e.g., blackberry sky) by the author's intended meaning of "me, the speck." Accept either answer with support.
6. It is ironic that a "simple one" could write a passage with abstractions and complex phrasings and comparisons, such as "colony of ants" and "pride of lions."

"Home"

1. "Back when homework was still just a myth"--explicit because it contains "was"
2. Back when homework was something I hadn't experienced.
3. "they played like my grandma"--The simile is effective in that it gives a more vivid picture of a team playing poorly.
4. "when homework was still just a myth / told by my brother / mean teachers were unheard of / and doing anything I didn't feel like / was a total joke"
5. Readers can infer that the narrator is self-effacing, humble.

"Song"

1. Answers will vary.
2. "thorny" and "barren"--Adjectives are usually placed before the nouns they modify, not after.
3. "briar as thick as tanned cowhide" and "brush as secretive as the moon hiding behind the sun...."
4. Alliteration--the repetition of the same sound usually at the beginning of several words in a series. "Briar," "bramble," and "brush" all begin with the consonant blend of "br."
5. Answers will vary.

"I'm Home"

1. "Sunday picnics, family reunions, and hopscotch afternoons"
2. "Tap, tap, tap"--onomatopoeia
3. "I look down at the old brick road and can swear it smiled at me, welcoming me and telling me to remember...."
4. Vivid verb: Inhale   Less effective verb: think about
5. "the lap of strawberries dazzling our tongues"
6. "The lap of strawberries" is an example of taste imagery, which enables the reader to almost experience what the author is describing.

"Home"

1. "The Teenage Mutant Ninja Turtles" is a TV show, which requires that it be enclosed in quotation marks. Since the passage already has been quoted, the double quotation marks must be replaced by single ones.
2. "tic-tac-toe" and "chips"--childhood
3. The ellipsis and a period are necessary since three periods represent omission, and the fourth period stands for the period at the end of the sentence.
4. The name of the TV show is not a question; the sentence is a question.
5. Answers will vary.

Dailies

☆ After I had checked over the clothes I had picked out, I headed toward the bathroom but stopped dead in my tracks. My worst enemy, my brother Alex, was making his way to my destination. He had a bad reputation of taking long showers and leaving the room with the lingering scent of his awful cologne. I looked at him, and he stared right back. It was like an old Western cowboy movie. Suddenly he shot me his don't-even-think-about-it look. So, of course, I retaliated with my world-famous-make-me look (Mescall, Meagan, "My Worst Enemy").

1. What can you predict will happen? Give support.

    A. Prediction:_____

    B. Support:_____

2. What are the comma rules for the following sentence?:

    A. First sentence:_____

    B. Second sentence (two commas/same rule):_____

    C. Fourth sentence:_____

    D. Sixth sentence:_____

3. Quote a figurative language device and tell its type.

    A. Device:_____

    B. Type:_____

4. Explain the rule for capitalizing "Western."_____

5. Give two common adjectives that could have been used instead of the hyphenated adjectives. Which do you like better and why?

    A. Common adjectives:_____,_____

    B. Better and why? _____

6. Quote a vivid verb and give a less effective one that could have been used.

    A. Vivid verb:_____

    B. Less effective verb:_____

7. Why does the author use "had" in the first sentence? What tense is this?

    A. Reason:_____

    B. Tense:_____

8. What is the tone of the passage? Give support.

    A. Tone:_____

    B. Support:_____

9. Write a short passage where you describe a typical scene at your house. Include one figurative language device and a hyphenated adjective.

    _____

    _____

    _____

    _____

    _____

    _____

10. What type of conflict does this passage represent?_____

Dailies

☆ I stopped, looked back at Jacob, and realized we didn't have a chance. We didn't have a chance to run to the shed, we didn't have a chance to distract them, we didn't have a chance to stealthily get to the house (Roeschen, Michael, "No Help in Sight").

1. What two Smiley-Face Tricks does the author use in this passage?

   _____&_____

2. How are the Smiley-Face Tricks effective? What mood do they create?

   _____

3. "Stealthily" is an adverb, which the author needed to describe that there was no way to get to the house, even secretly. Write a sentence using "stealthy", the adjective, that could fit the passage. Give a **context clue** within the sentence and underline it.

   _____

   _____

   _____

4. What can you infer about the narrator? Give support.

   A.   Inference:_____

   B.   Support:_____

5. From what point of view is this passage written?_____

Dailies

♥The inside of the bus rolling merrily down Oakdale Drive was dusty and hot and had that bitter, stale smell only sweat has. I steadily walked to the fourth seat from the back, right side, careful not to trip over shoes or backpacks or books that could be in my way, and plopped my stuff on the seat. It was then I heard a soft breathing in my ear, a little snotty sounding, like it was plugged up.

"Leave me alone, you punk!" I said in pieces to the dark-haired boy breathing on my neck.

"I am sick and tired of your little attitude!" And I meant every word. His little attitude loves to explode in my face like a timer going off for a cook to check her cookies before they harden and turn crispy.

"For once, I am actually happy that it's time to get off this bus!" I yell.

"Shut up, you know you like me. You know you wanna hold me and kiss me," he said slowing singing those words and dancing around me like a fly around sticky fly paper.

I swear, to the bottom of my heart, he was right.

"Fly away, little birdie, and leave me alone!" was what I said, though.

His eyes got wider, like they hurt with tears, and he got that little ear-to-ear, sly smile that I love to hate.

He mumbled a few words in my ear, something like, "I'll be back," in a macho-man tone, and I realized that his voice was both sweet and sour.

• • •

The inside of the bus rolling merrily down Oakdale Drive was dusty and hot and had that bitter smell only sweat has. I steadily walked to the fourth seat from the back, right side, careful not to trip over any shoes or backpacks or books that could be in my way, and plopped my stuff on the seat. I heard a soft breathing in my ear, a little snotty sounding, like it was plugged up.

"Get away, you punk! I am so not in the mood right now!"

"Oh, come on, you know you want me!"

Yep, I sure did. I guess you could say I was his I-love-to-pick-on girl and he was the one I love to hate (Green, Kathleen, "The One I Love To Hate).

1. This excerpt (beginning and end) from a short story is based on a paradox.

    A. Define "paradox":_____

    B. Explain the main paradox in the story:_____

_____

    C. Quote a minor paradox having to do with the boy's voice:

_____

2. Explain how this excerpt is an example of a full-circle ending:

_____

_____

3. A. Explain the use of the hyphens:_____

    B. Quote three instances where the author has used hyphens:

_____,_____,_____

4. Quote an example of the following comma rules:

    A. Interrupter: _____

    B. Direct address:_____

    C. Coordinate adjective: _____

5. Explain the rule for most of the paragraphing:

_____

6. Write a dialogue where you persuade someone to leave you alone. You must use specific details for effect, proper punctuation and paragraphing for dialogue, and have at least one line of a full-circle ending.

_____

_____

_____

_____

_____

_____

_____

_____

_____

_____

_____

Dailies

☆   It was like a drug. It caught me fair and square. It was like night; it shut the darkness into my life and caused a loneliness I had never known. Oh, how I missed my grandmother. None of the tears and sorrow the night let out could bring her back. Nobody felt like opening presents or turning on the festive house lights, for darkness covered the lonely, deserted road (Pelt, Gregg, "Grandmother").

1.   What is the conflict? Is it internal or external?

    A.   Conflict:_____

    B.   Type and explanation:_____

2.   What can you infer about the setting:_____

3.   Quote two similes:_____

    _____

4.   "Fair" and "square" are examples of what literary device?_____

5.   What is the comma rule for separating "lonely" from "deserted"?_____

✔   Rewrite the sentence, substituting the conjunction "and" for the comma. Which way is more effective? Why?

    _____

    _____

Dailies

☆   It was a satin dress with a flared skirt that skimmed the knees. Lavender and tight down to the waist, her satin dress. That was his reason. She had this all-eyes-on-me look that made me hate her even more. I didn't get it. What did guys see in this hazel-eyed, pure-skinned, one-of-a-kind Black Barbie doll? For an actual moment I thought I saw some saliva roll down my boyfriend Chris's chin. I wanted to bust his lip, but that wouldn't work because it was practically on the floor. I wanted to hurl (Hargrave, Brittany, "Barbie Doll").

1.   What is the tone of this passage? Support your answer.

    A.   Tone:_____

    B.   Support:_____

2.   Explain the conflict and type.

    A.   Conflict:_____

    B.   Type:_____

3.   What do you think is the most effective description the author uses to describe the girl?

    _____

4.   Explain the use of the hyphens:_____

5.   Explain why "Black Barbie" is capitalized:_____

6. What is the rule for making a *noun singular possessive*? Give an *example* in the passage.

   A. Rule:_____

   B. Example:_____

7. Quote the *fragment* and explain how it is *effective*.

   A. Fragment:_____

   B. Effective:_____

8. What is the *comma rule in the next to the last sentence?*_____

9. Quote the *hyperbole:*_____

10. Rewrite the passage from *Chris's point of view:*

    _____

    _____

    _____

    _____

    _____

    _____

Answer Key

*Accept other answers if supported.
*Answers to writing questions will vary.

"My Worst Enemy"

1.   A.   * There will be a "showdown" between brother and sister.
       B.   *"Suddenly he shot me his....So, of course, I retaliated with...."
2.   A.   Introductory adverb clause
       B.   Appositive
       C.   Compound sentence
       D.   Interrupter
3.   A.   "It was like an old Western cowboy movie."
       B.   Simile
4.   Refers to a part of the country
5.   A.   * Threatening & fearless
       B.   The hyphenated modifiers are more sophisticated and add humor.
6.   A.   Retaliated
       B.   Responded
7.   A.   The checking over the clothes happened before the action in the excerpt.
       B.   Past perfect tense
8.   A.   Humorous
       B.   *"my world-famous-make-me look"
9.   Answers will vary.
10.   External

"No Help in Sight"

1.   Repetition for effect & magic three
2.   The repetition adds to the suspense, while the magic three gives the passage a poetic effect.
3.   * The stealthy footsteps didn't escape our trained <u>radar</u>-like hearing, even though they thought they were so <u>secretive</u>.
4.   A.   *We can infer that the narrator is an adventurous type.
       B.   "We didn't have a chance to stealthily get to the house."
5.   First person

"The One I Love to Hate"

1. A. A statement that at first seems contradictory but on closer examination makes sense
   B. "Loving" to "hate" someone seems contradictory; however, in this excerpt the girl seems to "hate" the boy who annoys her, while, in fact, she "loves" him.
2. The author repeats some exact phrases from the beginning.
3. A. Hyphenated modifier
   B. "Dark-haired boy," "ear-to-ear grin," "I-love-to-pick-on girl"
4. A. "It was then I heard a soft breathing in my ear, little snotty sounding, like it was plugged up."
   B. " 'Fly away, little birdie, and leave me alone!'"
   C. "Ear-to-ear, sly grin"
5. Dialogue
6. Answers will vary.

"Grandmother"

1. A. The conflict is between the grandmother's death and the feeling of loneliness.
   B. External
2. Christmas Eve
3. "It was like a drug" & "It was like night"
4. Assonance
5. Coordinate adjective--two or more adjectives before a noun
   "...for darkness covered the lonely and deserted road"
   The original version is more sophisticated; it flows better without the conjunction.

"Barbie Doll"

1. A. Angry
   B. "I wanted to bust his lip...."
2. A. The conflict is between the narrator and the "Black Barbie doll," who has her boyfriend's attention.
   B. External
3. "What did guys see in this hazel-eyed, pure-skinned, one-of-a-kind Black Barbie doll?"
4. Hyphenated modifier
5. "Black" is a nationality, and "Barbie" is a specific brand name of a doll.
6. A. To make a singular noun possessive, add an apostrophe and an "s."
   B. "Chris's"

7.   A.   "Lavender and tight down to the waist, her satin dress."
        B.   It is effective because it emphasizes the features of the dress rather than the noun "dress."
8.   Compound sentence
9.   "I wanted to bust his lip, but that wouldn't work because it was practically on the floor."
10.   Answers will vary.

Dailies

☀Josh could tell that Brian was about to boil over, blow his cap, explode like a time bomb. Brian was steaming, and I mean steaming (Poston, Greg, "Incredible Journey").

1.　Quote a **magic three:**＿＿＿＿＿＿＿,＿＿＿＿＿＿＿,＿＿＿＿＿＿＿＿

2.　Quote a **simile:**＿＿＿＿＿＿＿＿＿＿＿＿＿＿＿＿＿＿＿＿＿＿

3.　Quote three **metaphors** and tell whether they are **implicit or explicit:**

　　A.　**Metaphor:**＿＿＿＿＿＿＿＿＿＿**Type:**＿＿＿＿＿＿＿

　　B.　**Metaphor:**＿＿＿＿＿＿＿＿＿＿**Type:**＿＿＿＿＿＿＿

　　C.　**Metaphor:**＿＿＿＿＿＿＿＿＿＿**Type:**＿＿＿＿＿＿＿

4.　Write **at least 50 words**, continuing the story of the **"Incredible Journey."** Pretend that these are the first two sentences of the narrative. Your job is to **interest an editor** in your work.

＿＿＿＿＿＿＿＿＿＿＿＿＿＿＿＿＿＿＿＿＿＿＿＿＿＿

＿＿＿＿＿＿＿＿＿＿＿＿＿＿＿＿＿＿＿＿＿＿＿＿＿＿

＿＿＿＿＿＿＿＿＿＿＿＿＿＿＿＿＿＿＿＿＿＿＿＿＿＿

＿＿＿＿＿＿＿＿＿＿＿＿＿＿＿＿＿＿＿＿＿＿＿＿＿＿

＿＿＿＿＿＿＿＿＿＿＿＿＿＿＿＿＿＿＿＿＿＿＿＿＿＿

5.　Write a **30-word (exactly) sentence** that further **characterizes Josh or Brian**. Tell which **method of characterization** you have used: appearance, environment, actions, speech, what others say, inner thoughts and feelings.

＿＿＿＿＿＿＿＿＿＿＿＿＿＿＿＿＿＿＿＿＿＿＿＿＿＿

＿＿＿＿＿＿＿＿＿＿＿＿＿＿＿＿＿＿＿＿＿＿＿＿＿＿

☼Leah McKay swished her hips as she was walking by my desk today. I know that doesn't sound strange, but I can't stand it when she does that. I mean I don't see why every guy in the world drools over her. So she has beautiful blonde, bouncy curls, buys her clothes from stores that I can't even pronounce, and was voted most popular at a school across town she doesn't even go to.

"Excuse me, but, Dena, what is the answer to number six?"

"Excuse me, but, Leah, my name isn't Dena. It's Serena, and if you can't get the answer to number six, that's your problem."

"Well, excuse me, whatever-your-name-is. I just asked what the answer is."

For somebody who's rich, beautiful, and popular, she must not be too smart because our teacher, who makes a pit bull on a rampage look like a cute little pug, was standing right there.

"Ms. McKay, were you asking Serena for the answer?"

"Well, see....Okay, I didn't want to have to say this, but we always get the answers off each other, ever since sixth grade."

She did it. I can't believe she did it. She told the fattest lie in the universe.

"Really?" Mrs. Tomato (the name all the kids call her) said, her eyes turning a strawberry red, that vein in her forehead popping to the tune of the tick-tock of the clock (Leal, Julia, "The Hair on Fire").

1. What does the **narrator** think of Leah McKay? **Support** your answer:

    A.   Opinion of main character:_____

    B.   Support:_____

2. How does the author use **humor** in the excerpt?

    _____

3. Quote a **hyperbole:**_____

4. Quote examples of the following **comma rules:**

    A.   **Direct Address:**_____

    B.   **Compound Sentence:**_____

    C.   **Series:**_____

5.   **Write a vignette persuading the reader to feel sorry for Leah McKay. Use dialogue, figurative language, and humor.**

_____

_____

_____

_____

_____

_____

_____

_____

6.   Write a **sentence of at least 30 words characterizing the narrator**. Explain which **method of characterization** you have used:

_____

_____

_____

7.   Explain the **conflict** in the passage and tell whether it is **internal or external.**

    A.   Conflict:_____

    B.   Type:_____

☼Emily and I lived on Apple Street, the most elegant of all streets. Only six houses settled on Apple Street, all beautiful, one-story houses. Willow trees stood like soldiers in everyone's back yard and front yard with only their hair-like leaves blowing in the wind (Bell, Amanda, "The Marshmallows in Hot Chocolate").

1. What is the rule for the **comma** in the first sentence?_____

2. To prove the **effectiveness of combining**, rewrite the first sentence, making it into **two sentences**:

    _____

    _____

3. **Which way is better**?_____**Why?**_____

4. Why is there a **hyphen** between **"one"** and **"story"**?_____

5. Quote two **similes:**_____

    &_____

6. **Write at least a 50-word paragraph describing your neighborhood. Use at least two similes:**

    _____

    _____

    _____

    _____

    _____

    _____

    _____

    _____

☼Why couldn't I have stayed in elementary school, where little kids got their pictures hung on the "Wall of Success" if they colored in the lines, where the extent of anyone's possibilities was to spell the word "Washington" correctly, where everyone was happy?
(Haifley, Glynis, "And Then There Was Math").

1. What specific **stylistic device** has the author used to make this passage sound **poetic**?

_____

_____

2. The author uses **specific details for effect**. Quote two:

   A._____

   B._____

3. Why are **"Wall of Success"** and **"Washington"** in **quotation marks**?

_____

4. Write at least a **50-word passage** where you begin: Why couldn't I have stayed in junior high.... Use at least **three specific details for effect** and **one figurative language device** that you will label. Use a **tone** similar to the author's.

_____

_____

_____

_____

5. In question 4, why does the word **"author's"** have an **apostrophe** if there is no word that the author "owns" that is **directly after the word**?

_____

✴"'You knew! You knew and you didn't tell me! How could you? I hate you! Do you hear me? I hate you!' she spoke her words so clearly that she didn't have to repeat herself, and I didn't have to ask what she was talking about because I knew" (Pruett, Amanda, "I Remember").

1. What is the **tone** of the passage? Give **support.**

    A. Tone:_____

    B. Support:_____

2. Why does the author use **quotes within a quote**?

    _____

3. What is the rule for the **comma** after "herself"?

    _____

4. Write at least a **50-word passage, with dialogue.** Be sure to use quotation marks correctly. In the passage, you will **reveal the "subject" being discussed. Be sure to make your dialogue sound natural and believable.**

    _____

    _____

    _____

5. Now write another passage of at least 50 words, where you will **assume the role of the original speaker and end the discussion. Use quotation marks correctly.**

    _____

    _____

    _____

Answer Key

*Accept other answers if supported.
*Answers to writing questions will vary.

"Incredible Journey"

1.   "boil over, blow his cap, explode like a time bomb"
2.   "explode like a time bomb"
3.   A.   "boil over"   (implicit)
      B.   "blow his cap" (implicit)
      C.   "Brian was steaming" (implicit) (Even though there is a "be" verb, the metaphor is implicit in that it compares Brian to something that can actually steam. It does not compare Brian to "steaming.")
4.   Answers will vary.
5.   Answers will vary.

"The Hair on Fire"

1.   A.   The narrator thinks Leah is snobby but not too smart.
      B.   "For somebody who's rich, beautiful, and popular, she must not be too smart."
2.   The author uses humor in her description of the teacher, in her dialogue regarding the misuse of the narrator's name, and in the description of Leah's "being voted most popular" at a school she doesn't attend.
3.   "She told the fattest lie in the universe."
4.   A.   " Excuse me, but, Dena, what...."
      B.   "I know that doesn't sound strange, but I can't   ...."
      C.   "For somebody's who's rich, beautiful, and popular...."
5.   Answers will vary.
6.   Answers will vary.

"The Marshmallows in Hot Chocolate"

1.   Appositive
2.   Emily and I lived on Apple Street. It was the most elegant of all streets.
3.   The author's original way is better since it is more sophisticated.
4.   "One" and "story" work together as a single adjective to modify "houses."
5.   "Willow trees stood like soldiers" & "their hair-like leaves"
6.   Answers will vary.

"And Then There Was Math"

1.   The author's use of repetition in the form of a magic three helps make the passage poetic.

2.   A.   "where little kids got their pictures hung on the 'Wall of Success' if they colored in the lines"

    B.   "where the extent of anyone's possibilities was to spell the word 'Washington' correctly"

3.   "Wall of Success" designates a specific place, and "Washington" must be in quotes as it is a word referred to as a word.

4.   Answers will vary.

5.   "Author's" needs an apostrophe as it refers to the "tone" that the "author" owns.

"I Remember"

1.   A.   Angry

    B.   "I hate you!"

2.   The passage is already quoted; therefore, the single quotes represent dialogue.

3.   Compound sentence

4.   Answers will vary.

5.   Answers will vary.

Dailies

☞ "Man, I got problems."

"YOU THINK YOU GOT PROBLEMS. YESTERDAY MY SISTER BRINGS HER I-WISH-I-HAD-BETTER-WEAVES FRIENDS BY THE HOUSE. THEY BE LIKE ACTIN' LIKE YOU GOTTA DO WHATEVER THEY SAY. THEN THEY LOSE THEY MIND."

"They done already lost they mind, what you talkin' about?"

"I MEAN ALL SUDDEN LIKE THEY WANNA TAKE THEY SHOE OFF, LIKE THEY ALL HAD ON ONE BIG SHOE OR SOMETHIN'."

"So, man, they just wanna be all comfortable like."

"YEAH, BUT THEY FEET SMELL LIKE YEAR-OLD HAM OR GYM SOCKS ON THURSDAY, YOU KNOW JUST WAITING FOR SATURDAY WASH. THEN THEY ACT LIKE IT'S THEY HOUSE AND THEY GO TRY TO FIX THEMSELVES A MEAL IN YOUR KITCHEN. THEY EAT YOUR MACARONI AND CHEESE, YOUR NEWLY BAKED CORNBREAD, AND DRINK YOUR KOOL-AID."

"Not your Kool-Aid, brother!"

"SEE, TOLD YOU I GOT PROBLEMS."

"I mean if I was you, and they was my sisters, I'd been moving like yesterday" (Disu, Taiwo, "I Got Problems").

1.   List two **smiley-face tricks** the author used to make this **dialogue effective:**

_____ **&** _____

2.   The author is trying to achieve **real-life dialogue**, rather than "standard" English usage. Underline three examples of **nonstandard speech and rewrite them in standard English.**

A._____

B._____

C._____

3.   Quote two sentences with a **direct address:**

A._____

B._____

4.   Explain the **rule for the hyphens** between " I-wish-I-had-better-weaves " and
      "year-old."

      _____

5.   Quote a sentence with an **introductory word:**_____

      _____

6.   Why does the author **change paragraphs?**_____

7.   Quote an **error in verb tense** and correct it:_____

8.   Define **subjunctive mood** and **correct the error** evident in the passage:

A._____

B._____

9.   Write a **similar dialogue** that you and your friend might have. Use at least two
      smiley-face tricks.

      _____

      _____

_____

_____

_____

_____

☞"Oh, that's so sweet," I said with a smile on my face, not noticing his grin from dimple to dimple. I bit down into the chocolate cupcake with vanilla icing and sprinkles when I felt the CRUNCH! My eyes widened wider than the Grand Canyon, my nose did the turn-up thing, and my mouth turned sideways as I looked down to see two little worms wiggle in my 'wonderful' cupcake" (Arthur, Peri, "Evil, Malicious, Adorable!")

1.   Quote a **hyperbole:**_____

2.   What can the reader **infer from the antagonist's grin?**

     _____

3.   Quote a **magic three:**_____

4.   Quote an **alliteration:**_____

5.   Study how the **author constructed the first sentence.** The dialogue is followed by a **speaker tag,** which most of us use, but the unusual part--the part that makes this good writing--is that the author **combines description in the form of a prepositional phrase followed by a participial phrase.** Write a piece of dialogue, using this same construction.

     _____

     _____

     _____

     _____

6.   Pretend that **you are the teacher**. Ask **one more question** about the passage--in terms of literature or grammar--and **answer it**.

_____

_____

☞He was sitting on a sofa in an apartment in his overalls. He was not very happy about the place, but he wasn't happy about the other one either. Black and white tiles that he used to play checkers with, red or maroon wallpaper, he never could tell the difference. One window, a window into another world. Big, ugly yellow-green blinds that need replacing, maybe with some baby-blue blinds. It was a color his eyes had never touched before. One small dank closet used for the master bedroom. A micro-sized closet space for the kitchen. It was so cramped that the refrigerator door wouldn't open all the way. There he was sitting on a sofa so old that the dinosaurs might have used it. He was sitting there staring at a thirteen-inch black and white television. It wouldn't be so weird if it was turned on, but to him it was turned on. It was showing back-to-back episodes of "See Your Cousin Drowned in the Lake." He just sat there while the whole world passed him by as he remembered his cousin. (Deming, Adam, "One Man's Life").

1.   List the **six ways an author can develop character:**_____

_____

☞On which **method does this author primarily rely?**_____

☞Quote **three examples** as proof:_____

_____

2. What is the **conflict** evident in the passage?_____

_____

_____

3. Quote a **fragment** and explain why the author has used this **fragment for effect**:

_____

4. Quote a **hyperbole** and explain why it is **effective**:_____

_____

5. What can the reader **infer about the character** from the second and third sentences?

_____

6. What is the "**window into another world**"?

_____

7. Quote a **compound sentence** and explain why this is a **particularly effective** sentence:

_____

_____

8. Write at least a **50-word passage** in which you **describe a character** based on one of the **six methods**:

_____

_____

_____

_____

☞HE SAID WE WEREN'T THE COUPLE WE USED TO BE. HE SAID WE WERE THROUGH. AND I THOUGHT WE WERE AT THE PEAK OF OUR RELATIONSHIP. APPARENTLY HE DIDN'T. COME TO FIND OUT FROM AN ANONYMOUS SOURCE, HE LEFT ME FOR HER. FROM THEN ON MY LIFE WENT DOWNHILL. MY GRADES WENT ROLLING DOWN A STEEP MOUNTAIN LIKE TUMBLEWEEDS IN THE WIND. IT WAS AS IF I HAD TURNED INTO THAT ONE ODD GIRL YOU'VE KNOWN FOREVER WHO HASN'T EVER CARED ABOUT HOMEWORK, PEOPLE, MUCH LESS HER OWN LIFE. LET'S JUST SAY THAT NOW I FINALLY UNDERSTOOD THAT GIRL. ALL MY FRIENDS TOLD ME TO GET OVER HIM, BUT I GUESS MY HEART DIDN'T LISTEN.

THERE'S THE GO-BELL. SIXTH PERIOD IS OVER. SLOWLY I SWING MY PURSE ON MY SHOULDER, PUT ON MY BACKPACK, AND WALK OUT THE DOOR, MY HEAD HANGING, MY SHOULDERS SLOUCHING. I SEE THEM TOGETHER, SIDE-BY-SIDE, HIM AND HER, JUST LIKE WE USED TO BE (HOLMES, REBECCA, "HAND in HAND").

1. Quote a **figurative language device** and identify its **type**:

A. _____ B. _____

2. A. What **tense** does the story begin in and to **what tense does it change?**

    _____

    B. **Why?**_____

3. Quote two **noun absolutes**: _____ &

    _____

4. What can you **infer about the statement**: "We weren't the couple we used to be"?

    _____

5.   Quote a **magic three:**

_____

6.   Write at least 50 words about a time **when your heart didn't listen to your head.**

_____

_____

_____

_____

_____

☞ **The ball was floating in the air like a lost bird or plane in the sky. I had nothing to do but run under that ball and catch it. It was like slow motion (Coleman, Sean, "The Game").**

1.   Quote two **figurative language devices and identify their types.**

A._____

B._____

2.   What can you **infer about what is happening in the passage?** Quote **support.**

A._____

B._____

3.   Write a passage modeled after this excerpt about an **everyday occurrence.** Be sure to use at least **three figurative language devices.**

_____

_____

_____

_____

_____

_____

_____

_____

_____

_____

_____

Answer Key

*Accept other answers if supported.
*Answers to writing questions will vary.

"I Got Problems"

1. Humor & hyphenated modifiers
2. A. "They be like actin'"--They acted like (as if)....
   B. "like you they slave"--like (as if) you are their slave
   C. "Women done already lost they mind"--Women have already lost their minds.
3. A. "Man, I got problems."
   B. "Not your Kool-Aid, brother!"
4. Both sets of words work as single adjectives, one modifying "friends" and the other "ham."
5. "See, told you I got problems."
6. Dialogue--new speaker
7. "Yesterday my sister brings"--"Yesterday my sister brought"
8. A. "I mean if I was you"
   B. Subjunctive mood is "I mean if I were you."
9. Answers will vary.

"Evil, Malicious, Adorable!"

1. "My eyes widened wider than the Grand Canyon."
2. Readers can infer that the antagonist's grin is a result of his mischief involving the cupcake.
3. "My eyes widened wider than the Grand Canyon, my nose did the turn-up thing, and my mouth turned sideways...."
4. "worms wiggle"
5. Answers will vary.
6. Answers will vary.

"One Man's Life"

1. Appearance, actions, speech, inner thoughts and feelings, what others say, environment
   *Environment
   *"Black and white tiles that he used to play checkers with," "One window, a window into another world," "Big, ugly yellow-green blinds"
2. Remembering the drowned cousin

3. "One window, a window into another world." The author perhaps wants to emphasize that the boy in the excerpt is in his own world, the world of memories. He's not looking out the window into "another world," as he has withdrawn into his mind.

4. "There he was sitting on a sofa so old that the dinosaurs might have used it." The hyperbole is effective in that it not only adds humor but completes the picture of the uninviting room.

5. Readers are told that the character is not happy and can infer that perhaps he is indifferent to his surroundings.

6. The "real world"--outside his apartment, outside his mind

7. "It wouldn't be so weird if it was turned on, but it was turned on to him." The author's repetition of "turned on" is effective because the second part of the compound sentence reveals further information about the character, that he is so oblivious to his surroundings that a "turned off" TV is the same as a "turned on" one. In both cases the boy sees "back-to-back episodes of 'See Your Cousin Drowned in the Lake.'"

8. Answers will vary.

"Hand in Hand"

1. A. "My grades went rolling down a steep mountain like tumbleweeds in the wind."
   B. Simile

2. A. The excerpt begins in past tense and ends in present.
   B. The narrator is giving background information from the past and then switches to her immediate present, which is even more poignant since we as readers witness what she is seeing.

3. "my head hanging" & "my shoulders slouching"

4. We can infer that the reason the narrator and her boyfriend "weren't the couple they used to be" was because he had found a new girlfriend.

5. "Slowly I swing my purse on my shoulder, put on my backpack, and walk out the door."

6. Answers will vary.

"The Game"

1. A. "The ball was floating in the air like a lost bird or plane in the sky."--simile
   B. "It was like slow motion."--simile

2. A. We can infer that a basketball, baseball, or football game is being played.
   B. The narrator is catching a ball; the title is "the Game."

3. Answers will vary.

Dailies

For each of the following excerpts, prove your knowledge of grammar, stylistic devices of writing, and literature by answering the questions that follow.

☺   Georgette looked furtively about the restaurant, ran her tongue and finally a finger over an area at the back of her mouth along the gum line, and at last, locating the nuisance, extracted one long, chili-bean red, perfectly manicured fingernail from between her teeth and with it a mischievous strand of Alaskan king crab (Teacher Sample, "Every Little Thing").

1.   This sentence contains a "magic 3" verb set (THREE VERB PHRASES WITH A MAIN VERB IN EACH). Write each verb phrase. (Hint: "locating" is not a main verb.)

   A._____B._____C._____

2.   What comma rule applies when separating these verb phrases?

   _____

3.   What comma rule applies when setting off the phrase "locating the nuisance"?

   _____

4.   Why is a comma used to separate "long" from "chili-bean red"?_____

5.   Why is there a hyphen between "chili" and "bean"?_____

6.   What is the capitalization rule regarding "Alaskan"?_____

7.   A.   What one word is used to show that Georgette's efforts to dislodge the piece of crab are being done in hopes that no one will notice?_____

   B.   In question 7A, why is the verb "are" used as opposed to "is"? With what word does it agree?_____

8.   Write a *sentence with a "magic 3" verb set* that paints a picture of something *you* do in a "secret" manner:

_____

_____

_____

9.   What might you be able to *infer* about Georgette and why?

_____

_____

10.   Rewrite the passage in *present tense:*_____

_____

_____

_____

Dailies

☺   Like all Southern mothers, my mother had determined early in our relationship that no matter what it took--all the family money, all the family patience, or with my stiff, white petticoats raised, all the swift lashes Mother could bring herself to administer with the family switch--I would learn one thing or they, and presumably I, would die trying. I would learn how to be a lady. A Southern lady (Teacher Sample, "Far from a Lady").

1.   Explain the two capitalization rules:

    A.   Southern:_____

    B.   Mother:_____

2.   What comma rule applies to the first comma used?_____

3.   What comma rule applies to setting off the phrase "and presumably I" in commas?

    _____

4.   Explain the use of dashes:_____

    _____

5.   Why is there a comma used to separate "stiff" from "white"?_____

6.   What is the fragment and why is it effective?

    A._____

    B._____

Dailies

7.   Rewrite the fragment incorporating it into the previous sentence:
     (You may use ellipses.)

     _____

     _____

8.   Write the "magic 3" that is used:_____

     _____

.9. What phrase in the "magic 3" is repeated for effect?_____
     What is the effect?

     _____

10. What conflict is referred to in the passage?_____

     _____Internal or external?_____

Dailies

☺   I would hold a teacup properly, which I learned on my first lesson simply meant with one hand, not my customary two. Little finger capriciousness I learned by watching varying degrees of it-- from Aunt Elizabeth's stubby pinkie suddenly flailing about as if she were sending some sort of code, to the more subtle movements of Aunt Ethel's upturned delicate little finger. From that finger I learned my mother had been right. Actions do speak more loudly than words. Aunt Ethel had missed out on everything that she deemed important--that is to say, a small place in the society of our small town and the affection and attention of her husband and children-- and somehow it showed in that finger. Her finger managed to look as important as she herself was not (Teacher Sample, "Far from a Lady").

1.   Why does the author use the phrase "more loudly" instead of "louder"?

_____

2.   Write an original sentence that correctly uses the adjective "louder."

_____

3.   Quote a simile used and explain its tone: A._____

    B.   _____

4.   Rewrite the second sentence so that it is in natural order (SUBJECT/VERB/OBJECT):

_____

_____

✔ Which way do you think is better? Why?_____

_____

5. Characterize Aunt Ethel by quoting a phrase from the passage and explaining which method of characterization it represents (APPEARANCE, ACTIONS, SPEECH, WHAT OTHERS SAY, INNER THOUGHTS AND FEELINGS, ENVIRONMENT).

_____

_____

6. Cite a comma usage and explain the rule:_____

_____

_____

7. Explain the use of the dashes:_____

_____

8. Write about someone's mannerisms that seem to you to be characteristic of their personalities. Use the excerpt as a model.

_____

_____

_____

_____

Dailies

☺   Mrs. Abner J. Meade's fingers were nothing like the fingers that wrapped themselves around Mama's china teacups. I could imagine Mrs. M's pinkie finger doing all sorts of dances mid-air. Or maybe hers would do nothing at all. They wouldn't have to. That would be it. She would sip tea, her lips barely touching the cup's edge, her little finger doing nothing, and she would be noticed (Teacher Sample, "Far from a Lady").

1.   Quote a personification:_____

2.   Contrast Mrs. Meade's fingers and the two aunts' in the previous selection. Give quoted support.

_____

_____

3.   Why would the apostrophe be placed after the "s" in the word "aunt" as opposed to before the "s"?

_____

4.   Use the word "aunt's" correctly in a sentence:_____

_____

5.   Quote two noun absolutes. [HINT: NOUN ABSOLUTES ARE NOUNS THAT HAVE NO GRAMMATICAL FUNCTION IN THE SENTENCE (NOT THE SUBJECT, DIRECT OR INDIRECT OBJECT, OBJECT OF PREPOSITION, ETC.) AND ARE FOLLOWED BY A PRESENT OR PAST PARTICIPLE. EXAMPLE: I WALKED INTO THE PRINCIPAL'S OFFICE, MY KNEES SHAKING. OR...I WALKED INTO THE PRINCIPAL'S OFFICE, MY HEAD LOWERED.]

_____ & _____

Name:_____Class:_____Date:_____

Dailies

☺ Mike said he remembered his mom's disappearance vividly, like the shiny red bike he got when he was six, with tassels on the handle bars that would fly up as he sped around the neighborhood, tooting his new horn and with the iridescent patches glowing after dark that his mom had decorated both bumpers and the hubs of his spokes with. The bike was his freedom and he remembered. And the shotgun from his granddaddy he got when he was ten, that had been his permission to be a man, to be grown-up enough to be trusted with life and death. But after that Mike always said that for his twelfth birthday he got a new mom (Teacher Sample, "Coronado Bayshore Motel").

1. Quote two participial phrases. (*HINT: In this case they are present participles-- "-ing" words--that are not the main verb and are used as a sophisticated method of varying sentence structure. Example: I walked into the principal's office, declaring my innocence.*)

_____ & _____

2. Rewrite the passage so as to delete the participial phrases but still retain the information from the phrases. (*You may use ellipses.*)

_____

_____

_____

✔ Which way do you think is better? Why?_____

3. Quote a metaphor in the passage and explain whether it is explicit or implicit. (HINT: EXPLICIT METAPHORS CONTAIN A "BE" VERB--IS, AM, ARE, WAS, WERE, BE, BEEN, BEING. EXAMPLE: "ALL THE WORLD'S A STAGE." IMPLICIT METAPHORS ARE IMPLIED, SUCH AS "BLACKBERRY SKY.")

_____

_____

4. Formal English requires that we not end a sentence with a preposition. Rewrite the sentence that violates this rule:

_____

_____

5. What is the tone of this passage?_____Explain:_____

_____

6. One compound sentence does not contain a comma. Write the sentence including the comma and speculate as to the reason why the author excluded it.

_____

_____

_____

7. What can you infer about Mike's mother? Give support.

        A.   Inference:_____

                           _____

        B.   Support:_____

                           _____

Answer Key

*Accept other answers if supported.
*Answers to writing questions will vary.

"Every Little Thing"

1. A.   "looked furtively about the restaurant"
    B.   "ran her tongue and finally a finger over an area at the back of her mouth..."
    C.   "extracted one long, chili-bean red..."
2. Series
3. Interrupter
4. Coordinate adjective
5. Hyphenated adjective
6. Proper adjective
7. A.   Furtively
    B.   "Are" is used because it is plural and agrees with the noun "efforts."
8. Answers will vary.
9. Readers could infer that Georgette has some money ("Alaskan king crab" and "perfectly manicured fingernail") and that, while her manners might not follow all the rules of etiquette, she cares what society thinks ("looked furtively about the restaurant").
10. Georgette looks furtively about the restaurant, runs her tongue and finally a finger over an area at the back of her mouth along the gum line, and at last, locating the nuisance, extracts....

"Far from a Lady"

1. A.   Proper adjective
    B.   Proper noun--person's name could be directly substituted
2. Introductory phrase
3. Interrupter
4. Parenthetical phrase--gives more information
5. Coordinate adjective
6. A.   "A Southern lady."
    B.   The fragment is effective in that it emphasizes that the narrator wouldn't learn to be just any type of lady--but a Southern lady.
7. I would learn to be a lady, a Southern lady.
8. "all the family money," "all the family patience," "all the swift lashes Mother could bring herself to administer...."
9. "all the family"--The effect is that it takes a whole family to make a Southern girl a

Southern lady.
10.   Becoming a Southern lady--external

"Far from a Lady"

1.   "More loudly" is an adverb phrase modifying "do speak." "Louder" is an adjective.
2.   * I am louder than you.
3.   A.   "as if she were sending some sort of code"
       B.   Humorous--comparing the way a woman holds a teacup to something such as a stranded person sending a code for survival
4.   I learned little finger capriciousness by watching....
       *The first is more sophisticated, more unusual.
5.   "Aunt Ethel had missed out on everything that she deemed important"--environment or what others say
6.   "I would hold a teacup properly, which I learned on my first lesson simply meant, with one hand,...."--nonrestrictive adjective clause--or interrupter
7.   Parenthetical phrases--giving more information
8.   Answers will vary.

"Far from a Lady"

1.   "fingers that wrapped themselves"
2.   Mrs. Meade's fingers were confident. They perhaps would do "all sorts of dances mid-air" or maybe "nothing at all." The aunts' motions, however, were more studied or more desperate: "suddenly flailing about" and "somehow it showed in that finger."
3.   Plural possessive
4.   * My aunt's house is beautiful.
5.   "her lips barely touching the cup's edge" and "her little finger doing nothing"

"Coronado Bayshore Motel"

1.   "tooting his horn" and "glowing after dark..."
2.   *...neighborhood. He would toot his new horn... The author's version is more sophisticated.
3.   "The bike was his freedom"--explicit (has a "be" verb)
4.   ...with which his mom had decorated both bumpers and the hubs of his spokes
5.   Sad/poignant--We know that something has happened to Mike's mother because "after that Mike always said that for his twelfth birthday he got a new mom."
6.   "The bike was his freedom and he remembered."--Short compound sentences do not require a comma, and, besides that, perhaps the author did not want any interruption. He wanted the sentence to "flow."
7.   A.   We can infer that at least at some point she had cared about Mike.
       B.   "his mom had decorated both bumpers and the hubs of his spokes"

Dailies

✓Maybe we can blast one past the pitcher's mound, rocket one over the infielder's glove, or even slam one out of the ballpark. Hitting a baseball hard and far isn't as easy as Sammy Sosa makes it look, and it's not as simple as counting to five either (Lumpkin, Kyle, "How To Play America's Favorite Pastime").

1.   Quote a **magic 3**:_____
_____

2.   A.   Quote three **vivid verbs**: _____,_____,_____

     B.   Give a **less effective synonym** for each:_____,_____,_____

3.   A.   Quote a **simile**:_____

     B.   Why is the phrase about Sammy Sosa not really a simile?_____
_____

4.   A.   Quote two **singular possessive nouns**:_____ & _____

     B.   Write a sentence using both of the above nouns in their **plural possessive** forms:
_____

5.   What is the **main idea** of the excerpt?_____

6.   Write at least a 50-word paragraph giving information about a **sport or recreation** you enjoy. Use at least **three vivid verbs and one simile**:

_____

_____

_____

✓It's the same thing every day. We go to school seven hours a day, five days a week, for almost forty weeks a year, just so that after we have agonized over all the in-class work, we can go home to do some more of that finger-cramping, eyes-squinting, brain-teasing labor that Mrs. Know-It-All calls homework. Who wouldn't love it if we could be thirteen and still be capable of holding a ball because we don't have arthritis from our death grips on our pens or pencils? Who wouldn't love it if we could be fifteen and go to the store and not spend an hour feuding with ourselves over what the change from a five-dollar bill should be because we're still wondering what a cosecant is? Who wouldn't love it if we could be seventeen years old and not be blind as bats from reading twelve novels in six weeks? Well, all we have to do is learn how to talk Mrs. I-Know-Everything out of those miserable nights of missing our favorite TV shows to do work we have already done before. All it takes is a little effort, pride, and dignity, and we will be homework-free. We all might want to follow these three steps to help us out some, to give us a little jump start. All we need to know is what to say, when to say it, and how to say it (Shannon, Jessica, "Play Time").

1. A. Explain what makes the author's introduction an **attention-getter**:_____

_____

    B. Quote an **example** to prove your point:_____

2. A. Quote the **thesis** of the essay:_____

_____

    B. Explain how the three points or aspects of the thesis are stated in **parallel terms:**
_____

3. Quote a **hyperbole:**_____

4. Explain what is so **effective about the author's progression** of being thirteen, fifteen, and finally seventeen:

_____

5.   A.   What can you **infer** about the author's attitude toward her teacher?

_____

    B.   Quote **proof** of your answer:_____

6.   Write an **introduction to a "how-to" essay** using the author's style to attract the reader's attention:

_____

_____

_____

_____

_____

_____

    ✓ "Sucking up" and being a hard worker can help and so can having good behavior. Remember when you volunteered to babysit that demon-possessed kid who never listened? Well, that's what teachers might think about you. How can you listen when you can't even stop conversing with your neighbor? Hold the gossip for lunch. Don't talk or interrupt a teacher when he or she is busy. It's forbidden. And don't draw repulsive monsters on your paper either. Then there's the screaming. Unless there's a bomb threat, hurricane, earthquake, tornado, or a roach as big as a Volkswagen crawling by your feet, don't scream in class. Even when your classmates start acting like chimpanzees, sit quietly and polish your halo. Your grades depend on it (Latchmiepersad, Viandra, "How To Be a Teacher's Pet").

1.   What is the rule for the **hyphen** between "demon" and "possessed"?

_____

2.   Quote an example of **humor**:_____

_____

3.   Quote a **simile that's also a hyperbole**:_____

4.   A.   What can you **infer** about the narrator's grades?_____

        B.   Quote **proof** of your answer:_____

5.   What is the **subject of the imperative sentence**: "Hold the gossip for lunch"?

    _____

6.   In at least 50 words, write your own version of **how to be a teacher's pet**:

_____

_____

_____

    ✓**Now you're getting somewhere. You've interrupted the lesson as frequently as you used to barge into your parents' conversation when—from your vantage point of the back seat on vacation— you'd ask every five minutes "Are we there yet?" Now that you've conquered verbal abuse, you can work on physical tactics. Even if it's just clicking your pen or tapping your pencil, it still can make your teacher have a nervous breakdown. The thing that really gets on teachers' nerves is if you dig through your backpack, but this can't be a silent, polite digging. You must rattle and shuffle and zip the zipper up and down and up and down almost as if the thing had a life of its own. When you click your pen—click, click, click—at a steady pace, that will make them as crazy as sharks on a feeding frenzy.**

    "Are you done yet!" your favorite teacher will boom.

    "No, not quite yet," you'll answer in your good-boy/girl tone, the one that says without saying, "How could you possibly accuse me of any impropriety?"

    Getting into trouble never felt so good (Norred, Brandon, "How To Get on Your Teacher's Nerves").

1.   How has the author used **dialogue** effectively in a "how-to" paper?

_____

_____

2.   A.   Quote three **vivid verbs** from one sentence:_____,_____,_____

        B.   **Rewrite the sentence** in a less effective way:_____

_____

3.   How is the last sentence **ironic**?_____

4.   Quote a **personification**:_____

5.   Why does the author use **dashes** in the second sentence?_____

_____

6.   Write a **humorous dialogue between a teacher and you**. Remember to use quotation marks and proper punctuation and to indent for each new speaker. Each of you must have at least two lines.

_____

_____

_____

_____

    We've all cried at least once in our lives. We've all made a puddle of tears on our pillows because a pet died, our parents are talking about getting a divorce in their marrying-you-was-a-mistake-and-I-can't-stand-you-anymore fights, or we just got in a "victory or death" war with our best friend and made a truce never to talk to each other again. We've all thought that there was no one who has been through what we have, who has felt our pain, who has experienced this knot in the rope of life (Adams, Alyssa, "How To Capture the Sea's Tears").

1.   Quote examples from the excerpt to which a **reader could relate**:

_____

2.   A.   Quote the **hyphenated modifier**:_____

_____

B.   What is the rule for the hyphen between **the last word in a hyphenated modifier and the noun it modifies**?

_____

3.   Quote a **cause and an effect**:_____

4.   A.   Quote a **metaphor**:_____

     B.   Is it **implicit or explicit**?_____

     C.   **How can you tell**?_____

5.   Why does the author put "victory or death" in **quotation marks**?

_____

6.   Write at least a 50-word descriptive paragraph where you appeal to the reader by **describing things we've all done**:

_____

_____

_____

_____

Answer Key

*Accept other answers if supported.
*Answers to writing question will vary.

"How To Play America's Favorite Pastime"

1. "Maybe we can blast one past the pitcher's mound, rocket one over the infielder's glove, or even slam one out of the ballpark."
2. A. "Blast," "rocket," "slam"
   B. Hit, send, knock
3. A. "It's not as simple as counting to five"
   B. A simile compares two "unlike" things; Sammy Sosa is in reality hitting a baseball. The comparison, then, would be between similar actions.
4. A. Infielder's & pitcher's
   B. Both infielders' and the three pitchers' equipment lay in the dugout.
5. While hitting a baseball is not easy, players still hope for the exceptional play.
6. Answers will vary.

"Play Time"

1. A. Most readers can identify with the complaints.
   B. "We go to school seven hours a day, five days a week, for almost forty weeks a year...."
2. A. "All it takes is a little effort, pride, and dignity, and we will be homework-free. We all might want to follow these three steps to help us out some, to give us a little jump start. All we need to know is what to say, when to say it, and how to say it."
   B. They are all noun phrases.
3. "death grips on our pens or pencils"
4. The author is appealing to the various stages of the reader's life by giving a scenario that fits each stage.
5. A. The author thinks that the teacher is a "know-it-all," who gives unnecessary work.
   B. "Mrs. I-Know-Everything...work we have already done before."
6. Answers will vary.

"How To Be a Teacher's Pet"
1. Hyphenated modifier
2. "Unless there's a bomb threat, hurricane, earthquake, tornado, or a roach as big as a Volkswagen crawling by your feet, don't scream in class."

3. "Even when your classmates start acting like chimpanzees, sit quietly and polish your halo."
4. A. We can infer that the narrator's grades are good.
   B. "'Sucking up' and being a hard worker can help and so can having good behavior."
5. Understood "you"
6. Answers will vary.

"How To Get on Your Teacher's Nerves"

1. The author's dialogue serves as a method of elaboration, giving specific details for "what to say" that can get on a teacher's nerves.
2. A. "Rattle," "shuffle," "zip"
   B. You must make noise with the zipper....
3. "Getting into trouble" doesn't usually feel good.
4. "as if the thing had a life of its own"
5. Parenthetical information
6. Answers will vary.

"How To Capture the Sea's Tears"

1. "a pet died, our parents are talking about getting a divorce..., or...we just got into a war with our best friend"
2. A. "marrying-you-was-a-mistake-and-I-can't-stand-you-anymore fights"
   B. A hyphen is not used between the last word in the group and the noun that is being modified.
3. "We've all made a puddle of tears on our pillows because a pet died...."
4. A. "this knot in the rope of life"
   B. Implicit
   C. No "be" verb
5. The author is not using "victory or death" literally and wants to emphasize its figurative usage.
6. Answers will vary.

Dailies

⇒During my younger years as a child, my father would contribute to one thing, the TV. While the family would sit at the table, each biting off our biscuits filled with eggs, cheese, and sausage, with glasses of orange juice with precisely five ice cubes floating in the middle of each, the table would be filled with silence. Any noise in the house my father would make, which came from the fourth room, two doors left from the bathroom. His room.

With the TV cranked loud and the remote next to the fan, my father ignored everyone and everything in the house, except for the TV.

Mom would often bring him supper because he would let the breakfast spoil, but all he did was put it on the brown dresser covered with a flowered pillowcase, next to the report I had wanted him to read, next to the fan, next to the TV remote (Pelt, Gregg, "The TV Remote").

1. Quote an example from the passage that makes the piece especially **poignant** and explain your answer.

    A. Quote:_____

    B. Explanation:_____

2. Quote a **repetition for effect** and explain the effect:

    A. Quote:_____

    B. Effect:_____

3. Quote an example of specific **details for effect** and write a less **effective, more** general **version:**

    A. Specific details:_____

    B. Less effective version:_____

4. Quote a sentence that exemplifies a **comma used for an appositive:**

_____

5.	Quote an example of a sentence with an introductory **phrase:**

_____

6.	Write at least a 100-**word passage with a theme of isolation**. Use **specific details and a "progressive" repetition for effect** (i.e., next to, next to, next to).

_____

_____

_____

_____

_____

⇨As if we don't do enough at school, there's the little thing the teachers lovingly refer to as "homework." I don't see its use. We kids spend eight hours of our day doing what the teachers call "preparing us for the future" and then they bombard us with homework! Parents, though, have it so much easier. They get to be in charge of the moola, you know, the money. Paying the bills and loans and whatever else adults deal with can't begin to compare to the year's worth of work we have every night trying to figure out polynomials.

Mother says, "Don't mess with me today; I had to balance the checkbook."

I think, "Geez! Take some Midol! I've got eighty-eight more problems to do!" (Cunningham, Amber, "Kids vs. Parents").

1.	What specifically is the **contrast** presented in the excerpt?_____

_____

2.	In your opinion, what is the **most effective verb** in the passage?_____

List **five verbs that would have been less effective**:_____,_____,

_____,_____,_____

3.	Why is "preparing us for the future" in **quotation marks**?_____

Dailies

4.   Quote a **context clue** in the passage:_____

5.   Quote a **hyperbole**:_____

6.   Write a 50-word (exactly) humorous **paragraph that gives a context clue for an unfamiliar word.**

_____

_____

_____

⇨The first thing I hope to change in twenty years is my appearance. Now at the age of thirteen I have acne that comes and goes whenever it wants to like Gina on an episode of "Martin." Besides that, I have a horrible habit of sucking my thumb, leaving me with the overbite of overbites. If that's not enough, now--thanks to my mother's I-always-know-best-for-my-baby attitude--I have short hair. Buzzed would be more the word. However, I've decided that when I get to be thirty-three, my appearance will be totally different. The acne will have been blasted away like Martians in a movie, the habit of sucking my thumb will have been voided from my memory, and that overbite will have been braced into a perfect row, shining like stars. And the whole issue of short hair...well, let's just say Mother will have to take a back seat (Curette, Margo, "The Old Me vs. the New Me").

1.   Quote two **similes** the author uses to create her humor:

       A._____

       B._____

2.   Why would "Martin" be in **quotation marks**?_____

3.   Quote an **idiom**:_____

4.   How does the author contrast **her view of her mother** when the author is 13 vs. 33?

_____

5.   Quote the magic **three sentences**:_____

_____

_____

6.   Write at least a **50-word humorous contrast of your appearance now vs. what you perceive it to be twenty or so years from now.**

_____

_____

_____

_____

⇨ LET'S FACE IT--NEITHER TEACHERS NOR STUDENTS HAVE HANDWRITING THAT ANYONE CAN READ. A DOG MIGHT AS WELL HAVE STEPPED INTO A PUDDLE OF INK AND STARTED DOING DONUTS ON OUR PAPERS IN THE EFFORT OF CAPTURING ITS OWN TAIL (KOHLES, BRAD, "ARTIFACTS AND BRATS").

1.   Good writing is supposed to **evoke images for the reader**. How does this very brief excerpt accomplish that?

_____

2.   Why would the author have used "**its own tail**" as opposed to "**their own tails**"?

_____

3.   The author could have garnered laughs from the dog stepping "into the puddle of ink...doing donuts on our papers." What does the author **add to the metaphor**, and **how does this extension elevate the humor?**

    A.   Addition to metaphor:_____

    B.   Effect on humor:_____

4.   What is the **main idea** of the passage?_____

5.   What does the **title suggest the excerpt is about**?_____

6.   Write a passage in which you illustrate **something that two very different groups have in common:**

_____

_____

_____

_____

       ⇒Has your mom ever given you that look--you know, the I-am-serious-if-you-don't-clean-your-room-you're-not-going-anywhere-all-weekend look? Well, I get it all the time. I'll be having a great day, ready to fly out the door to play when she yells, "Jennifer, is your room clean?"

    "Well, uh, you see...I...."

    "Go now!" she interrupts me like a brick wall popping up in my face.

    Stomping away, I get the usual I-hate-my-room-and-my-mom-who-is-getting-on-my-nerves feelings (Kilcrease, Jennifer, "The Look").

1.   What **Smiley-Face trick** does the author primarily use to achieve **her humor?**

_____

2.   Explain the author's use of **paragraphing:**_____

_____

3.   Identify the **conflict** and quote a passage that supports whether it is **internal or external:**
    A.   Conflict:_____

     B.   Quote:_____

4.   How could readers **identify with this passage**?_____

_____

5.   What can you **infer** about the author and what **prediction** can you make?

     A.   Inference:_____

     B.   Prediction:_____

6.   Write a **typical dialogue** between you and your father or mother, **predominantly using one Smiley-Face trick:**

_____

_____

_____

_____

_____

_____

_____

Answer Key

*Accept other answers if supported.

*Answers to writing questions will vary.

"The TV Remote"

1.   A.   * "my father ignored everyone and everything in the house, except for the TV"
       B.   Readers can feel the narrator's pain in being ignored.
2.   A.   "...Next to the report I had wanted him to read, next to the fan, next to the TV remote"
       B.   Not only does the repetition give the reader a vivid sense of setting but also of a progression from the least important to the father ("the report") to the most vital ("the TV remote").
3.   A.   "with glasses of orange juice with precisely five ice cubes floating in the middle of each"
       B.   with glasses of orange juice and ice
4.   "...my father would contribute to one thing, the TV."
5.   * "During my younger years as a child,"
6.   Answers will vary.

"Kids vs. Parents"

1.   The amount of work kids have vs. that of adults
2.   "bombard"
       *give, assign, dole out, dish out, throw at
3.   Obviously the author disagrees with the teachers' notions of "preparing us for the future"; therefore, she uses quotation marks to set off her sarcasm.
4.   "you know, the money"
5.   "the year's worth of work we have every night"
6.   Answers will vary.

"The Old Me vs. the New Me"

1.   A.   "like Gina on an episode of 'Martin'"
       B.   "that overbite will have been braced into a perfect row, shining like stars"
2.   Title of TV show
3.   "take a back seat"
4.   When the author is thirteen, her mother has the "I-always-know-best-for-my-baby attitude" whereas when the author reaches thirty-three she believes that her mother "will have to take a back seat."
5.   "The acne will have been blasted away like Martians in a movie, the habit of sucking

my thumb will have been voided from my memory, and that overbite will have been braced into a perfect row, shining like stars."
6.   Answers will vary.

"Artifacts and Brats"

1.   We can picture the type of marks made by the dog.
2.   "Its own tail" must agree with its singular antecedent, "a dog." "Their own tails" is plural and would have to have "dogs" as its antecedent.
3.   A.   "in the effort of capturing its own tail"
      B.   The ink and the donuts are funny, but the addition of the fruitless effort of "capturing its own tail" adds even more humor to the piece.
4.   Both teachers and students are guilty of having illegible handwriting.
5.   Old people vs. young people
6.   Answers will vary.

"The Look"

1.   Hyphenated modifiers
2.   New paragraph for each new speaker in dialogue
3.   A.   Mom's desire for a clean room and daughter's desire to go out
      B.   "I-hate-my-room-and-my-mom-who-is-getting-on-my-nerves"--external
4.   Most readers have had a similar experience with their mothers.
5.   A.   *Her room is usually messy.
      B.   *She will clean up her room.
6.   Answers will vary.

Name:_____Class:_____Date:_____

Dailies

       The beach is full of people and laughter. Children and their shovels meet at the same place every Saturday, scooping the same sand and rebuilding the same castle that took them hours to make and a second to be washed away by the roaring waters. The waves make the same fresh, crisp sound every time I step into the water as if they are greeting me, waiting for my presence. No clouds appear in the sky, for they are afraid and hide behind the bleeding yellow-and-red horizon. Dogs dance on tiptoes to please their masters and keep wide, white grins as they leap off the ground and receive what they dream of and look forward to every sunny Saturday afternoon--the frisbee (Curette, Kristen, "The Beach").

1.   What could be said to be **ironic** in the piece?_____

2.   What **repetition for effect** does the author use?_____

3.   Quote examples of the following **comma rules:**

      A.   **Coordinate adjective**:_____

      B.   **Compound sentence** using "for" instead of "and" or "but":

_____

      C.   An **appositive** that the author chose to punctuate with a **dash** rather than a comma:_____

4.   Quote an example of a **personification**:_____

5.   Quote another example of **figurative language** and explain its **type**:

A.   **Quote**:_____

B.   **Type**:_____

6.   The author uses **vivid imagery** to describe a beach scene. Using **imagery and figurative language, describe a place you like to go. (At least 50 words)**

_____

_____

_____

_____

_____

Storms sweep over
the deep blue sea
no more running, sloshing, or collecting shells
Fun has been replaced
Waves form waiting
to erase what's left
on the beach
Clouds move in
dark ones at that
and a young girl stands
dripping in her flowered suit
hair tied up
She's motionless
with only four words
planted on her lips
"Can I keep him?"
And the bird lies in her arms
as the storms sweep over
(Pruett, Amanda, "The Bird").

1.   What phrase does the author use to make her poem come **full circle**?

_____

2.   Quote an example of **personification**:_____

3. Authors can reveal **characterization** by describing a character's appearance, inner thoughts and feelings, what others say, environment, actions, and speech. Name two that you think the **author relied on most** and quote the phrases to **support your answer:**

A. Type:_____Quote:_____

B. Type:_____Quote:_____

4. A.   What can you **infer** about the girl?_____

    B.   Give **evidence**:_____

5. Explain two **conflicts** in the poem:_____&

    _____

6. **Write a poem** of at least ten lines, using the words "storms," "girl," "bird," "shells," and "erase." Use at least **one method of characterization** and **one example of figurative language.**

flowered dress, red
brown hair
blue eyes
the girl stood on the beach
like a lone wolf separated
from the rest of the pack
The day was supposed
to be filled with volleyball
mountainous sand castles
and scuba diving but that
was before the cloudless sky
turned night-black as a
symbol signifying lightning and thunder
and rain that were sure to come
Before the partying teenagers
ran to the shelter of their cars
not watching where they
were going and stomping
the defenseless, injured seagull
Before the waves started roaring
and the wind started howling
and the lone girl was the only
one to stop to help the seagull

(Keul, Ryan, "The Lone Girl")

1. A. What is unusual about the author's **placement of the adjective "red"**?
_____

    B. What is unusual about the **first three lines**?_____

_____

2. Why does the author use **"were"** instead of **"was"** in the line **"symbol of lightning, thunder, and rain that were sure to come"**?_____

_____

3. Quote a **cause and an effect**:_____

4. Quote an example of **figurative language** and tell its **type:**

A.   **Quote:**_____B.   **Type:**_____

5.   What is a **symbol** in the poem and of what is it symbolic?

A.   **Symbol:**_____B.   **Symbolism:**_____

6.   **Write at least 50 words (poem or vignette) based on a contrast.** Use the line "but that was before...."

_____

_____

_____

_____

_____

just another day at the
beach
children building
sand castles
from Styrofoam cups
one child splashing
while the other
whines
that sand got in
his eyes
but one child
undoubtedly
stands out from the rest
her one-piece multi-flowered
swimsuit
is silhouetted against the waves
crashing at her feet
a dark pink bow hangs
crooked

in her hair
she holds a small, injured
seagull in her arms
a rain cloud moves in
as her mother flashes the
camera
and the day ends
just another day at the beach

(Fitzwater, Megan, "Just Another Day at the Beach")

1.   How is it **ironic** that the author begins, ends, and titles the poem with "just another day at the beach"?_____

2.   A.   In what **tense** is this poem written?_____

     B.   Give three **examples** as proof:_____,_____,_____

3.   Quote two specific **details for effect:**

A._____B._____

4.   What is the rule for the use of the **hyphens**?_____

5.   What is the rule for the **comma** after "small"?_____

6.   Exchange with a partner **five words for things that could be found outside**. Write a **poem of at least ten lines** using the words, specific details for effect, and a hyphenated adjective.

Serene clouds paint the sky as though an artist is gently stroking at a blue canvas. The sea gleams and glitters like sugar crystals on blueberries. But as soon as the sun has time to shine on worriless children, merely playing in the sand, a darker force takes over, transforming the feather clouds into harsh, black monster clouds, as if hell has come from the heavens, crashing the gentle waves, turning laughter into panic.

The skies turn their focus on a lone seagull as it lies on the sandy beach, torn away from its flock. All the children run away, too busy for the lost seagull, except for the girl, her beauty apparent not only in the colorful flowers she wears but in her deep blue eyes, a reflection of the water before the storm takes over. She now carries the bird gently, hoping that maybe tomorrow will be filled with feathers and sugar crystals on blueberries once again (Shaver, Rachel, "Sugar Crystals on Blueberries").

1.   Quote examples of the following **figurative language devices**:

A.   **Implicit metaphor**:_____

B.   **Simile**:_____

C.   **Personification**:_____

2.   The last sentence has been combined using a **participial phrase** (an "-ing" word group used as an adjective). The original sentences could have been the following: "She now carries the bird gently. She hopes that maybe tomorrow will be filled...." Rewrite the sentences, combining them, and **using two methods** besides a participial phrase:

A._____

B._____

3.   Explain two **conflicts** in the poem:_____&

_____

4.   What could be considered **ironic** in the poem?_____

5. What two **details** do you know about the children?

_____&_____

6. **Write a 25-word (exactly) sentence** about an *impending storm.*

_____

_____

_____

Answer Key

*Accept other answers if supported.
*Answers to writing questions will vary.

"The Beach"

1. It's rather ironic that it takes "hours" to make a sand castle and only a "second" to destroy it.
2. "Same"
3. A. "fresh, crisp sound"; "wide, white grin"
   B. "No clouds appear in the sky, for they are afraid and hide behind the bleeding yellow-and-red horizon."
   C. "...what they dream of and look forward to every Saturday afternoon--the frisbee."
4. "Dogs dance on tiptoes to please their masters" or "The waves...as if they are greeting me..."
5. A. "No clouds appear in the sky, for they are afraid and hide...." or "bleeding yellow-and-red horizon"
   B. Personification
6. Answers will vary.

"The Bird"

1. "storms sweep over"
2. "Waves form waiting / to erase what's left / on the beach"
3. A. Environment: "Storms sweep over / the deep blue sea"
   B. Actions: "She's motionless.../And the bird lies in her arms"
4. A. We can infer that she cares about animals.
   B. "Can I keep him?"
5. The storm vs. having fun; nature's fury vs. its gentleness
6. Answers will vary.

"The Lone Girl"

1. A. The author places the adjective **after** the noun it modifies rather than before.
   B. It is unusual for three lines of descriptive phrases to be placed before the subject.
2. The verb "were" is used to agree with the plural subjects "lightning and thunder/and rain."

3. "Before the partying teenagers/ran to the shelter of their cars/not watching where they/were going and stomping/the defenseless, injured seagull"
4. A. "the girl stood on the beach/like a lone wolf"
   B. Simile
5. A. "volleyball/mountainous sand castles/and scuba diving"
   B. Fun
6. Answers will vary.

"Just Another Day at the Beach"

1. We wouldn't think that "just another day at the beach" involves injury of any kind and "rescue" by a child.
2. A. Present tense
   B. * "Building," "splashing," "whines," "stands," "is silhouetted," "holds"
3. A. "children building/ sand castles / from Styrofoam cups"
   B. * "but one child / undoubtedly / stands out from the rest / her one-piece multi-flowered / swimsuit/ is silhouetted against the waves"
4. Hyphenated modifiers
5. Coordinate adjective
6. Answers will vary.

"Sugar Crystals on Blueberries"

1. A. "feather clouds"
   B. "The sea gleams and glitters like sugar crystals on blueberries"
   C. "Serene clouds paint the sky"
2. A. * She now carries the bird and hopes that....
   B. *As she carries the bird, she hopes that....
3. Sun and peaceful clouds vs. Storm and black clouds; children who ignore the seagull vs. the girl who carries it
4. It's ironic that "as soon as the sun has time to shine on worriless children," that "a darker force takes over." We would think that the sun would reflect the children's mood, rather than be a part of destroying it.
5. "worriless" & "all the children run away, too busy for the lost seagull"
6. Answers will vary.

Dailies

A man pulls up
to a grocery store
walks inside
smirk on his face
Rolex on his wrist
corruption in his head
buys his groceries
using food stamps
stealing from the poor
to make the wealthy
wealthier
the exact opposite
of Robin Hood
He has no shame
no regret or remorse
He conducts his
daily life in a
shadow of lies
leaving the needy
to suffer and starve
in the slums
(Burnham, Brian, "Corruption").

1.   The author describes the man using a **magic three**. Quote it:

_____,_____,_____

2.   A.   What is the **allusion** that the author uses?_____

      B.   How does the author **"alter" the allusion**?_____

Dailies

3.   A.   Explain the author's use of **capitalization** of line beginnings:

_____

        B.   Why is "Rolex" **capitalized**?_____

4.   What **context clue** does the author give for the word "remorse"?_____

5.   What is the **theme** of the poem?_____

6.   Write at least a 15-line poem using the beginning lines "A man/woman pulls up to a _____." Use a **magic three** to describe the man/woman, at least one example of **figurative language** ("shadow of lies"), and one **allusion.**

        Anaconda (n): 1. A child-eating, stalking monster that allows no escape. It creeps up when no one sees it coming until it's too late. 2. A test.

        Deceased (adj.): The way students are while in school, completely dead and silent, completely unaware of their surroundings even when a teacher is yelling in their faces.

        Furor (n): "Shut up! Do your work! Sit down!" The loud outburst that occurs unexpectedly when students are quiet, concentrating, and doing their work.

        Nap (n): 1. The daily activity students do in first period. 2. What kids never did when they were little so they make up for it in high school. (Roeschen, Michael and Jose Campos, "Survival Guide").

Dailies

1.   Quote an example of the following **comma rules:**

      A.   **Series:**_____

      B.   **Coordinate adjective**:_____

      C.   **Interrupter**:_____

2.   Explain the reason for the **hyphen** in "child-eating":_____

3.   Quote an example of **humor:**_____

4.   The authors have used an **analogy** by describing a test as an anaconda. List at least **two characteristics** that the two have in common.

      _____&_____

5.   Are these "definitions" based on **fact or opinion?**_____

      Explain:_____

6.   Choose a common noun or adjective and write your **own version of the definition of the word:**

      _____

      _____

      _____

      Boys (n): 1. Of the male gender who always seem to leave the toilet seat up. 2. The people who never seem to do anything right and are always getting into trouble. 3. Immature creatures. 4. The part of the population that can be very easily tricked by a pretty face. 5. TV-remote-control lovers.

      Computer (n): 1. Machine used for e-mailing the cyber guy that girls are so in love with who has e-mailed them once but they've returned the message sixteen times. 2. Technological advance that allows students to type papers that need to be twenty pages or more for that teacher who has more dust on him/her than dinosaurs at a museum.

Opera (n): 1. Place where obese people sing music no one understands. 2. So-called music that makes human beings fall asleep.

(Hernandez, Alma and Julia Leal, "Survival Guide Dictionary for Everyday Kids").

1. A. From whose **point of view** are these entries written--a boy's or a girl's?_____

    B. Quote two examples of **proof:**_____&

    _____

2. Quote an example of a **hyperbole:**_____

3. Quote your favorite example of **humor:**_____

4. A. In the **source/footnote**, explain why the first author's name is inverted but the second author's is not:

    _____

    B. Also in the source/footnote, explain the rule for **capitalizing the title:**

    _____

5. Explain two **stereotypes** on which the authors play:

    _____&_____

6. Write your own **definition of the opposite sex**. Make sure you have at least **three parts to it and use humor:**

    _____

    _____

    _____

I have a passion for bagpipes
smile a lot
and think humming birds are beautiful
I have braces and straight hair
my mom's laugh
my dad's brown eyes
which I used to wish would
turn emerald-green overnight
People say I'm daring
but I hate roller coasters
But I still smile a lot
I still long for green eyes
and I won't always have braces
and I might get too old and tired
to appreciate hummingbirds anymore

✂

I have a dancer's posture
dimples I borrowed from my grandmother and
I lie sometimes for no reason
I blush when I'm nervous
I'm bad at pretending to like someone
I can't sing but I dream of
becoming a famous rock star
I write

I used to breathe in love
and pick sunflowers in a napkin
But I still can't sing
and I'll probably always catch
myself lying just because
and my posture
won't stay strong forever

and I may not always write
But maybe I'll start
picking sunflowers
in a napkin once again
(Shaver, Rachel, "Sunflowers").

1.   Explain how the author has **constructed** this poem:

_____

2.   List three aspects of the **author's appearance**:

_____,_____,_____

3.   A.   What could the author have meant as a **symbol**?_____

        B.   Of what is it a **symbol**?_____

4.   Since we can't "breathe in love," what type of **figurative language** would this
        exemplify and why?

        A.   Type:_____ B.   Reason:_____

5.   What is the **contrast** presented in the poem?_____

_____

6.   Write at least a **25-line poem about yourself**. Include your passions, what you are
        versus what you wish to be. Paint a vivid picture of yourself.

The quarterbacks were One-Armed Willie and Gator. We called Tony "One-Armed Willie" because of the freak accident he had involving his little brother and a lawnmower. Must I go on? You would think that he'd be immobilized, but he's not. He's the most sure-shooting, best darn thrower you ever did see.

We call Joe "Gator" because he squashes the defense he's against with one whiplash motion. Big Bear has always told us to nail the opponents' you-know-what's into the dirt. But Gator's always getting under Big Bear's skin and loving every minute of it because, as is Gator's nature, he's always taking his sweet time ending the quarter with his infamous gator-like play. Big Bear, as usual and as my dad always says, is sweating bullets over the outcome. He needn't have worried. We all knew.

The rest of the team was simple. Not too many questions were asked for fear of Big Bear and Mr. Death. Don't ask. Gator and One-Armed Willie

 were always the captains for the constant fighting between the two teams. If there had been an actual election of captains, there would have been no teams.

Once the captains were established, they picked us off one by one, like the prey of blood-sucking mosquitoes. I was always chosen first because of one simple fact--the football was mine. We were playing with my brand-new NCAA football that I had gotten for Christmas.

The game would start with a throw-off, after the combatants had taken sides. See, the only thing I objected to was playing on this street because Old Man River lived exactly in the middle of the end zones. Anything that goes in his yard doesn't come out (Student Writer, "Old Man River").

1.   Quote two **conflicts** in the excerpt:

A._____

B._____

Dailies

2.   Explain the following **grammar rules:**

A.   **Hyphen** between "One-Armed":_____

B.   **Dashes** after "skin" and before "because":_____

3.   How does the **excerpt's ending** grab the **reader's attention**?_____

_____

4.   Quote an **example** of the following:

A.   **Simile**:_____

B.   **Humor:**_____

5.   A.   From what **point of view** is the excerpt written (i.e., first person, third person,
             omniscient)?_____

B.   **Proof:**_____

6.   Write at least a **50-word beginning to a short story** involving two characters like
       "One-Armed Willie" and "Gator."

_____

_____

_____

_____

_____

_____

_____

_____

_____

Answer Key

*Accept other answers if supported.
*Answers to writing questions will vary.

"Corruption"

1. "smirk on his face," "Rolex on his wrist," "corruption in his head"
2. A. Robin Hood
    B. "stealing from the poor / to make the wealthy / wealthier"
3. A. The author's capitalization at the beginning of some lines indicates the beginning of sentences.
    B. Brand name
4. "regret"
5. Some people practice "corruption" with no remorse.
6. Answers will vary.

"Survival Guide"

1. A. "quiet, concentrating, and doing their work"
    B. "child-eating, stalking monster"
    C. "...completely dead and silent"
2. Hyphenated modifier
3. *"What kids never did when they were little so they make up for it in high school"
4. They are dreaded and creep up on you unexpectedly.
5. Opinion--They are the authors' humorous versions of the dictionary entries.
6. Answers will vary.

"Survival Guide for Everyday Kids"

1. A. Girl's
    B. Boys--"The people who never seem to do anything right and are always getting into trouble"
        Computer--"Machine used for e-mailing the cyber guy that girls are so in love with...."
2. "teacher who has more dust on him/her than dinosaurs at a museum"
3. *"place where obese people sing music no one understands"
4. A. The rule for footnoting authors is to invert the first author's name but not the others.
    B. Capitalize first, last, and all important words.
5. *Boys are "immature" and opera singers are "obese."

6.   Answers will vary.

"Sunflowers"

1.   The author states what she is like--her characteristics--what she is and what she is not. She also predicts what she might be like in the future in relation to her present traits.
2.   * "I have braces and straight hair," "my dad's brown eyes," "I have a dancer's posture"
3.   A.   Picking sunflowers
       B.   Childhood activity
4.   A.   Metaphor
       B.   "Love" is being compared to something we can "breathe in," easily and naturally such as air.
5.   * The narrator now versus the narrator in the future or her positive traits versus her negative traits
6.   Answers will vary.

"Old Man River"

1.   A.   * "But Gator's always getting under Big Bear's skin...because, as is Gator's nature, he's always taking his sweet time ending the quarter with his infamous gator-like play."
       B.   "See, the only thing I objected to was playing on this street because Old Man River....Anything that goes in his yard doesn't come out."
2.   A.   Hyphenated modifier
       B.   Parenthetical information
3.   We, as readers, want to know more about this "Old Man River."
4.   A.   "gator-like play"
       B.   "I was always chosen first because of one simple fact—the football was mine."
5.   A.   First person
       B.   "We" and "I"
6.   Answers will vary.

Name:_____ Class:_____ Date:_____

Dailies

★ We've all tried to figure out our parents. Just when we thought we had our moms pegged, they'd ground us for feeding FooFoo, our poor, overfed kitty, too many cat cakes--or whatever they're called. Then our dads would go off the wall because their sacred TV remotes were moved to the other side of their equally sacred couches. We all know that if our parents are like most parents, they are different in their appearances and lifestyles, but similar in at least a few ways (Whitaker, Jared, "Moms and Dads").

1. A. For what **mode of writing** is this an **introduction** (e.g., narrative, persuasive, comparison/contrast, descriptive, how-to)?

   _____

   B. Quote **proof:**_____

2. A. From what **point of view** is the piece written (i.e., first, third, etc,)?

   B. Quote **proof:**_____

3. Quote an **attention-getter** that the author uses:_____

4. Quote examples of the following **comma rules:**

   A. **Coordinate adjective**:_____

   B. **Appositive:**_____

5. If this essay would result in a **five-paragraph paper**, list what you think the **subject** of each of the five paragraphs would be:

A._____ B._____ C._____

D._____ E._____

6.   Write an **introduction** of your own for this **same mode of writing**, using a **subject of your own choice**. Remember to begin with an attention-getter and to conclude with a thesis statement that contains the three aspects you will cover.

_____

_____

_____

_____

_____

★Another difference between the two, besides their appearance, is their personality. My dad knows every play, pitch, and position in baseball. He's been glued to every double steal, fast ball, and left-field play in the history of the game. He's good in math--he's no Albert Einstein--but he'll pass. At least he knows when to invert and multiply. Not only that, my dad is an outgoing person. He could walk up to anyone and make friends. Like Will Rogers, my dad would say that "I never met a man I didn't like." As for Mom, she's a quiet-find-a-corner-and-just-stay-there-until-someone-starts-talking-to-her sort of person. She has her books and her thoughts to keep her company. As for sports, Mom doesn't give a whirlwind-hoop-slammin'-jumping-jack thing about baseball. Talk about someone who needs someone to elucidate or explain math to her. She doesn't know a subtrahend from a dividend and doesn't care to learn. Personalities of my parents--they are worlds apart (Free, Kayla, "Mom vs. Dad").

1.   This is the **second paragraph of a comparison/contrast paper**. Quote the transition word, the topic of the first paragraph, and the topic of this paragraph:

A.   Transition:_____B. First Paragraph:_____

C.   Second Paragraph:_____

2.   This paragraph is structured in such a way as to give the reader three points about "Dad" and then, conversely, the same three points about "Mom." **List the three points or aspects (subcategories) below:**

_____,_____,_____

3.   The author uses a **famous quote as support**. Cite the quote and explain how it adds to the author's point:

A.   Quote:_____

B.   Explanation:_____

4.   Cite an **unfamiliar or difficult word** that the author uses and give its **context clue:**

A.   Unfamiliar word:_____B.   Clue:_____

5.   Quote **examples** of the following:

A.   **Hyperbole:**_____

B.   **Humor:**_____

C.   **Assonance**:_____

6.   This paragraph is based on the difference between the author's mom and dad. **Write the first body paragraph for an essay that ties in with the introduction that you wrote for the first "Daily" in this section.** Remember that the topic sentence must contain the key statement of the paragraph followed by at least three subcategories and their supports.

_____

_____

_____

_____

_____

_____

_____

_____

_____

_____

★Hey, losers, want a date? Then listen to this advice. You've been moaning and groaning about not having a date--we've all heard it a million times before. Poor you, Friday everyone's going to some dance while you're stuck at home, sitting on the coach, eating grapes, watching "Cops." Boys, do you want to get out and get a girl? We guys are supposed to be the bold ones--right-- the "men." But yet some of us guys are not "man" enough to ask a girl if she can go out with us this Friday. Instead, we pass a note to Sally Sue, who passes it to Donna, who passes it to the "love of our life." Our dream woman unfolds the letter and reads in our almost illegible handwriting: "Will you go out with me to the dance this Friday? Circle 'Yes' or 'No.'" Step up to the plate, fellows. We can be women-magnets if we remember three tricks of the trade: forget shyness, put ourselves in the woman's situation, and ... (Pelt, Gregg, "Step Up to the Plate").

1. Quote the **thesis sentence** and fill in the **third "how-to" step of your own:**

_____

_____

2. Quote three examples of **commas used for direct address:**

A._____ B._____ C._____

3. Quote **examples** of the following:

A. **Hyperbole:**_____

B. **Assonance:**_____

4. A. Explain why "Cops" is in **quotation marks:**_____

   B. Give another **example of this same rule:**_____

Dailies

5. Explain why the **quote within a quote** is used for "_Yes_" or "_No_":_____

_____

6. **Write a body paragraph for a how-to essay** that uses the **third aspect** (the one you supplied) as its topic. Remember to have a topic sentence, complete with transition word and key idea, followed by at least three subcategories and supports.

_____

_____

_____

_____

_____

_____

_____

_____

★Billy wasn't really that bad of a kid. Sure, you can ask any teacher in the entire hall exactly how long his discipline report is (last time I heard it was two pages with a 10-point font). It is even rumored that Billy actually started D-Hall at our school (the first elementary to have it) although Jenkins, a goofy, nerdy fifth grader, claims he did for hacking into Mrs. Hybrid's computer and changing his grade a single point up (72 to 73). I think Jenkins is criminally insane for not changing it to an "A," but that's just me. In fact, Mrs. Hybrid can and must type faster now so that Jenkins will not see her password. Back to Billy, though. Although he supposedly started D-Hall and has the longest discipline report of all, he was just another striped-shirt, short-pants kid. Billy was the one that actually led everyone to the big "crime" of the elementary school (Burnside, Ben, "Green-Draped Problems").

1. How does this **"introduction"** to a narrative get the **reader's attention?**

_____

2. Why is the grade of an "A" put in **quotation marks**?_____

_____

3.   Quote examples of the following **comma rules:**

    A.   **Coordinate adjective**:_____

    B.   **Appositive**:_____

    C.   **Introductory word**:_____

    D.   **Interrupter**:_____

4.   A.   What is the predominant **method of characterization** that the author has used to describe Billy (i.e., appearance, inner thoughts and feelings, what others say, actions, speech, environment)?

_____

    B.   Quote **proof:**_____

5.   **Predict** what the **conflict** of the narrative will be and explain your answer:

A.   Prediction:_____

B.   Explanation:_____

6.   **In at least 100 words write the next episode of the narrative.**

_____

_____

_____

_____

_____

_____

_____

_____

_____

★It won't end. It will never end. The hands on the clock will keep ticking away, the teachers with bad breath will keep chitchatting about proportions and decimals, the homework will keep building and building, higher and higher, never stopping. I thought it would be different, simple, relaxing, unexplainable. No, the word I'm looking for now is boring. There are no friends to talk to or pass notes to, no doodling little Marvie the Martians on each other's papers, no more funny faces to giggle at. My last year here in junior high and I can't share any classes with any of my friends, especially Tommy Deekins. That guy had stolen my heart from the first day we met, but I have never gotten the courage to tell him how I feel about him. Okay, let's not get into that right now.

It's been thirty-seven minutes and forty-three seconds since I have been in this room listening to this teacher blabbering on and on about taking away negative three and then adding that to nineteen to get an answer of negative sixteen. Oh wow! Like this will pop up when I'm busy writing my next best-selling novel, <u>Oklahoma Runaway.</u>

"Daisy! Are you going to answer problem twenty-eight or not? We have been waiting for three minutes for your answer and explanation," old Mrs. B. sounding again like a knight slaying the dragons that captured the princess.

"Oh, am I bad? I didn't do that one." To tell you the truth, I didn't do any of my homework last night, I thought to myself.

"Fine, do twenty-nine for us." This woman is unrelenting.

"Sorry, no can do. Don't have that one either."

"So let's just say you didn't do any of last night's homework, right?" Her eyes were beating me into the ground. I never liked teachers staring at me like that. Too frightening for me.

"Uh, yeah, I guess you can say that."

"You're zapped for next Wednesday."

"Zapped! Wednesday? This can't happen. I have a basketball game that day. It's the championship game, and the team's counting on me to be there. You can't do this to me!" If only I had said that to myself--instead of aloud.

The bell had rung, and I entered the halls of doom. No one can think straight with all these rugrats pushing and shoving one another or just standing in the middle of the hall as if their feet are glued to the ground (Stoerner, Brianne, "More Than Friends").

1. Quote a sentence that is an example of a **contrast** of the "real" vs. the "imagined":

_____

2. Cite three examples of **irregular verbs** (i.e., verbs that do not form their past tenses using "-ed") and give the **present, past, and past participle forms** (i.e., form used with a helping verb--have, had, etc.).

A. Present:_____Past:_____PP:_____

B. Present:_____Past:_____ PP:_____

C. Present:_____Past:_____PP:_____

3. A. Explain the reason for **underlining** <u>Oklahoma Runaway</u>:

_____

B. Give **another example** of this rule:_____

4. Explain how this "introduction" to a narrative is an **expanded moment**:

_____

_____

5. A. Explain why "junior high" is not **capitalized**:_____

_____

B. Write an original sentence where "junior high" would be **capitalized**:

_____

6.   You have two choices. Write the **next 50 words of the present narrative** or **start a narrative of your own** with the lines "It won't end. It will never end."

_____

_____

_____

_____

_____

_____

Answer Key

*Accept other answers if supported.
*Answers to writing questions will vary.

"Moms and Dads"
1. A. Comparison/contrast
    B. "...they are different in their appearances and lifestyles, but similar in at least a few ways"
2. A. First person
    B. "We," "our," "us"
3. "Just when we thought we had our moms pegged, they'd ground us for feeding Foo Foo"
4. A. "poor, overfed Kitty"
    B. "Foo Foo, our poor, overfed Kitty, "
5. A. Introduction
    B. *Differences in parents' appearances
    C. *Differences in parents' lifestyles
    D. Similarities
    E. Conclusion
6. Answers will vary.

"Mom v s. Dad"
1. A. Another
    B. Appearance
    C. Personality
2. Sports, math, relationship to others
3. A. " 'I never met a man I didn't like.' "
    B. The author compares her father to Will Rogers in that both have "never met a stranger." Both are friendly and outgoing.
4. A. Elucidate
    B. Explain
5. A. "He's been glued to every double steal, fast ball, and left-field play in the history of baseball."
    B. "At least he knows when to invert and multiply."
    C. "Subtrahend from a dividend"
6. Answers will vary.

"Step Up to the Plate"
1. *"We can be women-magnets if we remember three tricks of the trade: forget shyness, put ourselves in the woman's situation, and ..." (Answers for the third aspect will vary.)
2. A. "Hey, losers,"

        B.   "Boys,"
        C.   "Step up to the plate, fellows"
3.   A.   "We've all heard it a million times"
        B.   "moaning and groaning"
4.   A.   Title of a TV show
        B.   "Friends"
5.   Quotation marks are already used to enclose what is written on the note; therefore, words referred to as words within the note must be enclosed in single quotation marks.
6.   Answers will vary.

"Green-Draped Problems"

1.   It uses humor and specific details that surprise the reader.
2.   Grades are enclosed in quotation marks to highlight or emphasize them, just as words referred to as words.
3.   A.   "goofy, nerdy fifth grader"
        B.   "Jenkins, a goofy, nerdy fifth grader,"
        C.   "Sure,"
        D.   "Back to Billy, though."
4.   A.   What others say or actions
        B.   "You can ask any teacher in the hall exactly how long his discipline report is"
5.   A.   "The big 'crime' of the elementary"
        B.   Billy's "crimes" have escalated, and we can predict that soon he will pull off the biggest caper of all.
6.   Answers will vary.

"More Than Friends"

1.   "It's been thirty-seven minutes and forty-three seconds since I have been in this room listening to this teacher blabbering on and on [real]....Like this will pop us when I'm busy writing my next best-selling novel [imagined]...."
2.   A.   Build, built, built
        B.   Steal, stole, stolen
        C.   Tell, told, told
3.   A.   Titles of books are underlined.
        B.   *<u>Dandelion Wine</u>
4.   The author "expands the moment" in math class, adding her thoughts, details about conversation, etc.--rather than simply telling the reader that she was zapped.
5.   A.   It's not a specific "junior high."
        B.   I go to Gentry Junior High.
6.   Answers will vary.

Dailies

✎My hands, I've never known what to do with them. Mama always said to put them in my pockets or fold them in my lap or hold my purse in front of me--all lady-like--with both hands. But Mr. Avedon he said for me to just look natural and I ain't got no pockets and they got me astandin' and they done took my purse away so it's like my hands are birds or something. I can feel they want to fly, lift right on up over my shoulders, over my head, lift right on out of this place. But I'm gonna try to keep 'em steady, real quiet like I wait when Henry passes my room at night, real quiet so he'll fly right over my shoulders and my head and right on out of the house. I'm going to try to keep 'em steady with this here man paying for my services and all.

I told him right off that I weren't no model and I didn't want no picture taking--didn't have no one to give no picture to anyways-- but he said I'm a fine model and besides I'd get me fifty dollars. I ain't really sure how much fifty dollars are or what I'd buy with a fifty dollars. Maybe Ethel'll let me get one of them doughnuts she's always eatin'. I seen where she gets 'em that time I tripped and blacked my eye up good and broke them ribs. I don't remember falling over nothing. Henry just laughed and told me to shut up, old fool. And I seen Ethel licking the chocolate frosting off and then sticking that big fat old tongue of hers inside and scooping out the filling. Looks like whipped clouds, that filling. I'd like to take my hands and let them fly through them clouds and my tongue could settle on that chocolate and I'm getting tired of astandin' up here now and my hands are aching for me to let them loose.

If Mama were only here she'd know what to do. I could push my hands in my pockets where they'd be safe and Mama'd let me set down and rest and she'd pat my lap-hands and she'd go get my purse and I could hold it and find my comb and I don't remember what else Ethel done put in there, but if Mama was here we'd have our tongues out licking away on that chocolate and our hands dipping deep into them doughnut clouds and I wouldn't give Ethel none and I'd ask Mr. Avedon if he could take Henry away and it's my hands.

I've never known what to do with them but I'll try to keep 'em steady. I'll try, really I will (Teacher Model. "My Hands").

1.   The narrator's language is true to her upbringing, to herself. Quote three examples of **nonstandard grammar:**

A.   **Double negative**:_____

B.   **Incorrect verb usages (Hint: 3)**:_____

C.   **Noun followed by a repetitive pronoun** (e.g., My mother she):_____

D.   **"Them" used as an adjective** (instead of correctly as a pronoun):

`_____

E.   **Subjunctive verb error** (e.g., If I was here--incorrect-- vs. If I were here--correct):

_____

2.   The narrator makes an **allusion** to Mr. Avedon, a famous photographer. What can you **infer** that the narrator is doing in the passage?

A._____   B. **Clues**:_____

3.   What can you **infer** about Henry and Ethel?

A._____

B.   **Clues:**_____

4.   Quote two **magic 3's:**

A._____,_____,_____

B._____,_____,_____

5.   A.   Look up the word **"poignant"** and write its definition:_____

_____

B. Quote three examples of something **poignant** from the passage:

1._____

2._____

3._____

6. This passage was inspired by the author's **viewing of a picture**. Using a picture as your inspiration, **write a passage revealing the character of one person in the picture.** You may choose to use inner thoughts and feelings, environment, speech, appearance, what others say, and/or actions.

_____

_____

_____

_____

_____

_____

_____

_____

✏See, at first I couldn't bring myself to lie. I had never really lied about anything except to tell Annie, no, she didn't look fat in her new poodle skirt, the circular one that stood out way more than it was supposed to, due to her fat hips, or to assure her brother Hank he could still get into Heaven even if he had killed old man Bower's cat with his new slingshot--one smooth, round stone right between the eyes. Nobody really liked that old alley cat Elmo anyway, and old man Bower probably deserved a little sadness. He dished out enough. What with all those years' worth of Girl Scout cookies he refused to buy and all those times we got shooed out of the ravine, not only was one dead cat all right, maybe one wasn't enough, I'd tell Hank. It's not as if Annie and I peddled Chocolate Mint Wafers every day and it's not as if Hank hadn't given Elmo sufficient warning to shut that dern howling up or pay for it and it's not as if it was old man Bower's personal ravine just because it backed up into his property. And besides if he hadn't always been fiddlin' around out in his shed, sharpening his old tools or cleaning his old paintbrushes or if he hadn't been spying on us out in his back field, raking leaves into piles near as tall as he was, piles like big brown tepees just waiting for a couple Indian braves like us to test 'em out, if he hadn't been fussing around all the time, maybe he'd still be the proud owner of one live cat (Teacher Sample, "The Coronado Bayshore Motel").

1. The rule for **punctuating appositives** is that if the appositive is only one word, a comma is not necessary. **Cite two appositives** from the passage to which the author applies this rule:

    _____ & _____

2. Quote three **specific details** that the narrator uses as reasons for why Bower "deserved a little sadness."

A. _____

B. _____

C. _____

3. A. What is the **tone** of the passage? _____

    B. Quote three examples of **proof:** _____,

    _____, _____

4. Quote the following examples of **figurative language:**

A. **Metaphor:** _____

B. **Simile:** _____

Dailies 5

5. Quote **specific details** about the skirt, cat, and cookies.

A. **Skirt:**_____

B. **Cat:**_____

C. **Cookies**:_____

6. Begin a vignette with the line: "At first I couldn't bring myself to lie." You might want to tell a few "white" lies that you've told and perhaps end the passage with a "real" lie. Use **figurative language and specific details for effect.**

_____

_____

_____

_____

_____

_____

_____

✎Virgil didn't come from our two-story houses with the Sears aluminum siding. His lawn wasn't mowed weekly by a father in Bermuda shorts and trimmed meticulously by a mother in a large-brimmed straw hat like what's-her-name on "Father Knows Best." His yard wasn't filled with matching lawn furniture, clay pots of geraniums, and a charcoal grill for Sunday afternoon hamburgers, but with rusted oil barrels and trash cans and steel piping, the kind used to drain roadways and subdivisions, piping that there on Virgil's lawn was rolled onto its sides or propped up against each other like giant, sprawling tinker-toy structures, toppled, destroyed, and abandoned by kids no longer interested.

And daily we watched the only goats we had ever seen up close-- in someone's yard, that is--poking their heads into the hollowed-out cylinders, looking for food in the mornings or perhaps a pool of rainwater left standing from a night's shower. Or curling up--funny, angular bodies and whiskered faces half in, half out--as refuge from the strong Texas afternoon sun.

We all studied with curiosity the growing number of discarded ovens and refrigerators and pieces of cars--like the cab of a Checker taxi, #99--and parts of buildings torn from their original surroundings that found their way onto Virgil's lawn.

I'll never forget the morning Daddy was driving me to school when he stopped the car, lit his unfiltered Camel, and pointed out the window to yet another addition to the Polks' yard, namely the peacock-blue booth, evidently from some diner. An entire booth with its wall-mounted jukebox and all, just like the booth we'd all pile into at the Nip and Sip, drinking root beer floats, eating cheeseburgers, and feeding an endless supply of nickels and dimes into a machine that looked very much like the one sitting under the hundred-year-old oak in Virgil's yard (Teacher Sample, "Virgil and Room 117").

1.   Quote one clue for the **place of the setting** and at least three clues for the **time:**

A.   **Place**:_____ B.   **Time:**_____

_____,_____

2.   What are the **rules** for the following used in the passage?

A.   **Dashes:**_____

B.   **Hyphen** (e.g., peacock-blue):_____

3.   Quote three examples of **contrast** of the narrator's environment and Virgil's:

A.   Narrator:_____

     Virgil:_____

B.   Narrator:_____

     Virgil:_____

C.   Narrator:_____

       Virgil:_____

4.   If an author has done a good job with description, the reader should be able to **envision the scene**. Draw the picture of Virgil's yard that the author paints--even if you have to use labeled stick figures.

5.   Quote one example of a **singular possessive noun** and one of a **plural possessive noun:**

A.   **Singular Possessive**:_____ B.   **Plural P.**_____

6.   In at least 50 words, **describe a place so well that a reader could literally draw it.** Concentrate on your **use of specific details for effect.**

_____

_____

_____

_____

_____

_____

Dailies

✎I was nineteen when the thing with the doctor happened.

How it happened was that the three of us had all piled into Mama's Le Sabre to take Daddy to Park Place Hospital in Houston, where Daddy had agreed to have tests made to see if maybe Dr. Dan was wrong, where perhaps Daddy would learn that he had some sort of temporary malfunction of his nerves like he got, say, whenever his mother would come at Christmas and wouldn't leave till March.

Or maybe like the time Uncle Fred tried for one whole year to teach me "The Bells Are Ringing" on Grandma Wilson's melodeon in our front room. Of course, we never realized how we might be wearing out our musical welcome, how we might be getting on Daddy's nerves, until mid-lesson--my last lesson, I might add--with me hovered over the keyboard, pumping away at the pedals, and Uncle Fred in the straight-back needlepoint chair drawn up beside me, Fred bent over me so as to redirect my fingers at every mistake, and, believe me, plenty of redirecting was going on.

Then without precedence Daddy appeared, scooted in beside me on the velvet bench, positioned his hands over mine in such a way that it became clear he wanted mine to drop aside for a moment, and proceeded to play not only the, by then, infamous litany of ringing bells but everything from "Five Foot Two, Eyes of Blue" to Rachmaninoff's "Prelude in C-Sharp Minor." He then lit one of his unfiltered Camels, closed the keyboard, stood up, and walked down the hall to the study.

And you know what, I could've smoked one of those Camels myself when he got done. I never even knew that he knew how to play, except it made sense, his mama teaching piano lessons up in Peoria, Illinois, when he was a boy. And you had to know Daddy. He didn't do it to show off or to best his beloved only child. I saw right away that when you've got all that way down deep inside you and someone's banging away like they've never even heard of rhythm, day after day, right down the hall from where you're studying your physics or your calculus or your light particles as they relate to speeding bullets--one of which you've probably been fantasizing has Uncle Fred's name on it--when you've been subjected to all that, you just want to hear it done right. Just once. That's all (Teacher Sample, "The Thing with the Doctor").

1. List three **adjectives** for the narrator's father and **quote support:**

A. Adjective:_____Quote:_____

B. Adjective:_____Quote:_____

C. Adjective:_____Quote:_____

2. What can you **infer** from the following: "and, believe me, plenty of redirecting was going on"?

    _____

3. Quote an example of **humor** involving Uncle Fred:_____

    _____

4. **Look up the following words** and **write synonyms** that could have been used: "litany," "precedence," "melodeon," and "subjected."

    _____,_____,_____,_____

5. State the **capitalization rules** for the following words:

A. **Titles of songs** (Which words are capitalized?):_____

B. **Christmas:**_____

C. **March:**_____

D. **Uncle Fred:**_____(When do you not capitalize "uncle"?)

    _____

6. This excerpt is based on **contrast.** Write at least 50 words where you show your readers a distinct **difference in the way you do something and the way someone else does.** Use specific details for effect and humor.

    _____

    _____

    _____

_____

_____

_____

_____

✎Mama had cruised down Hawthorne Drive, past the Finnigans' and the Brownings', past old man Bower taking his nightly constitutional, wearing his orange hunting cap and carrying a walking stick he had whittled out of a branch of some sort, carrying this stick more like a batter up to the plate, as if he could swing it at something, as if it mattered. You couldn't see the crazy old man in his crazy old cap, Mama always said, until you were up on him so close you almost knocked him into next week.

And that stick. The only animals for miles were a couple of Persians, a crippled dachshund, Elmo the alley cat, and Blackie, who by that time Daddy had rigged to Mama's clothesline. Bower didn't have to worry about Blackie. Daddy had planned that dog's every move within an inch of his life. That old dog was too tired from sleeping, relieving himself, and trying to get to the azaleas that old man Bower held no more interest for him than Daddy's boxer shorts or Mama's slingshot brassieres hanging from the same clothesline old Blackie himself was.

That night Mama had just swung into our driveway and started the final trek down an acre's worth of oyster-shell drive to the house when we noticed all the lights were out, which was never the case with a father who had a whole world to fix. Just as Mama and I were contemplating this phenomenon, we were almost blinded by two sort of strobe light apparatuses coming from the garage, cutting the darkness with swirling beams of white light.

As we slowed our runway approach, we realized Daddy was attached to both of them as kind of a cross between the ballet dancers we had just come from—pirouetting, arms high overhead in a perfect letter "o," then low to his sides in a graceful, swooping motion--and old man Bower the time Mama actually grazed him a little on our way home from eating our customary Sunday night liver and onions at the cafeteria.

That Sunday, we weren't expecting the old man out so soon. It was still light a couple of hours before you usually spotted him, head swiveling left and right, stick hoisted up over his shoulder. And Mama and I had been talking about the ballet company when, the next thing we knew, Bower was flailing his stick at us as if we were a swarm of killer bees, all this right before he sort of darted into the ditch, his feeble old body taking the hedge like the slow motion replays of the Olympic high jumps.

Of course we helped him out, and, of course, we brushed him off, Mama trying to feel his legs and ribs for broken bones. And, yes, we offered him a ride home, which--of course--he refused, understandably, I guess. And luckily we talked him out of calling the police, Mama saying all the while Judge Karl Scheele, her brother, would see to it that this never happened again, as if Judge Karl Scheele, her brother, were going to ride with us to the cafeteria or the ballet company or to wherever Mama and I might be coming back from on our way to seeking out old men to run down in the streets (Teacher Sample, "Check the Pattern").

1. Quote **examples** of the following:

A. **Repetition for effect:**_____

B. **Simile:**_____

C. **Humor:**_____

D. **Magic 3:**_____,_____,_____

2. **Summarize** what happens in the passage:

A. Beginning:_____

B.   Middle:_____

C.   End:_____

3.   What is **ironic** about Bower's notion about the stick?_____

4.   What **details** are used to describe the ballet dancers?_____

_____

5.   Why is the **apostrophe after** "Finnigans" and "Brownings" instead of **before**?

_____

6.   **Exchange five words with a neighbor to use in a vignette.** Use figurative language, specific details for effect, humor, etc.

_____

_____

_____

_____

_____

Answer Key

*Accept other answers if supported.
*Answers to writing questions will vary.

"My Hands"

1. A. "I ain't got no pockets"
   B. "they done took my purse," "I weren't no model," "I seen"
   C. "But Mr. Avedon he said"
   D. "Maybe Ethel'll let me get one of them doughnuts"
   E. "but if Mama was here"
2. A. Posing for a picture
   B. "they got me astandin'"
3. A. They both mistreat the narrator.
   B. "when Henry passes my room at night, real quiet so he'll fly right over my shoulders and my head and right on out of the house" & "I wouldn't give Ethel none"
4. A. "Mama always said to put them in my pockets or fold them in my lap or hold my purse in front of me"
   B. "lift right on up over my shoulders, over my head, lift right on out of this place"
5. A. Affecting or moving the emotions; keenly distressing
   B. 1. "didn't have no one to give no picture to anyways"
      2. "I ain't really sure how much fifty dollars are"
      3. "Henry just laughed and told me to shut up, old fool."
6. Answers will vary.

"The Coronado Bayshore Motel"
1. "her brother Hank" and "that old alley cat Elmo"
2. A. "Spying on us in his backfield"
   B. "What with all the years of Girl Scout cookies he refused to buy"
   C. "All those times we got shooed out of the ravine"
3. A. Humorous
   B. "It's not as if Annie and I peddled Chocolate Mint Wafers every day," "It's not as if Hank hadn't given Elmo sufficient warning to shut that dern howling up or pay for it," "she didn't look fat in her new poodle skirt, the circular one that stood out way more than it was supposed to, due to her fat hips"
4. A. "Indian braves"
   B. "piles like big brown tepees"
5. A. "the circular one that stood out way more than it was supposed to, due to her fat hips"

B. "he had killed old man Bower's cat with his new slingshot—one smooth, round stone right between the eyes"

C. "It's not as if Annie and I peddled Chocolate Mint Wafers every day"

6. Answers will vary.

"Virgil and Room 117"

1. A. "His yard" and "strong Texas afternoon sun"

   B. "like what's-her-name on 'Father Knows Best' ", "just like the booth we'd all pile into at the Nip and Sip...feeding an endless supply of nickels and dimes into a machine", & "Bermuda shorts"

2. A. Parenthetical phrases adding more information

   B. Hyphenated adjective

3. A. *Narrator: "His lawn wasn't mowed weekly"

   Virgil: "rusted·oil barrels and trash cans and steel piping...on Virgil's lawn"

   B. *Narrator: "lawn...trimmed meticulously by a mother in a large-brimmed straw hat"

   Virgil: "the only goats we had ever seen up close—in someone's yard, that is"

   C. *Narrator: "just like the booth we'd all pile into at the Nip and Sip" or "matching lawn furniture"

   Virgil: "yet another addition to the Polks' yard, namely the peacock-blue booth, evidently from some diner"

4. Pictures will vary.

5. A. Virgil's

   B. Polks'

6. Answers will vary.

"The Thing with the Doctor"

1. A. Musical—"proceeded to play not only the, by then, infamous litany of ringing bells but everything from 'Five Foot Two, Eyes of Blue' to Rachmaninoff's 'Prelude in C-Sharp Minor.'"

   B. Brilliant—"studying your physics or your calculus or your light particles"

   C. Complex--"I saw right away that when you've got all that way down deep inside you"

2. Readers can infer that the narrator wasn't very good at her piano lessons.

3. "speeding bullets—one of which you've probably been fantasizing has Uncle Fred's name on it"

4. Same responses (recitation or recital); introduction of something (introduction); a small reed organ (organ, piano); to be exposed to (been made to listen)

5.   A.   First and last words and all important words
       B.   Holiday
       C.   Month
       D.   Name of relative--"Uncle" would not be capitalized if it were preceded by a possessive pronoun (e.g., my uncle) or in any other case where the person's name cannot be directly substituted.

6.   Answers will vary.

"Check the Pattern"

1.   A.   "crazy old man in his crazy old cap"
       B.   "carrying his stick more like a batter up to the plate"
       C.   "you almost knocked him into next week"
       D.   "as if Judge Karl Scheele, her brother, were going to ride with us to the cafeteria or ballet company or to wherever Mama and I might be·coming back from...."

2.   A.   The narrator discusses what a hazard old man Bower is.
       B.   The night of the actual story the narrator and her mother noticed that a "phenomenon" had occurred at their house--"all the lights were out."
       C.   The excerpt flashes back to the time the narrator and her mother actually "grazed" old man Bower on their way home from the cafeteria.

3.   It's ironic that the old man is so obsessed about carrying the stick--as if he could be in danger of something he could actually swing at--since "the only animals for miles were a couple of Persians, a crippled dachshund, Elmo the alley cat, and Blackie, who by that time Daddy had rigged to Mama's clothesline." The real danger, ironically, is from the narrator's mother and her driving, something a stick held by an old man couldn't handle.

4.   "pirouetting, arms high overhead in a perfect letter 'o'"

5.   Plural possessive

6.   Answers will vary.

Name:_____ Class:_____ Date:_____

Dailies

After fourteen years
of endless instructions
on how to do things the "right" way
After fourteen years
of waging wars
over slug-sized problems
After fourteen years
of running to Mom
to avoid thousands of bruises
but getting them anyway
in the end
After fourteen years
of death threats
if I lay a finger on his stuff
After fourteen years
of pillows that fly
and coincidentally
smack me in the face
Finally
after fourteen long years
my brother goes off to college

(Kohles, Brad, "Departure").
(Inspired by "Breaking Drought" from <u>Out of the Dust</u> by Karen Hesse)

1. A. What is the fourteen-year-old **conflict** in the poem?_____

    B. What can you **predict** might be a "new" conflict?_____

2. Quote an **implicit metaphor:**_____

3. A. Quote an effective example of **alliteration**:_____

    B. Quote an **assonance**:_____

Dailies

4.   Quote a **hyperbole**:_____

5.   Why is "Mom" **capitalized** but "brother" in lower-case?_____

_____

6.   Write a poem using a **refrain** (e.g., "after fourteen years") **based on a conflict**
      with someone in your family. Include a metaphor, an alliteration, and a
      hyperbole.

In my closet
There's a box
Filled with a billion photos
Some when I was a baby
When I got my first tooth
Some when I started school
When I carried my Elmo lunch kit
And some when I went to church
A princess in my puffy gowns
There are some with the entire family
During Christmas and Thanksgiving
Some with me waking up
Looking like a witch
And acting like one

Ready to cast a deadly spell
The list goes on forever
But the memories remain
Waiting to be looked at
Waiting to be touched
Waiting in a box
In my closet

(Latchmiepersad, Viandra, "Photos").
(Inspired by "Boxes" from <u>Out of the Dust</u>).

1. Explain the following **capitalization** rules:

    A. **Elmo** (but not lunch kit):_____

    B. **Christmas and Thanksgiving**:_____

    C. Why are "princess" and "witch" not **capitalized**?_____

    _____

2. What **prepositional phrase** does the author use to make her poem have a **full-circle ending?**

    _____

3. Quote a **magic three**:_____,_____

    _____

4. A. Quote a **simile**:_____

    B. How does the author use **details for effect** to make the simile more interesting?

    _____

5. Quote two **hyperboles**:_____&_____

6. **Brainstorm a list of items that could be in your closet** and write a poem of at least **ten lines**, using a **full-circle ending**, a **simile with details**, a **magic three**, and one **hyperbole.**

I know that whenever someone says "winner"
They think of her
They picture her as the queen of first place
Trophies flying around her
Medals thrown everywhere
Every drip of joy and hope that trickles down my
way
She catches it
Making it one of her own
I can feel her beady eyes
The torture of them looking right through me
Her devilish mouth screaming out those words
Like fireballs burning my face all over again
"You got second place, huh?"
That one little sentence making me feel so small
She was the only rock I would trip on every time
I had a chance to reach first place
I can sometimes still feel those words pinching me
I can also see the scars
But I know that the race has just begun

(Wadhwani, Tehniya, "The Winner").
(Based on "Me and Mad Dog" from Out of the Dust).

Dailies

1. What **details** does the author use to illustrate that others think of "the winner" as "queen of first place"?

A._____B._____

2. Explain how the author's one line of **dialogue** is effective:

_____

3. Quote an **explicit metaphor** and explain its meaning:

A. Quote:_____

B. Meaning:_____

4. A. What **vivid verb** does the author use to describe what "those words" do to her?

_____

   B. What would be a **less effective verb**?_____

5. A. What can you **infer** about "the winner's" personality?

_____

   B. Quote **proof**:_____

6. **Write a poem about you and _____.** You might want to begin with the line "I know that whenever someone says_____/they think of _____."
Include **figurative language, vivid verbs, and at least one line of dialogue.**

It all started off normal
a normal you're-my-friend-so-come-spend-the-night day
We were just playing outside
collecting bugs
digging through the grass
tramping through ant piles
and breaking down bushes
just to find some bugs
just some of those six-legged things
It was just a normal day
then it turned into a war
a contest of who can collect the most bugs
We were fighting over logs of bugs
over patches of weeds
bugs everywhere
flying as if pilots
the smell of grub in the air
the look of war surrounding us
the feeling of it in our hands
Grasshoppers, spiders, ants, beetles, and rolypolies
crawled, flew, jumped, and rolled
It was a battle
It was a war
It was...
It was two friends and a game

(Whitley, Trey. "The Battle, the War, the Game").
(Based on "Rabbit Battles" from Out of the Dust).

1. A.   What is the rule for the **hyphen** between "six-legged"?

    _____

    B.   Write **another phrase** that would be an example of this rule:

    _____

2. A.   Explain the rule for making "bush" **plural**?_____

    B.   List other word endings that **require this same rule**:

    _____

3. A.   What **repetition for effect** has the author used?

    _____

    B.   What is the **rule for the commas** separating "grasshoppers," "spiders," etc.?

    _____

4. What is the **irony** involved in the poem?_____

5. Quote an effective **simile**:_____

6. This poem is based on collecting bugs. **Write a poem or a vignette** about **something you have done with a friend that "started out normal" but escalated into something else.**

Dailies

The ovens are on and the bread is baking
It's time for bread again
The woman comes with her "little basket,"
as my mom says,
loaves of bread overflowing
stacked on top of each other
It's time for bread again
It's like the seasons
It's bread time again
like it's summer again
The brown loaves
light as feathers
sell
They sell until there are the last two
and my mom pounces on the opportunity
and she takes it
in a how-do-you-make-homemade-bread-like-this voice
the bread
the ritual
the taste
spectacular

(Paulk, Dallas, "The Bread").
(Based on "Harvest" from <u>Out of the Dust</u>).

1.   A.   What can you **infer** about the **setting** (time and place) of this poem?

_____

       B.   Quote **proof**:_____

2.   What **analogy** does the author use for "bread time"?_____

3.   What line do you think creates the best **visual imagery**?

_____

4.   Quote another **Smiley-Face Trick** the author has used:

_____Type:_____

5.   A.   Explain the rule for making "loaf" **plural:**_____

      B.   List **two other words** that follow this rule:_____

6.   **Rewrite the ending of the poem,** changing the last four lines.

Answer Key

*Accept other answers if supported.
*Answers to writing questions will vary.

"Departure"

1. A. Older brother vs. younger brother
    B. The younger brother might miss the older brother (internal conflict).
2. "slug-sized problems"
3. A. "waging wars"
    B. "death threats"
4. "endless instructions"
5. "Mom" is capitalized because her name can be substituted, but "brother" is not because it is preceded by a possessive pronoun.
6. Answers will vary.

"Photos"

1. A. Capitalize the brand name but not the product.
    B. Holidays
    C. They are common nouns, not the names of a specific "princess" or "witch."
2. "In my closet"
3. "Some when I was a baby," "Some when I started to school," "some when I went to church"   Note: The next "some" phrase is in a new sentence that begins with "There" and would not be included.
4. A. "Some with me waking up / Looking like a witch"
    B. The author's details make the image of the witch even more vivid: "And acting like one / Ready to cast a deadly spell."
5. "Filled with billions of photos" & "The list goes on forever"
6. Answers will vary.

"The Winner"

1. A. "Trophies flying around her"
    B. "Medals thrown everywhere"
2. The one line of dialogue is precisely what the narrator does not want to hear. Her goal is to be the winner, not second-place.
3. A. "She was the only rock I would trip on every time"
    B. "The queen of first place" is the narrator's only obstacle.
4. A. Pinching

B. Hurting
5. A. We can infer that she is the type who gloats over her victories.
   B. "Her devilish mouth screaming out those words..../That one little sentence making me feel so small"
6. Answers will vary.

"The Battle, the War, the Game"

1. A. Hyphenated modifier (modifying "things")
   B. "you're-my-friend-so-come-spend-the-night day"
2. A. When a word ends in "sh," add "es" to make it plural.
   B. "s," "ch," "x," or "z"
3. A. "It was a battle/It was a war/It was..../It was two friends and a game"
   B. Series
4. It is ironic that a "normal" day turns into a "war."
5. "bugs everywhere/flying as if pilots"
6. Answers will vary.

"The Bread"

1. A. * The weather is getting colder.
   B. * "like it's summer again"
2. "It's like the seasons"
3. "The brown loaves / light as feathers"
4. "in a how-do-you-make-homemade-bread-like-this voice"--Hyphenated modifier
5. A. Some words ending in "f" are made plural by changing the "f" to "v" and adding "es."
   B. Thieves; lives
6. Answers will vary.

Dailies

i see beautiful people all around me
the freer the will the more i am drawn
.... i want escape
i want to do something outrageous just to break the rules
i want to be free of any definitions that attempt to confine me
i want to be anything delirious
crazy
edgy
pushing
past any boundaries you thought you had of me
i want to try everything
i was told not to try
i want to go mad with delight
insane with rage
i want to bite the bullet and smile
jumping cliffs
daring to be immortal   (Student Writer, "i")

1.   What effect does the author's decision not to **capitalize** the personal pronoun "I" have on the poem?

_____

2.   State the **theme** of the poem:_____

3.   Quote a **paradox:**_____

4.   List five **irregular verbs** and give their **three principal parts** (present, past, past participle):

A._____,_____,_____   D._____,_____,_____

B._____,_____,_____   E._____,_____,_____

C._____,_____,_____

5.   A.   What can you **infer** about the narrator's life?_____

     B.   Quote **proof:**_____

6.   Write a **17-line** (exactly) poem beginning with the line " i want." Try experimenting with **line divisions** and **shape** as the author has done.

There she stood, stage frightened, frozen
Her hair light blonde, her face red,
Full of embarrassment
The room began to snicker
As everyone broke out in chatter
The song began to play: 1, 2, 3, 4
Toe Touch, Hurkey, Toe Touch
Her legs wouldn't move
The music played faster
Longer and longer
A never-ending game she couldn't win
Then her heart fell to her stomach
Her one true best friend was laughing at her
How could she
Then from out of the audience flew food
And the horrible sound of booing spread through
The auditorium like wildfire
The only thing to do now was run and never look back
(Moore, Reagan, "Jitters")

1.   What rule of **capitalization** regarding poetry has the author used?

_____

2.   **Summarize** what happens in this narrative poem:

A.   Beginning;_____

B.   Middle:_____

C.   End:_____

3.   What is the **climax or turning point** of the poem?

_____

4.   Look up the term **"metonymy"** and explain what line exemplifies this literary device:

_____

5.   Quote three **specific details for effect** that the author uses to make the reader empathize with the narrator's plight:

A._____B._____C._____

6.   Write a **free verse poem** involving a time **you were embarrassed or frightened.**

Dailies

She watches him walk by
As he puts his baseball cap on
And takes a sip of his Dr. Pepper
She looks around at the other boys
And realizes no one stands out as much as he
She stares at his new tennis shoes
To see his initials
Printed in small letters
On the toe of each shoe
He and his friend toss a tennis ball around
When his friend throws it over his head
The boy follows the path of the ball
And looks down to see the girl
Sitting on her beach towel
Under the umbrella
Smiling
Looking at his tennis shoes
Then up at him
"Finally," he thinks,
"The girl of my dreams has noticed me."
(Lewis, Angie, "Tennis Shoes")

1. What is the rule for the author's use of **"he"** (fifth line) as opposed to "him"?

_____

2. Why does the author use **quotation marks** in the last two lines?

_____

3. What is the rule for the **commas** in the next to the last line?

_____

4. What can you **infer** about the setting?_____

5. How could the ending be said to be **ironic**?

_____

6.   Write a poem about **someone noticing you.**

"Put that book down!
Why are you reading when you don't have to?"
Everyone asks me this
but no one understands my reasons
so I tell them a story
about a yellow car
that didn't get supreme gasoline and
was having such a bad day
that the heavens started to give out rain
and Godzilla came and the
Japanese yelled "Godzilla!"
at one thousand words per minute
and the ape stepped on every car
but
the yellow car
then

Rambo appears and drives away in the car
The car is then ashamed that he had complained,
Now being driven by the infamous Rambo and all,
"Did I mention that the car had complained?"
"No, and none of this makes sense."
I pick my book back up
(Burnside, Ben, "The yellow car")

Dailies

1. Quote a **cause and an effect**:_____

2. Quote an example of **humor**:_____

3. Quote three **elements of fantasy**:

A._____B._____C._____

4. How does the poem come **full circle**?_____

5. What is the real **conflict** expressed in the poem?_____

6. Write a **"fantasy" poem** that begins with **dialogue**.

_____

_____

_____

_____

_____

_____

_____

Someone is mending his faith
We are ripping out the stitches
claiming the path of least resistance
paying too much in a country called free
Too often we are falling through the cracks
The bruises harden our skin and the scars heal more slowly
Anger thick like syrup swallows us whole
and no longer do we inhale love
but thrive on the thought of its existence
just another hole left by the stars.
Broken words and unfinished sentences
lace the rooms with a palpable tension.
Sometimes I want to drown in this man's skin
but instead I find myself smothered already

by the stale stench of emptiness
coating our sideways glances, our fragments of feeling
But one night I feel buttery hands brush my cheek
"We're okay," he confides in me, his voice like the ocean,
rising, then receding again all in delicate sprays of foaming emotion
He turns away
"We're okay," I confirm
And the stars fill the sky   (Shaver, Rachel, "Confirmation")

1.   Why would it be grammatically incorrect to write "someone is mending their faith"?

_____

2.   Quote an example of each of the following **figurative language devices**:

A.   Simile:_____

B.   Metaphor:_____

C.   Personification:_____

D.   Alliteration:_____

3.   The poem expresses **two conflicts**. Explain each.

A._____

B._____

4.   What is the grammatical rule for the author's using **"more slowly"** as opposed to **"slower"**?

_____

5.   Explain the following lines: "and no longer do we inhale love/but thrive on the thought if its existence/just another hole left by the stars."

_____

6.   Write a poem that contains **two conflicts**.

Answer Key

*Accept other answers if supported.
*Answers to writing questions will vary.

"i"

1. The author's use of the lower case "i" adds to the theme. The author feels not yet fully realized as a person; therefore, not important enough to capitalize.
2. See answer 1.
3. "I want to go mad with delight"
4. A. See, saw, seen
   B. Draw, drew, drawn
   C. Break, broke, broken
5. A. We can infer that the narrator wants to grow and be freer or different.
   B. "i want to escape"
6. Answers will vary.

"Jitters"
1. Capitalize the first lines of poems.
2. A. The character in the poem is on stage, frightened and embarrassed.
   B. She couldn't perform her dance, and the audience not only booed her but threw food.
   C. She ran off the stage.
3. "Her one true best friend was laughing at her"
4. "The room began to snicker"--It's not the "room" but the "people" in the room.
5. A. "The room began to snicker"
   B. "Her legs wouldn't move / The music played faster / Longer and longer"
   C. "And the horrible sound of booing spread through / The auditorium like wildfire"
6. Answers will vary.

"Tennis Shoes"
1. The sentence has an omitted verb. It would read: "no one stands out as much as he **does**."
2. The quotation marks represent inner dialogue.
3. Direct quotation--separating speaker tag from dialogue
4. We can infer that the setting is the beach, as the girl is "sitting on her beach towel /Under the umbrella." However, it could be at a tennis court with the girl watching from the sidelines--on her towel, under an umbrella.
5. It's ironic in that the girl is admiring the boy, not realizing that she is "the girl of [his] dreams."
6. Answers will vary.

"The Yellow Car"

1. "But no one understands my reasons / so I tell them a story"
2. "the / Japanese yelled 'Godzilla!' / at one thousand words per minute"
3. A. "a yellow car.../ was having such a bad day"
   B. "Godzilla came"
   C. "Rambo appears"
4. The poem begins with an order for the narrator to put down his book; it ends with his picking the book back up again.
5. No one understands the narrator's desire to read.
6. Answers will vary.

"Confirmation"

1. "Someone" is singular; therefore, a singular pronoun (he/she) must be used in agreement. "Their" is plural and would require a plural antecedent.
2. A. "his voice like the ocean"
   B. "Someone is mending his faith / We are ripping out the stitches"
   C. "Anger...swallows us whole"
   D. "stale stench"
3. A. One conflict is the narrator against her "country called free," where hatred exists instead of love.
   B. Another conflict is the narrator versus the man she loves. She tells us that "sometimes I want to drown in this man's skin," but we learn that "instead I find myself smothered already / by the stale stench of emptiness."
4. "More slowly" is the adverb form and in this case modifies the verb "heal." "Slower" is an adjective.
5. The author is stating that love is not in abundance now, that it's another void in our lives. However, the thought of it holds promise.
6. Answers will vary.

Dailies

♡Sometimes I wish that all my problems would just disappear into thin air. But they won't disappear; they'll just keep holding onto me. It's like they're an annoying person that clings to me, follows me around, turns up around every corner. The trouble is that now they seem to be metamorphosing . They're tadpoles turning into frogs--just getting bigger and bigger (Odom, Ed, "Go Away!").

1. The author uses **figurative language** to **compare** his problems to what two things?

_____&_____

2. The author uses a **semicolon** to avoid a **run-on sentence**. Rewrite the sentence, using three other ways to avoid a run-on.

A. **Period:**_____

B. **Comma & conjunction:**_____

C. **Subordinate clause:**_____

3. Quote a **magic three:**_____,_____,_____

4. A. What is the **tone** of the piece?_____

   B. Give **support.**_____

5. Using a **context clue**, determine the meaning of "metamorphosing":

_____

6. Write at least a 50-word piece **comparing your problems to something.** Use figurative language and a magic three.

_____

_____

_____

_____

_____

"Whose turn is it to bag the papers?" yells Dad.

"I did it last time."

"No, I did it, you liar."

"Uh huh."

"Yes, I did. It was right before vacation."

"No, because I did."

"You're full of it."

"Do the newspapers, Brad."

"Darn it!"

Typical day at my house.

My brother and I express our brotherly love for each other daily

(Kohles, Brad, "Brotherly Love").

1. What is **ironic** about the last sentence (and the title)?_____

_____

2. What is the rule for **paragraphing dialogue**?_____

_____

3. Quote examples of the following **comma rules**:

   A. **Direct address**:_____

   B. **Introductory word**:_____

4. Why is "Dad" **capitalized** and "brother" is not?_____

5. A. What could be considered a **symbol** in the piece?_____

    B. Of what could it be **symbolic**?_____

6. Write a **dialogue** (of at least 50 words) that represents a "typical" day at your house. Observe rules for paragraphing, punctuating, etc. You may use **"speaker tags"** (e.g., "yells Dad.")

    _____

    _____

    _____

    _____

    _____

♡I fell down in excruciating pain. It was a million needles being jabbed into my side. The hot metal slamming up against my hip at what was like the speed of sound felt like a baseball player's vicious swing connecting with a 100-mile-per-hour fastball (Kader, Michael, "The Big Decision").

1. A. What can you **infer** has happened to the narrator?

    _____

    B. **Support** your answer:_____

2. A. Why is an **apostrophe** used in "player's"?_____

    B. **Write a sentence** using the word "players'":_____

    _____

C.   **Write a sentence** using the word "players": _____

_____

3.   Quote two **similes:** _____ & _____

4.   The line "It was a million needles being jabbed into my side" could be considered an example of two types of **figurative language**. Tell the types and explain.

A.   Type: _____ Explanation: _____

B.   Type: _____ Explanation: _____

5.   Quote a **fact and an opinion** from the passage:

A.   **Fact**: _____ B.   **Opinion**: _____

6.   To emphasize the **importance of figurative language**, rewrite the paragraph in **literal language**.

_____

_____

_____

_____

♡I see him across the dance floor. It's the first slow song. I stand alone, longing for a partner. But he's with someone else, dancing swiftly to the beat of the music, holding on to that snobbish little blonde. Her eyes are blue, blue and green, a deadly combination. I sigh heavily when the song is over, wishing it could have been me. I had watched his every move--a step to the left, a step to the right. Oh, I've lost him.

    I wander around, searching desperately. Has he left? Will I get my dance? Ah, yes, there he is, but who is that casually chatting with him now?

Dailies

The D.J. starts another slow song. He takes her hand while asking her to dance. She blushes with a grin capable of reaching across the state of Texas and even farther. What a cheap way to ask someone to dance; it's got to be the oldest in the book. I would have loved it. Still smiling, she flips her jet-black hair while laughing. I want to barf with disgust. I can feel that gagging feeling creeping slowly like a caterpillar, up my throat.

Quickly, I walk to get a drink to cure my jealousy--I mean my gagging feeling--my eyes still glued on them (Holmes, Rebecca, "A Blonde, a Cat, and Me").

1.   What could be considered **ironic** in the excerpt?_____

_____

2.   Quote **examples** of the following:

A.   **Hyperbole**:_____

B.   **Humor**:_____

C.   **Simile**:_____

3.   The author's **sophisticated sentence structure** is the result of various methods of **sentence combining**. Quote examples of the following:

A.   **Noun absolute** (e.g., I say a little prayer, my hands folded. The word "hands" is the noun absolute followed by a past participle, "folded.")

_____

B.   **Present participial phrase** (i.e., an "-ing" word group used as an adjective):

_____

4.   Explain the following **grammar rules:**

A.   **Hyphen** (between "jet" and "black"):_____

B.   **Dashes**:_____

C.   **Farther versus further:**_____

5. Explain one possible **theme** of the excerpt:_____

6. The excerpt is effective as it is filled with **details of the moment**. Write at least 50 words describing a moment when **you were jealous of someone**. Try to use at least one of the methods of sentence combining and figurative language:

_____

_____

_____

_____

_____

_____

_____

♡Can't sleep! Can't sleep! Can't sleep! My brain is pounding, my heart thumping, the clock ticking. I'm going to burst sooner or later, and they know it. I'm going to have it dragged out of me like a beaten-down opossum on the side of the road, all smushed and squashed with the lie I've told. I'm going to have to drip it out, drip by agonizing drip, out of my leaky-faucet mouth. Wait, maybe they know already. Maybe they know about the crisp sound of the weapon I used and the look on their colorful faces as they doubled over in pain. Their twig-like bodies were vulnerable to my touch.

I still think of it every waking hour of every day. I still get those dreams at night that I have so vividly dreamed from the very first day. It was five years ago. I was so young and naive. "They" dared me, "they" being Mario and Bernice, my two best friends.

"Go! Go! Just do it! Don't think! Do it!" Mario hissed in my ear. He was the one with this brilliant idea. He thought it up, he planned it out, but he didn't want to execute it. I was his guinea pig to see how much trouble he would get into if he did it. He was a filthy, hideous, mischievous little snake that was always coming up with these sorts of adventures.

Dailies

7

"Yeah, Sammie, come on. You've got it in ya, don't ya?" Bernie knew I was glad to help out a friend. Truth was, I was a doormat back then, and sometimes I still let people I don't even know walk over me like I have "Welcome" printed on my forehead. I wasn't sure what I should do. I could either be a wimp and disappoint my buddies, who thought I was cooler than that, or I could suck it up through a straw and do it (Ponder, Danielle, "Murder of the Colors").

1. For the following **verbs,** give their three **principal parts** (i.e., present, past, past participle):

A. **Burst**:_____,_____,_____

B. **Drag**:_____,_____,_____

2. Using **context clues,** determine the meaning of the following words:

A. **Naive**:_____ B. **Vulnerable**:_____

3. Quote two **magic threes**:

A. _____,_____,_____

B. _____,_____,_____

4. Quote examples of the following **figurative language devices:**

   A. **Implicit metaphor**: _____

   B. **Explicit metaphor**:_____

   C. **Simile**:_____

5. Using the title and any other clues, what can you **infer** the "murder" was?

   A. **Inference**:_____

   B. **Clues**:_____

© 2002 by M.E. Ledbetter

145

6. This excerpt is based on a **dare.** Write at least 50 words that could serve as the **beginning of a short story about someone being pressured into carrying out a harmless prank.** Use figurative language, magic threes, and one unfamiliar word.

_____

_____

_____

_____

_____

Answer Key

*Accept other answers if supported.
*Answers to writing questions will vary.

"Go Away!"

1. an "annoying person" & "tadpoles turning into frogs"
2. A. But they won't disappear. They'll just keep holding onto me.
  B. They won't disappear, and they'll just keep holding onto me.
  C. *Since they won't disappear, they'll just keep holding onto me.
3. "that clings to me, follows me around, turns up around every corner"
4. A. Frustration
  B. *"The trouble is that now they seem to be metamorphosing."
5. "tadpoles turning into frogs"--becoming something else, changing form
6. Answers will vary.

"Brotherly Love"

1. The poem is about a dispute between brothers, not "brotherly love."
2. Begin a new paragraph for each new speaker.
3. A. "'Do the newspapers, Brad.'"
  B. *"'Yes,....'"
4. "Dad" can be replaced by the father's name, whereas "brother" cannot since it is preceded by a possessive pronoun.
5. A. newspapers
  B. everyday objects that can be a source of disagreements
6. Answers will vary.

"The Big Decision"

1. A. We can infer that the narrator hit or was hit by a metallic object.
  B. "The hot metal slamming up against my hip"
2. A. "Player's" is singular possessive; the player owns the "swing."
  B. *The players' equipments was waiting for them.
  C. *The players ran onto the field.
3. "The hot metal slamming up against my hip at what was like the speed of sound" & "felt like a baseball player's vicious swing"
4. A. Metaphor--comparing the pain to needles
  B. Hyperbole--exaggerating the pain by saying a "million" needles
5. A. "I fell down"
  B. "in excruciating pain"

6. Answers will vary.

"A Blonde, a Cat, and Me"

1. It's ironic that the narrator says, "What a cheap way to ask someone to dance; it's got to be the oldest in the book. I would have loved it." The statement that it's "cheap" and the "oldest in the book" would make the readers assume that the narrator would want no part of it; however, she states that she "would have loved it."

2. A. "a grin capable of reaching across the state of Texas"
    B. "Quickly, I walk to get a drink to cure my jealousy--I mean my gagging feeling...."
    C. "I can feel that gagging feeling creeping slowly like a caterpillar, up my throat."

3. A. "Quickly, I walk to get a drink to cure my jealousy...my eyes still glued on them."
    B. "I stand alone, longing for a partner."

4. A. Hyphenated modifier
    B. Parenthetical insertion
    C. "Farther" implies distance; "further" implies depth.

5. Sometimes our love is unrequited.

6. Answers will vary.

"Murder of the Colors"

1. A. Burst, burst, burst
    B. Drag, dragged, dragged

2. A. inexperienced, innocent--"young"
    B. capable of being hurt--"Their twig-like bodies"

3. A. "My brain is pounding, my heart thumping, the clock ticking."
    B. "He thought it up, he planned it out, but he didn't want to execute it."

4. A. "leaky-faucet mouth"
    B. "He was a ...little snake" or "I was his guinea pig..." or "I was a doormat"
    C. "twig-like bodies"

5. A. Breaking of crayons
    B. *"colorful faces," "doubled over," "twig-like bodies," "Murder of the Colors" & the fact that the narrator was young

6. Answers will vary.

Dailies

◊As I walk through the door thinking about my weekend ahead, I hear an explosion. After a moment of silence, I realize that it wasn't an explosion; it was my dad's yelling, and here he comes, his face like a cherry without the stem.

"Michael, two 'F's'!"

"Huh?" I say.

"I didn't stutter, son. Two 'F's' on your report card!" His sound waves knock me back at least ten feet. "I'm taking the cable out of our TV!"

"Like it ever works anyway," I think.

"No computer!"

"I've lived without it for five months," I almost smile but decide against it.

"No video games!"

"Like I play them." This is almost getting funny.

"No friends!"

Now he's got me right where he wants me. Alone. My body drops like a sack of manure. I am manure. Now this definitely isn't funny

(Kadar, Michael, "The Explosion").

1. A. In general, how can readers **identify** with this dialogue?_____

_____

   B. List two phrases the author has used that could sound **familiar** to teenagers:

_____&_____

2.   A.   In what **tense** is the piece written?_____

       B.   List five **verbs** as proof:_____,_____,

_____,_____,_____,

3.   Quote examples of the following **figurative language devices:**

       A.   **Hyperbole**:_____

       B.   **Simile**:_____

       C.   **Metaphor**:_____

4.   A.   What is the rule for the **single quotation marks** surrounding the "F's"?

_____

       B.   What is the reason for the **apostrophe** and the "s" in "F's"?

_____

       C.   What is the reason for the **semicolon**?_____

5.   A.   If this were a short story, what would be the **climax or turning point**?

_____

       B.   **Why**?_____

6.   Write at least a 100-word **dialogue** that incorporates what **someone says** and what **someone else thinks** but does not actually say. Use figurative language and humor.

_____

_____

_____

_____

_____

_____

_____

♧I know that she hates me. I know that when she thinks of me, her lips curl with disgust. I know this, but I still like her.

"Will you go with me to the dance?" I ask, waiting for a reply. I know what it will be, but I just have to ask. I've seen her with all the guys. But I'm not jealous. I'm covetous! I'm not angry. I'm furious! I'm not enraged. No, not me. I'll just go on with my life....

"Sure. I have been waiting for you to ask me for the past week."

"All right. See you tomorrow," I stammer.

Well, I guess I don't really know everything. And you know what? When the big day comes, the day of the dance, my mom takes me to pick up my girl--my girl--embarrassingly playing Peter Frampton on the radio.

"Please turn that off."

"No, I like this song."

And when the girl of my dreams gets into the car, you'll never believe it! She starts singing along. Man, I really don't know everything! (Odom, Ed, "I Don't Know Everything")

1. What two parts of this vignette could be considered **ironic**?

_____ & _____

2. Why does the author use **four periods** in the second paragraph?

_____

3. On what **repetition for effect** is this piece based?_____

4. What **synonyms** does the author use for a **humorous effect**?

_____

5.   A.   What can you **infer** about the narrator's age?_____

Dailies

B.   **Clues**:_____

6.   Write at least a 50-word piece based on the lines "I know everything" or "I don't know anything."

_____

_____

_____

_____

_____

_____

♧The gray LeSabre makes its way down the final stretch, a whole 100-yards-long journey, and into the driveway. It's my grandparents. This time I'm going to be the first one to say "Hi." But it's too late. Here comes Schroeder, making his way around to the other side of the car, a wizard transforming between our house to my grandparents' car. My dog is the slowest dog in the world. How does he do it? How does he get all the lovin' first?
(Paulk, Dallas, "Schroeder").

1.   This piece is based on the **"surprise" ending.** Who do you **infer** Schroeder is when he is first mentioned?_____

2.   What effect does the author's **word choice** of "final stretch" and "journey" have on the piece?_____

3.   Quote examples of the following **figurative language devices:**

A.   **Hyperbole**:_____

B.   **Metaphor**:_____

4.   A.   Why is the **apostrophe** after the "s" in "grandparents'"?_____

    B.   Write a sentence using "grandparent's": _____

_____

    C.   Write a sentence using "grandparents": _____

_____

5.   What is a **cause and an effect**? _____

6.   Write a piece based on a **"surprise ending."** Start with the line: From the minute I laid eyes on her/him, I knew I had to have her/him." Your job will be to make the **object of your desire something other than a person. Use figurative language.**

_____

_____

_____

_____

_____

_____

_____

♣"ALYSSA ADAMS, GET OUT OF THERE RIGHT NOW AND FEED THOSE ANIMALS!"

THAT'S MY MOM, AS QUIET AS A SNAIL WITH ITS MOUTH TAPED SHUT! (I DON'T EVEN KNOW IF A SNAIL HAS A MOUTH!) SHE'S TRYING TO GET ME OUT OF MY ROOM AND OUTSIDE BECAUSE I RAISE ANIMALS, AND I NEED TO FEED THEM, WALK THEM, AND WATER THEM.

"I'M NOT GOING TO BEG YOU! BLAH, BLAH, BLAH!" SHE SHOUTS LIKE A COMMANDER GIVING INSTRUCTIONS TO HER LOWER-RANK SOLDIERS" (ADAMS, ALYSSA, "THE SUPER SUMMER").

1.   Quote examples of the following **comma rules:**

    A.   **Compound sentence**: _____

B.   **Series**:_____

C.   **Direct address**:_____

2.   The author not only uses two **similes** but adds **details** to them as well. Quote the similes and **underline the details for effect**:

A._____

B._____

3.   Quote a **fact and an opinion** from the passage:

A.   **Fact:**_____B.   **Opinion:**_____

4.   What **humor** has the author used as part of the **dialogue** with which the reader can identify?_____

5.   From what **point of view** is the passage written (FIRST PERSON, THIRD, OMNISCIENT)?

_____**Clues**:_____

6.   In at least 50 words, **predict** what will happen next. ADD TO THE STORY, USING DIALOGUE AND FIGURATIVE LANGUAGE:

_____

_____

_____

_____

_____

_____

_____

_____

Dailies

Rachel was the name I was born with
And it will stay with me the rest of my life
No matter how stupid I think it sounds
Rolling off other people's tongues
Though I wish for something more exotic
Like Desiree or Alexa
Names that come with flashing neon lights

I used to have a way of dreaming about filling up
Gucci models' stilettos
Instead of Foley's-brand boots
Only causing my feet to look clumsy
Making me trip over my confidence

My world was my back yard
Home to my personal creations and fantasies
Mud pies, lizard burials
Me a famous actress
Six-hundred-dollar earrings dangling from my ears
Servants kissing my feet

Satisfaction, I thought, did not
Lie in my plain-as-stripes life
But in entering my refuge
That polka-dot door at the back of my mind
Where I found someone else
Someone not Rachel

I didn't intend to like who I was
But year by year
Experience by experience
Sometimes contentment reflected
From my eyes instead of disappointment
When I saw my face, mind, and body
Begin to grow out of their elementary, simple form

The thing about Rachel
Maybe someday I can really invite her in
Fix her a drink
Play her favorite music
Because I might like what I find out
(Shaver, Rachel, "Plain as Stripes")

1.   **Summarize** what happens in this poem:

A.   Beginning:_____

B.   Middle:_____

C.   End:_____

2.   What **figurative language devices** would the following lines exemplify?

A.   "it sounds rolling off other people's tongues":_____

B.   "Making me trip over my confidence":_____

C.   "That polka-dot door at the back of my mind":_____

3.   What can you **infer** about the Foley's-brand boots?_____

4.   What **magic three** does the author use in talking about this "new" Rachel?

_____,_____,_____

5.   A.   What is the rule for the **comma** after "elementary"?_____

     B.   Why is the **apostrophe** before the "s" instead of after the "s" in "people's"?

_____

6.   Write a **poem about your name**. Tell about names you have wished for, fantasies you have had, and "personal creations" (e.g., mud pies, lizard burials). Then **come to terms with your name** at the end of the poem. Use the back of this paper.

Answer Key

*Accept other answers if supported.
*Answers to writing questions will vary.

"The Explosion"

1. A. Most readers have had similar discussions regarding grades.
   B. "'I'm taking the cable out of your TV,'" "'No computer!'", "'No video games!'"
2. A. Present tense
   B. Walk, hear, realize, comes, say, knock, think, smile, is getting
3. A. "I hear an explosion."
   B. "his face like a cherry"
   C. "I am manure."
4. A. Grades are enclosed in quotation marks, but--in this case--single quotation marks are used since the grade is part of a dialogue.
   B. An apostrophe and an "s" are used to make letters plural.
   C. The semicolon connects two clauses.
5. A. The turning point would be when the father declares that Michael will be allowed no friends.
   B. Up to that point, all the other punishments have meant nothing to Michael. The "no friends" decree results in Michael's saying, "Now he's got me right where he wants me."
6. Answers will vary.

"I Don't Know Everything"

1. "I know that she hates me....I know this, but I still like her." & "'Please turn that off....And when the girl of my dreams gets into the car...she starts singing along."
2. The first three periods are ellipses indicating that something has been omitted. The fourth period represents the period at the end of the sentence.
3. "I know"
4. "covetous," "furious," "enraged"
5. A. We can infer that the narrator is old enough to date but not old enough to drive.
   B. "...my mom takes me to pick up my girl..."
6. Answers will vary.

"Schroeder"
1. At first, we infer that Schroeder is a person, possibly a sibling of the narrator.
2. The phrases have a humorous effect in that they poke fun at the simple act of pulling into a driveway, making it more important (like a race or a laborious journey) than it is.

3.   A.   "My dog is the slowest dog in the world."
     B.   "a wizard transforming"
4.   A.   "Grandparents'" is plural possessive; both grandparents own the car.
     B.   *My grandparent's purse was left behind.
     C.   *My grandparents are coming to visit.
5.   The grandparents are coming for a visit (cause), and the narrator wants to be the first to greet them (effect).
6.   Answers will vary.

"The Super Summer"

1.   A.   "She's trying to get me out of my room and outside because I raise animals, and I need to...."
     B.   "feed them, walk them, and water them"
     C.   "'Alyssa Adams, get....'"
2.   A.   "That's my mom, as quiet as a snail <u>with its mouth taped shut</u>!"
     B.   "She shouts like a commander <u>giving instructions to her lower-rank soldiers</u>"
3.   A.   "That's my mom"
     B.   "as quiet as a snail"
4.   "'Blah, Blah, Blah!'"
5.   First person--my, me, I
6.   Answers will vary.

"Plain as Stripes"

1.   A.   The narrator wishes for a more exotic name.
     B.   The narrator dreams of a life that is not "plain as stripes" and enters the "polka-dot door" of her mind to find another part of herself.
     C.   The narrator has come to like her new name (this new person) and perhaps someday will "invite her in."
2.   A.   Metaphor
     B.   Metaphor
     C.   Metaphor
3.   We can infer that the "Foley's-brand boots" are plain, ordinary--just the opposite of the exciting "Gucci models' stilettos."
4.   "Maybe someday I can really invite her in," "Fix her a drink," "Play her favorite music"
5.   A.   Coordinate adjective
     B.   "People" is already plural; therefore, to make a plural that does not end in "s" possessive, add an apostrophe and an "s."
6.   Answers will vary.

Dailies

✔It might have been a dark and stormy night or a bright and sunny day or a rain-drenched evening, but all I know was that it existed. I wish it had never happened. It cursed my life for...well, not forever, just for my time left as an eighth grader.

Lima beans and ketchup, peach and red, earthworms and whipped cream. Yes, gross combinations, not even relatively close to the combination made three weeks ago today. Everyone knew I was after him; I guess she didn't. I'm not surprised she didn't know; the part of her brain which enabled her to think had been missing for quite some time now. The other part was there all right and in full power with her flirtatious moves and those kisses they sneaked. I'm sorry, but he might as well kiss a toilet seat. It already looked like she had kissed a weed whacker so it was easy to imagine how disgustingly weird, and not to mention painful, that looked. I just wanted to run over there to them, toilet disinfectant in one hand, soap in the other, and go on a cleaning rampage on the inside of his mouth. I could probably scrub and rinse it twenty times and still not be satisfied, if you know what I mean.

I turned away just in time to miss the hug that brought him to her, her to him, them together. That was the other thing that made me squirm all over--when they touched. Whether it was a little pat-pat on the shoulder, a finger-linked handshake that lasted longer than it should, or a full-fledged, wrap-around, dos-a-dos hug. I'm always surprised that his skin doesn't run away from its point of contact, jump off his body, shuddering, screaming, "Agony, torture, pain, please have mercy, and just burn me now!" (Holmes, Rebecca, "Lima Beans and Ketchup").

1.   How does the author's first sentence **parody** a "famous" beginning?

_____

_____

2. A. What **details for effect** does the author give to prove that "the combination made three weeks ago today" was gross?

_____,_____,_____

B. To what can you **infer** the "combination" she speaks of refers?

_____

3. The piece is based on **humor**. Quote three instances that you think are particularly effective:

A._____

B._____

C._____

4. Quote a **personification**:_____

5. A. What can you **infer** about the "other woman" from the way the author **characterizes** her?

_____Quoted **proof**:_____

B. What can you **infer** about the narrator?_____

Quoted **proof**:_____

6. Write at least a **100-word vignette in a humorous tone** about a time **you were jealous.** Try to use some of the author's Smiley-Face Tricks.

_____

_____

_____

_____

_____

_____

_____

✔I wish this could begin with once upon a time, but it doesn't. Maybe once upon a never or maybe once upon a time I would like to erase, forget. But however the story begins, I'll always know that the aching in my heart that has been here since childhood not only remains but grows where the walls are colliding without any air to breathe.

I live with my mother and my little brother on an old dirt road where silence is heard and always about like a plague. And even now, when I look down upon the dirt road, I start to wonder if the Pre-Cambrian days are still welded inside these rocks, for this very road is as old as a clear sky in the city. Willow trees stretch to the ground and yawn deep inside each other. Butterflies seem to float past, skipping over this desolate road, up and over the canopy of trees that embrace this burden with fierce force, and fly away with no worries, failing to leave behind their vibrant color as a gift for the empty field. There is no color. No life. Only the low humming of a whispering wind on fall evenings, vocalizing with the sun, also hiding behind clouds, for it, too, I'm sure fears this road (Daughtery, Lindsey, "Disappearing Butterflies").

1. How is the author's beginning a **"twist"** on the traditional "once upon a time"?

_____

2. Explain the author's image of "the walls are colliding without any air to breathe":

_____

3. A. Quote a **paradox** in the second paragraph:

_____

   B. Explain how this could, in fact, **be true**:

_____

4. Explain what the author means by the following line: "I start to wonder if the Pre-Cambrian days are still welded inside these rocks."

_____

5. A. Quote a **fragment for effect:**_____

   B. What is its **effect?**_____

6. Writing at least 100 words, **begin a short story with the line**: "I live with...."
   Use imagery, figurative language, symbolism, whatever "tricks" you can to make your passage come alive for the reader.

_____

_____

_____

_____

_____

_____

_____

✔When the dust settled, we examined each other, looking like we had just gotten back from war, back from foreign countries to search for the perfect girl. Or across a sea to find our long-lost brothers or through a forest thicker than an elephant's skin. Feeling like we were crammed up in an elevator, all our clothes in disarray, our hair tied in knots, our skin sweaty, we all continued looking for a small clearing where we could put our treasured Skittles into a tree stump so once and for all we could see the heavens rain Skittles (Hinton, Andrew, "Raining Skittles").

1. What is the **extended metaphor** on which the piece is based? (In other words, what is the author suggesting he and his friends are?)

_____

2. What is the **rule for the first comma**?_____

3. A. Quote your favorite **simile**:_____

   B. Quote your favorite **magic three**:_____,

   _____,_____

4. What is the author's **surprise ending**?_____

5. A. What can you **infer** about the age of the narrator and his friends?

   _____

   B. Quoted **proof**:_____

6. This piece fools the reader, making us think one thing when almost the opposite is true. **Write 100 words, using the author's idea of a complete** reversal at the end.

_____

_____

_____

_____

_____

_____

_____

_____

✔My legs were sticks as I tried hard to get home out of the storm. Gradually it got worse, worse, worse. I mean like golf-ball-size hail worse, stinging rain worse, boiling-mad thunder worse. I was a racer, my challenging opponent a whirling, twisting, claw-bearing, clothes-ripping, brain-throwing cyclone right behind me and gaining fast like a bear catching up with his dinner (Cummingham, Amber, "The First Day of Summer").

1. A.   What is the **conflict** in the piece?_____

    B.   **Internal or external**?_____

2. A.   Quote two **explicit metaphors**:_____&

    _____

    B.   Quote an **implicit metaphor**:_____

3. How has the author used **hyphenated adjectives** to add to the **imagery**?

    _____

4. What **progression** does the author use (i.e., a repetition for effect) to add to the
    intensity of the piece?

    _____

5. Write at least a 50-word passage about a **conflict with the "elements."**

    _____

    _____

    _____

    _____

✔I remember thirteen.   Thirteen, the age to be free to do anything your impulses suggested. I never thought I would grow old. I thought every year I could go to a fountain of youth and regenerate my adolescence. I thought I could always stay young, but now I'm 63, and I think I lost some trips to the fountain. I look in a mirror and see more wrinkles than I do hair. My once milky chocolate mane has turned into vanilla frosting over the years. I never thought of wearing orthopedic shoes or how my once-brown eyes could lose their gleam. My hands are wrinkled, my skin spotted with freckles like a dalmatian, and as pale as the moon. I used to be soft--like the clouds--with skin so smooth all the boys would admire it. Now I'm like wood left too long in the sun. I'm still the same person I used to be 50 years ago. I still do crazy things--like ride my bicycle without hands. The most exciting part is when people look at me like I'm crazy, but I don't care. I just feel the wind go through me and laugh (Villarreal, Michelle, "Who Am I?").

1.   A.   Look up "Fountain of Youth" and explain the origin of the **allusion:**

_____

      B.   What **humor** does the author use regarding the Fountain of Youth?

_____

      C.   Why has the author not **capitalized** "fountain of youth"?

_____

2.   What **details of appearance** does the author use to **characterize** herself in her older state?

_____,_____,_____

3.   A.   What **action** does the sixty-three-year-old narrator do that the once-thirteen-year-old narrator did?

_____

      B.   Of what would this action be **symbolic**?_____

4.   A.   Quote a **fragment:**_____

_____

      B.   **Rewrite the fragment**, making it a sentence:_____

_____

5.   What is the **conflict** of the piece?_____

6. This passage is based on **contrast—13 versus 63**. Write at least 100 words contrasting the present you with a future you.

_____

_____

_____

_____

_____

_____

Answer Key

*Accept other answers if supported.
*Answers to writing questions will vary.

"Lima Beans and Ketchup"

1.   It pokes fun at the cliche "It was a dark and stormy night."
2.   A.   "Lima beans and ketchup, peach and red, earthworms and whipped cream."
      B.   We can infer that the combination is the narrator's boyfriend and his new girlfriend.
3.   A.   "the part of her brain which enabled her to think had been missing for quite some time now"
      B.   "he might as well have kissed a toilet seat"
      C.   "It already looked like she had kissed a weed whacker"
4.   "the hug that brought him to her"
5.   A.   We can infer that "the other woman" has no scruples when the author writes about her "flirtatious moves" and that contact with her might require a "cleaning rampage."
      B.   We can infer that the narrator is jealous.
6.   Answers will vary.

"Disappearing Butterflies"

1.   The narrator states that she wishes she "could begin with once upon a time," but she can't.
2.   She feels trapped, like walls are closing in on her.
3.   A.   "where silence is heard"
      B.   The narrator's environment is so lifeless that even silence has a sound.
4.   The narrator tells us that she lives on an "old dirt road." By the narrator's comparing the age of the road to the "Pre-Cambrian days," she is saying that perhaps nothing has changed for millions and millions of years. That these very rocks of which she speaks date back to that time.
5.   A.   "No life."
      B.   It emphasizes how desolate the road is.
6.   Answers will vary.

"Raining Skittles"

1.   The narrator and his friends are like soldiers having "gotten back from war."
2.   Introductory adverb clause

3. A. "Feeling like we were crammed up in an elevator"
    B. "all our clothes in disarray, our hair tied in knots, our skin sweaty"
4. The narrator and his friends aren't soldiers but kids.
5. A. We can infer that the narrator and his friends are perhaps primary-school-age children.
    B. "where we could put our treasured Skittles into a tree stump so once and for all we could see the heavens rain Skittles"
6. Answers will vary.

"The First Day of Summer"

1. A. Narrator versus storm
    B. External
2. A. "My legs were sticks" and "I was a racer"
    B. "boiling-mad thunder worse"
3. The hyphenated adjectives emphasize the power of the storm.
4. "golf-ball-size hail worse, stinging rain worse, boiling-mad thunder worse"
5. Answers will vary.

"Who Am I?"

1. A. A mythical spring, sought in the Bahamas and in Florida by Ponce de Leon and others...would cure ills and renew youth
    B. The narrator thought that she would never grow old, that she would be able to go to some sort of "fountain of youth."
    C. The author's fountain of youth is not the mythical fountain. It is not used as a proper noun.
2. "more wrinkles than hair," "once milky chocolate mane has turned into vanilla frosting," "orthopedic shoes"
3. A. "ride my bicycle without hands"
    B. "being young at heart"
4. A. "Thirteen, the age to be free to do anything your impulses suggested."
    B. * Thirteen is the age....
5. Narrator versus aging
6. Answers will vary.

Dailies

☀The water was rustling like leaves in spring. I felt a cold breeze come in when I unzipped my tent door. I crawled out onto the sun-roasted dirt. I walked over to the river and, before I had even rubbed the sleep out of my eyes, I spotted what must have been the biggest trout I had ever seen. I ran over, snagged my rod, put a worm on the hook, and cast my line toward the speckled trout.

"Come on, fish, bite it. I know you want to eat that worm. Come on," I whispered. "I got you now! Yes!"

I reeled him in, knowing he would be at least five pounds.

It was then that I heard the footsteps. I slowly turned my head to see what it was, and that was the moment I saw my first bear" (Barfield, Justin, "The Bear").

1. With what **figurative language device** does the author begin the piece?

_____

2. How is the quotation a **divided quotation**?_____

_____

3. Quote the sentence that contains **commas in a series:**

_____

4. A. What **adjective** does the author use to describe the dirt?_____

   B. Write a **less effective adjective**:_____

5. A. What could be considered **contradictory** in the piece?

_____

   B. How could what the author describes be a **fact**?

_____

6. **Continue the story for at least 50 more words.** Use *sensory details* and *dialogue.*

_____

_____

_____

_____

☼I'm not so stupid. I can tie my shoes and count by two's. I can do the occasional math problem. I'm just the same as everybody. I put my pants on one leg at a time. Who's stupid now? I can ride a bike and talk on a mike without stuttering. It might not be that hard, but I can do it. Who's stupid now? (Barnett, Trey, "Who's Stupid Now?")

1. A. Why does the author use an **apostrophe** in "two's"?_____

   B. Write **four other examples** (besides numbers) that follow this same rule:

   _____,_____,_____,_____

2. This excerpt could be the basis for a **poem**. What **refrain** would the author use?

   _____

3. Quote two examples of **assonance** that the author uses:

   _____& _____

4. A. Explain the difference between **"who's"** and **"whose."**

   _____

   B. Write a sentence of exactly 25 words, using **"whose."**_____

   _____

5. Quote a **fact and an opinion** from the excerpt:

   A. Fact:_____

B.   Opinion:_____

6.   Using **slash marks (/)** divide the passage at appropriate places for a **poem**. Now **add one more stanza**, giving examples of "who's stupid now."

☼There I was all alone in the lonely outdoors without a drop of water to my name. Gazing far and wide for lakes or anything at all that consisted of water, I realized that my eyes were as tired as a bear during winter, my mouth as dry as the Sahara Desert, and my body as slow and weak as a helpless kitten let loose in the city. I looked up at the ominous sky, waiting until it rained, waiting until the sky would give me back my life (Flores, Jovanny, "The Outdoors").

1.   One sophisticated method of sentence combining is the use of a **participial phrase** (an "-ing" word group that works as an adjective).

     A.   Quote a **participial phrase** used by the author:

_____

     B.   **Rewrite the sentence,** combining it by using another method:

_____

2.   Quote a **repetition for effect** that the author uses:_____

3.   What **series of similes** works effectively?_____,

_____,_____

4.   A.   Quote an example of **personification**:_____

      B.   Explain why this is an example of this type of **figurative language**:

_____

5.   A.   What is the **conflict**?_____

      B.   Is it **external or internal**?_____

6.   Write a 50-word passage about **an individual versus nature:**

_____

_____

_____

☼As the sun falls into the darkness, the dinosaurs go to sleep. Then the earth starts to shake as they scatter in different directions. Some of the T-Rexes stomp on the nests of the plant-eaters like humans squashing bugs. The three-horns stab the big-mouths, the big-mouths bite the flyers, the flyers peck the long-necks, and what was once a peaceful part of the day turns into chaos and confusion. What were nests before are now, in a heartbeat, food for meat-eaters. All is lost now that the meat-eaters are devouring the plant-eaters and the wetness of the plant-eaters' tears (Free, Kayla, "The Dinosaurs").

1.   Why would it have been **redundant** for the author to have written "darkness of the night"?

_____

2.   A.   What is the **rule for the first comma**?_____

    B.   Write a **sentence of your own** that follows this rule:

_____

3.   A.   What word serves as a **context clue** for the meaning of "chaos"?

_____

    B.   What can you deduce that "chaos" means?_____

4.   A.   Quote a **progression** that the author uses:

_____

    B.   What is the **rule for the commas** in this sentence?_____

5.   Cite a **cause and an effect**:_____

_____

6.   Using your answer for **question 4A**, **write your own sentence** (consisting of at least 30 words) **based on a progression**.

_____

_____

_____

☼The old man just sat there staring at his glass of water. It was the first time I had seen him in years. The waiter at Chili's was getting angry. He had been asking him what he wanted for a good, solid two minutes now. At this point, the waiter had this if-you-don't-order-I'm-going-to-stab-you-with-this-fork look.

"Sir, what do you want to eat?"

The old man looked at me. "Oh, hey, Brandon. Didn't see you sitting there."

Finally the waiter yelled at him, and the whole restaurant was quiet.

The old man looked at the waiter and said, "I'm not hungry" (Wash, Brandon, "The Old Man").

1. A. What is the overall **tone** of the piece?_____

   B. Quote **proof:**_____

2. A. What can you **infer** about the old man?_____

   B. Cite **evidence:**_____

3. A. Quote your favorite line that the author uses to **characterize the waiter:**

   _____

   B. Which **method of characterization** does this exemplify (e.g., appearance, what others say, environment, speech, actions, inner thoughts and feelings)?

   _____

4. Quote two **comma usages and give their rules:**

A._____ Rule:_____

B._____Rule:_____

5. Cite a **cause and an effect**:_____

6. Write a **100-word vignette** beginning: "The old man sat there..."

_____

_____

_____

_____

_____

_____

Answer Key

*Accept other answers if supported.
*Answers to writing questions will vary.

"The Bear"

1.   Simile
2.   It is divided by the speaker tag, "I whispered."
3.   "I ran over, snagged my rod, put a worm on the hook, and cast my line toward the speckled trout."
4.   A.   "Sun-roasted"
      B.   *Hot
5.   A.   "I felt a cold breeze come in when I unzipped my tent door. I crawled out onto the sun-roasted dirt."
      B.   It could be even hotter in the tent so that the "fresh" air in comparison seems "cold."
6.   Answers will vary.

"Who's Stupid Now?"

1.   A.   An apostrophe is used to make a number plural.
      B.   Letters (a's); words referred to as words (You have too many "and's" in your paper.); symbols (&'s); years (1900's)
2.   "Who's stupid now?"
3.   "shoes and two's" & "bike and mike"
4.   A.   "Who's" is a contraction for "who is," whereas "whose" is the possessive case of "who."
      B.   Answers will vary.
5.   A.   * "I can tie my shoes"
      B.   * "I'm not so stupid."
6.   Answers will vary.

"The Outdoors"

1.   A.   * "Gazing far and wide..."
      B.   *When I gazed far and wide....
2.   * "waiting until"
3.   "my eyes were as tired as a bear during winter, my mouth as dry as the Sahara Desert, and my body as slow and weak as a helpless kitten...."
4.   A.   "the sky would give me back my life"
      B.   A human quality--giving back--has been given to the sky.

© 2002 by M.E. Ledbetter

5.   A.   Narrator versus outdoors

      B.   External

6.   Answers will vary.

"The Dinosaurs"

1.   Night **is** dark.

2.   A.   Introductory adverb clause

      B.   * When I get home, I start on my work.

3.   A.   Confusion

      B.   The opposite of peaceful; confusion, disorder

4.   A.   "The three-horns stab the big-mouths, the big-mouths bite the flyers, the flyers peck the long-necks...."

      B.   Series

5.   Because of all this violence, "what was once a peaceful part of the day turns into chaos and confusion."

6.   Answers will vary.

"The Old Man"

1.   A.   Sad yet humorous

      B.   " The old man just sat there staring at his glass of water." (Sad)

            "At this point the waiter had this if-you-don't-order...look." (Humorous)

2.   A.   We can infer that the old man is forgetful or confused.

      B.   "He had been asking him what he wanted for a good, solid two minutes now."

3.   A.   See answer 1B.

      B.   Appearance

4.   A.   * "good, solid"--coordinate adjective

      B.   * " 'Sir,'" --direct address

5.   When the waiter yelled, "the whole restaurant was quiet."

6.   Answers will vary.

Dailies

✂ He was so beautiful. So beautiful, in fact, that I wanted to scream out in agonizing pain just how beautiful he was. His eyes, green and wide open, stared as if seeing the world for the first time. His hands had the strength of a thousand men. His hair, which had the tendency to fall just a little over his left eye, was the loveliest shade of dark brown, and you could just run your hand right through it and you felt like you've never felt anything so wonderful. But the best thing about him was his soul. He had a million people and a million emotions in him and he was one in a million. And he loved me. Me.

Why did he care so much about me, though? I'm not special. I'm a nobody, invisible almost to myself. And one day, if it were something I did or said, I don't know what it was, but he just popped into my life like a good luck fairy. He made everything the way it should be. He was the Yang to my Yin, he was Sonny and I was Cher, I was the Dharma to his Greg. Bad analogies, I know, but very true nonetheless. When my parents were fighting, he made me forget my troubles and analyze the good things about my family. When I failed a test, he told me I was the smartest girl he knew. And when I felt down about myself, he told me I was the beautiful one, the apple of his eye (Ponder Danielle, "Beautiful").

1. The author has used several **repetitions for effect**. Quote two passages that contain repetition and explain each one's effect:

A. Passage:_____

Effect:_____

B. Passage:_____

Effect:_____

2. Quote a **hyperbole** that is effective in painting the picture of the **male character**:

_____

3.   Quote a **hyperbole** that helps characterize the **narrator:**

_____

4.   A.   Look up the term **"Yin and Yang"** and explain why the author uses this **allusion:**

_____

        B.   What other **allusions** does the author use?

_____

5.   Quote a **magic three** that involves **cause and effect:**

_____

_____

6.   Write a **character sketch** of at least 100 words about someone you know who **makes you feel good about yourself.** Try to use some of the author's Smiley-Face Tricks.

_____

_____

_____

_____

_____

_____

He was an eighty-three-year-old, my-way-or-the-highway, beer-drinking, cigar-smoking, cowboy-hat-wearing man that just so happened to be my great-grandfather. He was my mom's grandfather, the one who practically raised her. She had told me so many stories of him from when she was little that I felt I knew him, although I had never met him. He sounded like the perfect grandpa, and to my mom he was. I always wanted to meet this family legend, and when I was eight I got my chance.

There we finally found ourselves, face-to-face, but the only problem was that he was an old wrinkled little seventy-eight-year-old man, not the young, handsome dude I'd heard about all my life. So after the truth had set in, I thought he would be like most seventy-eight-year-olds--just rocking in a rocking chair. Boy, was I wrong! After only twenty minutes of being with him I, too, saw that young man in my mother's stories. He even chased his dog, and-- believe me--his young, fast dog got a run for his money. Then Grandpa saw me standing there laughing. He turned to me and said, "Hey, boy, you want to see if you can outrun me? You want to play too?" So I did. We ran and played as if he were an eight-year-old like me.

When we had made the return seven-hour distance from his house to ours, I was sad. But then years passed, and I learned to live without him. Until the news. The stroke, the heart attack, the Alzheimer's.

Finally, the seven-hour trip for the last time. This time to the hospital. After all the family's tears, he said, "Hey, boy, I'm gonna need someone to chase after my dog when I'm gone. You did a good job of it last time. You want to play?" So like last time I said "sure" and promised I would chase his dog until I died or the dog died, just like Grandpa had done that day.

He told me he didn't want anyone else to see him after me. He'd said everything he'd needed to say and saw everyone he needed to see. He also told me he was so happy that I was the last one he'd be with.

Since that day I've never had an honor like I had that day. And I never will. I got to be the last he saw, the last one to say goodbye to him, the last one who heard his words (Campos, Jose, "His Final Goodbye").

1.   How does the author **grab the reader's attention in the first line**?

_____

2.   **Summarize** what happens in this selection:

A.   Beginning:_____

B.   Middle:_____

C.   End:_____

3.   A.   What is the **tone** of the piece?_____

      B.   Quote **proof:**_____

4.   What **humor** has the author used?_____

5.   How does the author's ending come **full circle through dialogue**?

_____

6.   Write a **beginning for a character sketch** that is based on a list of **hyphenated modifiers.**

_____

_____

_____

_____

✂ My dad's stubbornness ate away at my mom's soul. He never wanted to do anything my mom suggested or said to do. She had shackles on her feet, was a prisoner in her own home. She wanted to know what happened to a love she once knew. My mom would soon find out that love that was as precious as gold was no more.

The parents of my neighbors, Jerry and Dana, went through the same thing. We never kept secrets from each other--best friends to the end--so they told me all the things to look out for in case my parents were thinking of getting a divorce. I'd know I was in trouble when words like "separating" and "time to think" and "finding myself" started floating around the house. Another sign, according to them, was if there is extra space in my parents' closet or suitcases with clothes in them.

Friday. I had always loved Friday. But not this Friday. This Friday turned out to be the most disquieting day of my life. All the signs that I was afraid of came true. There were bags with my dad's clothes in them and extra space in their closet (Greenridge, McNeil, "Lust and Love").

1.   Quote two **characteristics** that you find out about the **narrator's father:**

A._____

B._____

Dailies

2.   A.   What can you **infer** about the **narrator's mother**?

_____

      B.   Quote **proof**:_____

3.   Quote an **appositive**:_____

4.   Quote two **possessive nouns**:_____ &_____

5.   A.   Quote the **magic three**:

_____,_____,_____

      B.   How can the reader **identify with this passage**?

_____

6.   The author writes about **"signs" of divorce**. Write at least 50 words about **"signs of_____."** Your tone does not have to be the same as the author's. You might want to experiment with a humorous tone.

_____

_____

_____

    ✂ I step out of the car to feel the familiar crush of grass under my feet. I look through the curtains to catch a glimpse of the lost face of my best friend Kristen. I've known her since I was five, and even though life has separated us, we've been best friends ever since. I walk down the stone-filled pathway, memories flashing through my head. I remember when we sat in Kristen's front yard and watched her parents carefully put these same well-rounded stones in place. I lean over and pick a clover and remember what luck they used to bring. I wrap it in a handkerchief and place it in my purse for safekeeping. I continue walking and finally ring the doorbell, thinking about how many neighbors we had disturbed while playing the game "ding-dong-ditch."

Dailies

The door opens, and the lost face of my best friend becomes known again. Time shifts, and we are fourteen again, trailing guys at the mall or crawling out of our window to meet each other to sit at our special place and discuss everything fourteen-year-old girls discuss. Inevitably we'd be caught by our parents, and inevitably we'd promise never to do it again. Until the next time.

"Hey," her voice sounds so soft and familiar (Smith, Catherine., "A Clover, a Handkerchief, and a Boy").

1.   Cite two uses of **commas** and explain the rules:

A.   Quote:_____

        Rule:_____

B.   Quote:_____

        Rule:_____

2.   How is the last line an effective **ending** to the narrator's reverie?

_____

3.   **Titles** can make a reader want to read a piece. How is this title an interesting one?

_____

4.   A.   What is a **symbol** in this passage?_____

        B.   What does it **symbolize**?_____

5.   This excerpt is based on a **series of flashbacks**. Quote your favorite:

_____

6.   Write what could be the **beginning of a short story** by using a **series of flashbacks**.

_____

_____

_____

_____

_____

_____

Superman

tough and strong
tall and intelligent
waiting for the nerve
to ask that one girl
in the blue sequined
dress
if she wanted
to dance with him
waiting for the barfly
to pass out
and open the seat
next to her
so he could talk to her
waiting for
the hamburgers
to hurry up and cook
so he could show her
that he was more
than just a crime-fighting
superhero
he was a gentleman too
(Hollaway, Angela, "Superman").

1.   Explain how this poem is based on **incongruities** by giving two examples:

A._____

B._____

2.   What is **ironic** about the whole premise of this poem?

_____

3.   A.   Quote **four adjectives** that the author uses to **characterize Superman:**
          _____,_____,_____,_____

          B.   Write an **adjective** that you can **infer** about Superman from the narrator's
                    characterization of him:_____

4.   A.   From what **point of view** is this poem written?   (i.e., first person, third
                    person, omniscient)

          _____

          B.   Cite **proof:**_____

5.   Quote a **fact** and an **opinion** from the poem:

A.   Fact:_____

B.   Opinion:_____

6.   **Exchange five words with a neighbor to use in a poem.** (The author was
          given the following words: barfly, superman, hamburger, dress, and sequins.)
          Write a free verse poem using the words. (You may change the form of the
          words--e.g., "sequins" to "sequined.")

Answer Key

*Accept other answers if supported.
*Answers to writing questions will vary.

"Beautiful"

1. A. *"He was beautiful. So beautiful...."
        The author wants to emphasize his beauty.
    B. *"He had a million people and a million emotions in him and he was one in a million."
        Again, the author wants to aggrandize him, to highlight his complexity.
2. "His hands had the strength of a thousand men."
3. "I'm a nobody, invisible almost to myself."
4. A. *"Yang" is "bright, positive, and masculine," whereas "Yin" is "negative, dark, and feminine." The author is saying that they complete each other.
    B. *Sonny and Cher; Dharma and Greg
5. "When my parents were fighting, he made me forget my troubles....When I failed a test, he told me I was the smartest girl he knew. And when I felt down about myself, he told me I was the beautiful one...."
6. Answers will vary.

"His Final Goodbye"

1. The hyphenated adjectives not only add humor to the piece but paint a picture of a type of person that we all know in some way or another.
2. A. *The narrator finally gets to meet the legend, his great-grandfather, and in their playing together the narrator is able to see "that young man in my mother's stories."
    B. *Years later the narrator learns that his great-grandfather has had not only a stroke but also a heart attack and has been diagnosed with Alzheimer's.
    C. * The narrator is the last one to see his great-grandfather, who makes him promise to "chase after my dog" forever.
3. A. *Grateful
    B. *"Since that day I've never had an honor like I had that day."
4. "my-way-or-the-highway, beer-drinking, cigar-smoking, cowboy-hat-wearing"
5. The first time the narrator meets his great-grandfather, the grandfather asks, "You want to play?" The author comes full circle by having the grandfather ask the same question on the final visit.
6. Answers will vary.

"Lust and Love"

1. A.   "My dad's stubbornness"
    B.   "He never wanted to do anything mom suggested or said to do"--inconsiderate
2. A.   *We can infer that the narrator's mother didn't stand up for herself or that she felt powerless to do so.
    B.   *"She had shackles on her feet, was a prisoner in her own home."
3. "The parents of my neighbors, Jerry and Dana,...."
4. dad's & mom's
5. A.   "I'd know I was in trouble when words like 'separating' and 'time to think' and 'finding myself' started floating around the house."
    B.   *Many readers have gone through a divorce in the family and recognize the phrases themselves.
6. Answers will vary.

"A Clover, a Handkerchief, and a Boy"

1. A.   *"I've known her since I was five,...."--compound sentence
    B.   *"I continue walking and finally ring the doorbell, thinking about...."--interrupter or participial phrase that modifies the subject
2. *The narrator has been remembering all the times spent with her friend Kristen; therefore, Kristen's answering the door with her "soft and familiar" voice is the perfect ending to the daydreaming sequence.
3. *First of all, it's a magic three, which adds to the "poetry" of the piece. However, its real attention-getting quality lies in the fact that most readers want to know what these three things have to do with each other.
4. A.   clover
    B.   luck
5. *"thinking about how many neighbors we disturbed playing 'ding-dong-ditch'"
6. Answers will vary.

"Superman"
1. A.   *Superman is "tough and strong," but he is "waiting for the nerve / to ask that one girl...."
    B.   We have trouble picturing a girl in a "blue sequined / dress" seated next to a "barfly" as well as Superman "waiting for the barfly / to pass out" and "waiting for the hamburgers to cook."
2. *The irony is that Superman is even in a bar.
3. A.   "tough and strong / tall and intelligent"
    B.   *We can infer he is patient in that he is "waiting" as opposing to using his "powers" to get what he wants immediately.
4. Omniscient--the author knows what Superman is waiting for.

5. A. *"that one girl / in the blue sequined / dress"
    B. *"he was a gentleman too"
6. Answers will vary.

Dailies

→ My room became my get-away when I was a child because of my parents' fighting constantly over stupid things. Why was my father home late? Who participated more in cooking supper that night? Who supports the children more? My room took me to a place far, far away from there, away from the turmoil, away from the crying, and away from my parents. Sometimes I would dream of being in a land that consisted of only Mario, Luigi, and mushrooms that made you ten feet taller, and then I would take on the evil dragon-prince Bowser. And nothing was greater than flying away on a magical carpet with Aladdin, with the horrible sorcerer so close that I could smell, feel, and even hear his disgusting breath.

When I returned to the real world, that I-hate-it-here-I-want-to-go-back-to-my-dreamland, the old feeling, returned to my thoughts. The constant shouting and breaking of glass were waiting for me there. The words "I hate you" were being thrown around the room like a hot potato. No longer was I on earth; now I was in the fiery pits and it wasn't getting any colder (Odom, Edward, "Childhood").

1. Quote three **allusions** the author uses to make his piece more interesting and give the **background of the references** (tell what the allusions mean):

a.   Allusion:_____Background:_____

b.   Allusion:_____Background:_____

c.   Allusion:_____Background:_____

2.   A.   Quote the **hyphenated modifier:**_____

_____

      B.   To prove its effectiveness, **rewrite the sentence,** replacing the hyphenated modifier with a **single, more common adjective:**

_____

3.   Explain why the **apostrophe** is after the "s" in the word "parents'":

_____

4.   A.   What is the **author's tone**?_____

        B.   Quote a **passage that supports** your answer:_____

_____

5.   A.   Quote an example of **figurative language**:_____

_____

        B.   **Identify its type** (simile, metaphor, etc.):_____

6.   In at least 100 words, write about **a time you needed a special place** for your own private "get-away."

_____

_____

_____

_____

➜ *"Now, pay attention!"*

Teachers, what do they know with their don't-give-me-attitude looks? I would always stare into space, hoping I would see something besides my teacher's huge cowlick. School was my favorite place to daydream; how else could I make the epitome of boredom seem exciting? Going to school was like going to one of my fantasy concerts, where I was the star, and my cheering, clapping, waving fans were awestruck each and every day. But even being famous wasn't always easy, so I would sometimes slip away during all the fraction/proportion nonsense to the meadows, where I could taste the twirl of wind on the tip of my tongue and the sprinkle of rain rolling down my cheeks. Math class was always simple to get away from, as was Texas history, where I, too, almost got shot at the Alamo. Even so, I would rather dream my way into la-la land than learn. To me, then, it was all about "where you go, not what you know" (Martinez, Sophia, "Taking a Stroll on Sandra Dee's Path").

1. A. Who can you **infer** is the speaker of the first line?_____

    B. What is your **clue**?_____

    C. Why is this line in **quotation marks**?_____

2. Humor appeals to readers. Quote an example of **humor** used in this piece:

    _____

3. A. Quote an effective example of **imagery**:_____

    _____

    B. Explain to what **sense** your example appeals:_____

4. A. Why is the word "Texas" **capitalized** but not the word "history"?

    _____

    B. Explain the rule for **capitalizing courses** in school:_____

    _____

5. Quote the author's **theme:**_____

6. In at least 50 words, write about a time that you **daydreamed in class:**

    _____

    _____

    _____

    _____

➡️Here I am hiding amongst the trees. I am the James Bond of kids in my tree house. The darkness swallows me. I am waiting for the enemy to pass my secret lair. Only one other person knows of this tree house--my friend, who is on top studying the surroundings. Our house in the trees is invisible from the ground. We have to take the secret way up. Two trees down, behind the big pile of brush, there is a hole in the rotting tree where we enter. We stand up, grab the rope and jump, putting our feet on the wall of the tree, walking up its side while pulling ourselves up with the rope. From there we grab onto the cable swing and glide, glide, glide like birds across to the tree house. We are safe, as we know that the only way to get down is to swing from the rope to the trampoline.

But out of nowhere comes the enemy! He runs the direction in which, as a diversionary tactic, I throw the rock. I grab the rope and swing down, heading for the trampoline. I hit the tarp and bounce off, falling on my knees onto the surprisingly pillow-soft ground. Taking off like a jack rabbit toward the garage, I snatch the secret box and sneak with an I-can't-get-caught slyness to the concealed entrance, where my friend is waiting for me. We tie the box to the rope, and my friend begins to pull like he's the strongest man in the world. He then lowers the rope, and I climb.

As we sit and take a break in the chilled Mountain Dews and fresh double-fudge brownies and chocolate cookies, we both know that once again James Bond has completed his mission in the tree house (Kadar, Michael, "Don't Get into Poison Ivy!").

1. A. On what **metaphor** is the passage based?_____

    B. How does the author come **full circle** with his **extended metaphor**?

    _____

2. A. In what **verb tense** is the passage written?_____

    B. List **five verbs** to support your answer:_____,

    _____,_____,_____,_____

3.   A.   Quote a **repetition for effect**:_____

     B.   How does it **add to the piece**?_____

4.   Quote a **personification**:_____

5.   Quote a sentence that illustrates **specific details for effect**:

_____

_____

6.   In at least 50 words, write a passage about a **super-hero** you pretended (or could have pretended) to be.

_____

_____

_____

_____

→At my grandma's I was the war hero. Dropping like mere flies, the jet planes would crash into the earth as I shot them down with my BB gun. I called them jet planes; my grandma called them pesky pigeons that ate all of the squirrels' food. But I still knew my mission was to shoot any plane that got too close to the feeder. I wasn't just destroying planes; I was capturing tanks as they waddled across the grass. There were usually six or seven in a row heading for safety under the porch. I was the war hero at my grandma's, and I always got a reward (Barnett, Trey, "Running Wild").

1.   A.   Why is the word "grandma's" not **capitalized**?_____

_____

     B.   **When would you capitalize "grandma's"** other than at the beginning of a sentence?

_____

2.   Quote an example of an effective **alliteration** that the author used:

_____

3.   Explain the use of the two **semicolons**:_____

_____

4.   A.   Explain why "waddled" is an especially good **verb choice**:

_____

       B.   Give three **synonyms** for "waddled" that would be **less effective choices**:

_____,_____,_____,

5.   Explain the rules for **"too," "two," and "to."**

       A.   Too:_____

       B.   Two:_____

       C.   To:_____

6.   In at least 50 words, write a **humorous memory** you have of being at a relative's house:

_____

_____

_____

_____

➜I remember walking down the middle of the barn and touching each horse on the nose. There were rows and rows of them. My favorite, Amy, was always in the stall closest to the door. She was light, almost white-gray with dark grayish-black spots. I would always take her out to ride before beginning my stroll down the barn to see new foals, old mares, and hyper yearlings. On the ride through the pasture, I could hear the wind rustle its melody and almost taste the sweet spring flowers. I could feel the water splash my feet as Amy pranced through freshly poured drops of heaven.
Once Amy and I had explored everything there was to explore on our daily

adventure, I'd take her back to her stall and fall half-asleep on the great pile of hay. Listening to her munch, I would take in the other horses neighing at each other, with the occasional cow's bellow, and my dog panting beside me with one eye open to protect me from those pesky enemies who--without fail--broke my dream by calling me to supper.

　　Of course, those pests always lectured about how going barefoot around our farm leads to illness.　But who ever listened to them?　The dirt made me feel free, the hay comfortable, and the barn's old, creaking wood secure (Adams, Alyssa, "I Am Going to the Barn").

1.　　Quote an **appositive:**_____

2.　　A.　　Quote the use of another **comma:**_____

_____

　　　　B.　　What is the **comma rule** for your example?_____

3.　　Explain the use of the **hyphen** between "grayish" and "black":_____

_____

4.　　A.　　What can you **infer** the "drops of heaven" are?_____

　　　　B.　　Who are the **"pesky enemies"**?_____

　　　　C.　　Of what **figurative language device** would these be an example?

_____

5.　　**Summarize** what is happening in the passage.　Remember to state briefly the beginning, middle, and end.

A.　　Beginning:_____

B.　　Middle:_____

C.　　End:_____

6.　　Write a sentence that begins "On the ride through the..." and that includes at least **two examples of imagery:**

_____

Answer Key

*Accept other answers if supported.
*Answers to writing questions will vary.

"Childhood"

1.   A.   "Mario"--Super Mario Brothers Video Game
      B.   "Luigi"---Super Mario Brothers Video Game
      C.   "Mushrooms that made you 10 feet taller"—Super Mario Brothers video game
2.   A.   "I-hate-it-here-I-want-to-go-back-to-my-dreamland"
      B.   *When I returned to the real world, that familiar feeling returned to my thoughts.
3.   Plural possessive--Both parents are fighting.
4.   A.   *Anger
      B.   "I-hate-it-here"--referring to the "real world" of his parents' fighting
5.   A.   "I would take on the evil dragon-prince Bowser."
      B.   Metaphor
6.   Answers will vary.

"Taking a Stroll on Sandra Dee's Path"

1.   A.   A teacher
      B.   "Teachers, what do they know"
      C.   It's dialogue; a teacher is speaking.
2.   *"hoping I would see something besides my teacher's huge cowlick"
3.   A.   *"to the meadows, where I could taste the twirl of wind on the tip of my tongue and the sprinkle of rain rolling down my cheeks"
      B.   *Taste and touch
4.   A.   "Texas" is always capitalized, but "history" is only capitalized if it has a number after it (e.g., History III).
      B.   Language courses (e.g., Spanish, English, etc.) and courses with numbers after them are capitalized (e.g., Algebra IV); all other courses are not capitalized.
5.   "Even so, I would rather dream my way into la-la land than learn."
     "To me, then, it was all about 'where you go, not what you know.'"
6.   Answers will vary.

"Don't Get Poison Ivy"

1.   A.   "I am the James Bond of kids in my tree house."
      B.   He repeats the image by saying that "once again James Bond has completed his mission in the tree house."

2. A. Present tense
    B. *Am hiding, swallows, am waiting, knows, is
3. A. "glide, glide, glide"
    B. *The repetition helps the reader envision the process of gliding.
4. "The darkness swallows me."
5. *"Two trees down, behind the big pile of brush, there is a hole in the rotting tree where we enter."
6. Answers will vary.

"Running Wild"

1. A. "Grandma's" is not capitalized as it is modified by the possessive pronoun "my." In this sentence, "grandma's" cannot be replaced by her name (e.g., my Louise).
    B. "Grandma's" would be capitalized if it can be replaced by the person's name (e.g., We went to Grandma's to eat);
2. "Pesky pigeons"
3. The semicolons avoid run-on sentences by separating two independent clauses.
4. A. *The pigeons would "waddle" because they would be full of the "squirrels' food."
    B. Walked, traveled, ran
5. A. Also, in addition to; an excessive amount
    B. Number
    C. Preposition (e.g., Go to the store.)
6. Answers will vary.

"I Am Going to the Barn"

1. "My favorite, Amy,"
2. A. *"She was light, almost white-gray"
    B. *Coordinate adjective
3. Hyphenated adjective--implies that she was a whitish-gray horse
4. A. Rain
    B. *Parents, siblings, etc.
    C. Metaphor
5. A. *The narrator remembers being in the barn with her favorite horse, Amy.
    B. *Amy and the narrator would explore the pasture.
    C. *After their return, Amy would be fed, and the narrator would fall half-asleep until she was called in to supper and lectured once again.
6. Answers will vary.

Dailies

➡️We all have some sort of fire stored in us, some type of rage that usually expresses itself in uncontrollable mood swings. However, have we ever thought of fighting that fire with a little bit of its own medicine? Men and women taking charge, parents taking charge, younger siblings trying to take charge are only some of the reasons we teenagers might want to fight fire with fire. All it takes is a little bit of understanding, a speck of time to listen, and a teensy-weensy bit of bonding.

✄

After we have taken the time to understand and to listen, the final step is bonding, especially with the younger siblings. We all know of those nonsensical, non-stop sibling fights. And we all know that the older ones always  lose to those miniature, loud-mouth twerps with their missing teeth and their bowling-ball tummies. "Mom, Sarah's not letting me see her stuffed bunny!"

"Sarah!"

"But, Mom!"

Sound familiar? But we could always do something. Sure, we could tell them they could **see** it. That's what they wanted, isn't it? But you **see** with your eyes, not your hands. You still could let them **see** but tell them that it'll cost them and bribe as much as you can from them. And what about those they-hit-first-but-they-still-win fights. Sure, we could "bond" our fists with their faces, and that's what we've done in the past, knowing that the scolding we'll receive will be well worth it if we give them a hard enough punch before a parent comes to their rescue. Now, though, perhaps we should "consider the source," walking away, with a sophisticated you're-not-worth-the-trouble attitude. Sometimes the best "bonding" is the I'll-bond-by-myself-you-bond-by-yourself technique. Ah, sibling bonding (Mitchell, Sarah, "How To Fight Fire with Fire").

1.   How does the author use an **adage** as an attention-getter in her introduction?

2. What is the **thesis** of this "how-to" paper?

_____

3. The second paragraph is actually the author's third body. What **special transition** does the author use to **remind the readers of the two other points of the paper?**

_____

4. A. How does the author effectively use **dialogue** without making the paper a narrative?

_____

B. List two **rules of dialogue** that the author follows:

_____&_____

5. A. How does the author use humor to **characterize** younger siblings? Quote two examples:

_____&_____

B. How is the author's last solution about "bonding" **ironic?**

_____

6. Write an **introduction for a "how-to" paper** based on a **famous saying**. Be sure to include an attention-getter and your thesis, complete with three aspects or points to be covered.

_____

_____

_____

_____

_____

→We have all seen one. A catfish. We might not have known it at the time, we might not have been able to distinguish it from any other fish in the sea, but it was there all along. We have all looked at it and walked on by. The thing we probably didn't know was that with good teaching, a catfish can learn to sing for its supper. Of course, we all thought the proverbial "hell would freeze over" before a catfish learned how to sing, but perhaps the goal is not as impossible as it sounds. Teaching a catfish how to sing is a lot of hard work, full of long hours and grueling training, but it is well worth the effort. We have to gather our equipment, lure in a catfish with a good voice, and teach it the song.

✂

Besides gathering the equipment in order to teach a catfish how to sing for its supper, we must lure in just the right catfish, one with a good voice. We might want to consider putting our Gourmet Cuisine English worms on the hook of our Mickey Mouse rod and reel, as we must remember that this must be a special fish. After plenty of catfish are surrounding us--or actually our Gourmet Cuisine--we need to hold auditions to see which catfish has the best croak. A tenor voice is what we'll need if our catfish will be singing a song by the Beach Boys, but perhaps a bass with its smooth, low range would be just the thing for crooning out those love songs. Next, we have to hold rehearsals so our catfish's voice will sound skilled and honed to perfection. After all, singing for one's supper takes practice. Finally.... (De La Cerda, Megan, "How To Teach a Catfish To Sing for Its Supper").

1.   Obviously the author's paper is based on the **"impossible" or fantasy**. Cite three instances of the impossible:

_____,_____,_____

2.   How are the three aspects or steps in the thesis statement in **parallel structure**?

_____

3.   A.   What **fragment for effect** does the author use? _____

        B.   What is the **effect** on the reader?_____

        C.   **Rewrite the first several lines** without using a fragment:

_____

4.   A.   What can you **infer** about why the author uses the word "proverbial"?

_____

        B.   How is the author's use of the word "bass" a **pun**?

_____

5.   What are the **capitalization rules** for the following?

        A.   Mickey Mouse (but not "rod and reel"):_____

        B.   Gourmet Cuisine English worms:_____

        C.   Beach Boys:_____

6.   **Finish the author's second paragraph** by giving a **third step and support**.
        You might want to add a **concluding sentence** as well.

_____

_____

_____

_____

_____

_____

→School is to fun as a whale is to small. School is hard, school is frustrating, school is annoying, and it gets on every student's very last nerve until even that breaks. School is like going to work, except we get no reward or payment for everything we put up with. School causes pain, worry, and stress, yet learning is supposed to be fun. So how do we turn this torture, this agony, into fun? We need friends, goals, and confidence to discover enjoyment in school.

One of the first things we need to enjoy school is friends. Friends can help us when things go wrong. It's nice to have someone else who can share our feelings, somebody else who has forgotten the meaning of "free time," or somebody else who has visions of seeing the teacher doing the same work himself. Friends can help us with our problems and give us advice on how to solve three times "x" squared multiplied by the cube root of 350,250, how to be a poet and not know it, and even how to dump a lover. We also need friends to support us. They can encourage us, make us feel better. Lots of times all that's necessary is a little joke to make your day outshine the sun. Friends are important (Kohles, Brad, "How To Enjoy School").

1. A. Cite what you think to be the best example of **specific details for effect**:

    _____

    B. **Rewrite** the example using **general terms**:

    _____

2. Cite a **cause and an effect**:

    _____

3. What **analogy** does the author use in the introduction?

_____

_____

4. A. Quote a **hyperbole:**_____

    B. What **adage or saying** has the author used for **humorous effect**?

_____

5. What simple method does the author use to **conclude the first body paragraph**?

    _____

6. The author's next paragraph will be about "goals" in school. **Write a paragraph that informs students how to have goals.** Remember to begin with a transition word and a topic sentence followed by at least three examples and supports for each.

    _____

    _____

    _____

    _____

    _____

    _____

    _____

    _____

➡We all want money. We all love money. Some people might not have as much as other people. We've all heard the saying "money doesn't grow on trees." Well, yes it can. We can grow a money tree by following a few simple steps. All we have to do is obtain a silver dollar minted in the year of your birth, locate one red-headed friend to carry the dollar in his or her pocket for one day--for good luck--and then bury it. Our money tree will grow in no time.

✄

After obtaining the special silver dollar and finding our red-headed friend, the next step in growing our own money tree requires some dirty work, as in working in dirt. After traveling in the pocket of a redhead for twenty-four hours, the coin must be buried six feet

© 2002 by M.E. Ledbetter

into the ground. Our backyard must be the location for planting because we might want to keep our money tree a secret. We'll need to walk around our yard to find a spot where there is plenty of sunlight and the ground is soft. If the ground is as hard as a rock, we'll never make it down six feet. Of course, we'll have to use a shovel to dig our hole, as digging can be hard on our nails. Since the hole must be exactly six feet deep, measuring will be required, preferably by using a metal tape measure that is at least six feet long. Once we are sure that the hole is the correct depth, we must drop the coin into the deep, dark abyss. The visual image that we will create as the coin travels down the dark shaft will cause us to hear the coin hit the bottom with a soft thud, just as if it had landed on a tuft of cotton. We'll then need to let out a deep sigh and begin refilling the hole with dirt, patting the last of the dirt in a mound and letting nature take its course (Heinrich, Michael, "How To Grow Money").

1. What is the **grammar rule** for the author's use of "his or her" instead of "their" in the line "locate one red-headed friend to carry the dollar..."?

_____

2. Explain the **pun** in the topic sentence of the second paragraph:

_____

3. Why would it be **grammatically incorrect** if the author had written the following: After traveling in the pocket of a redhead for twenty-four hours, you...?

_____

4. What is the rule for placing a **comma** after the word "deep" in line twelve of the second paragraph?_____

5. A. What word(s) acts as a **context clue** for the meaning of "abyss"?

_____

B. What can you **infer** that "abyss" means?_____

6. Write a **concluding paragraph** that contains an attention-getting device and that restates the thesis and the three steps in the process.

_____

_____

_____

➜In the beginning God created man, then man created sports, and then sports created the fan. Since the beginning of time, when one Neanderthal first hurled a large chunk of rock at another, we have been captivated by the success and failure of the athlete. We idolize our sports heroes, placing them on a pedestal and paying them incredible amounts of money to catch a ball, and we do it for the fans. Fans range in shape and size and "technique." There are fans who quietly applaud their heroes, and there are those who paint themselves, wear Viking helmets, and stand bare-chested in snow. We only need to know three steps, though, to be a fan of sports: choose a sport, choose a team, and learn how to cheer like a Houston cheerleader.

✄

After we have chosen a sport and team, perhaps the most important step is to learn how to cheer. Now, there are only a few select body types that can fit into cheerleader uniforms, so if we are not of this nature, we'll just have to learn all the tricks to cheering correctly. First, we must understand that our team can do no wrong. If something happens to affect our team negatively, then it must be the other team's fault or, more likely, THE REF'S. The referee can be our team's best friend or worst enemy so it is imperative that we pay close attention to the action and cheer, boo, or throw things accordingly. Also, it is necessary that we learn all the important cheers that apply to our team. Some teams have highly sophisticated cheers, such as Yale's "Boolah Boolah," and the Aggies' "Whoop," while Harvard is known for "Annihilate them! Decimate them! Make them relinquish the ball!" We must make certain to study and memorize these cheers so as not to embarrass ourselves. Also, when cheering, we must be careful to cheer only at appropriate times. Cheering while the other team scores or, even worse, after everyone has already left the arena can lead to much reddening of the face, unless--of course--our team's colors are red, in which case nobody know but us (Hales, Zac, "How To Be a Sports Fan").

1. How does the author use a **progression** as an attention-getter in his introduction?

    _____

2. Cite three examples of **humor** in the introduction:

    A._____

    B._____

    C._____

3. Explain the use of the **colon** in the thesis statement:

    _____

4. Quote the sentence in the second paragraph that is quite sophisticated in that it is an example of a **magic three within another magic three:**

    _____

    _____

    _____

5. Cite two examples of **comma usage** and state their **rules:**

    A._____Rule:_____

    B._____ Rule:_____

6. Practice writing a **magic three by giving advice on how to choose a sport**. If you can, try a magic three within a magic three.

    _____

    _____

    _____

Answer Key

*Accept other answers if supported.
*Answers to writing questions will vary.

"How To Fight Fire with Fire"

1. *The author uses the adage "fight fire with fire" as an attention-getter, as she addresses the teenage audience and explains who the "other side" is and how to give them some of their "own medicine."
2. *The thesis is stated in the last two sentences. When provoked, teenagers might want to walk away or react in a thinking way instead of with anger.
3. "After we have taken the time to understand and to listen"
4. A. The author uses snippets of conversation to prove her point; therefore, dialogue is used as a method of elaboration.
   B. A new paragraph for each new speaker & quotation marks
5. A. *"missing teeth" & "bowling-ball tummies"
   B. *Walking away from trouble is usually not considered "bonding"; however, the author's point is that sometimes--ironically--the most effective "bonding" is done alone.
6. Answers will vary.

"How To Teach a Catfish To Sing for Its Supper"

1. *"with good teaching, a catfish can learn to sing for its supper," "one with a good voice," "hold auditions"
2. "Gather," "lure," and "teach" are all verbs.
3. A. "A catfish."
   B. *The author's first sentence makes the reader wonder what "one" is; therefore, it gets the reader's attention.
   C. *We have all seen a catfish.
4. A. *Perhaps by using the word "proverbial" the author is letting us know that she is not using the phrase "hell would freeze over" as a cliche but as an adage. She also might be mitigating her use of "hell."
   B. "Bass" refers to a type of voice as well as a type of fish.
5. A. Capitalize a brand name, but not the product.
   B. Same as above
   C. Musical group
6. Answers will vary.

"How To Enjoy School"

1.   A.   * "Friends can help us with our problems and give us advice on how to solve three times 'x' squared multiplied by the cube root of 350,250."
   B.   * Friends can help us with math problems.
2.   * If friends encourage us (cause), they can make us feel better (effect).
3.   "School is to fun as a whale is to small."
4.   A.   * "it gets on every student's very last nerve until even that breaks"
   B.   * "how to be a poet and not know it" (a variation of the adage)
5.   * The author comes full circle by repeating the point of his first body in a simple sentence.
6.   Answers will vary.

"How To Grow Money"

1.   "His or her" is singular and agrees with "one."
2.   "Dirty work" is a pun in this instance in that the work is actually with "dirt."
3.   * It would be a dangling modifier since "you" have not traveled "in the pocket of a red-head for twenty-four hours"; the "coin" does the traveling.
4.   Introductory adverb clause
5.   A.   * deep
   B.   a deep hole or space
6.   Answers will vary.

"How To Be a Sports Fan"

1.   * We have all heard the phrase "in the beginning God created man," but the author creates a humorous picture by writing about the creation of sports and the sports fan.
2.   A.   "when one Neanderthal first hurled a large chunk of rock at another"
   B.   "paying them incredible amounts of money to catch a ball"
   C.   "there are those who paint themselves, wear Viking helmets, and stand bare-chested in snow"
3.   Introduce a list
4.   "Some teams have highly sophisticated cheers, such as Yale's 'Boolah Boolah,' and the Aggies' 'Whoop,' while Harvard is known for 'Annihilate them! Decimate them! Make them relinquish the ball!'"
5.   A.   * "After we have chosen a sport and team,"--introductory adverb clause
   B.   * "First,"--introductory word
6.   Answers will vary.

Dailies

♡My mom sinks. She knows nothing can float without air so she exhales slowly, allowing herself to become enveloped in a suffocating layer of tension and worry evidenced through the circles under her eyes, her fidgeting hands. She's been pounding on the bathroom door for ten minutes now, slowing down to melodramatic drum beats, echoing her defeat as she collapses to her knees, veins popping out of her arms like rivers penetrating throughout her skin. She continues to pummel at the door, like trying to bruise concrete. I get the faint hint of water running steadily, fast and powerful, tiny needles of death splattering on the tub's bottom, ricocheting against the tile wall. Tears of fright are frozen to my mom's face. Purposely, I kick over the plastic pink trash can. Kleenexes, one dead Crest toothpaste tube, and pink plastic wrappers spew everywhere, but my mom manages to avert her eyes, glazed over with fear, in my direction, the door now etched with impending doom from her terrified fingernails.

"Daddy's in there," she whispers in some strange new voice. "Trapped. He's passed out in a locked bathroom and the water's still running."

Sound waves hesitate for a moment, and when her words finally catch up with my ears, shock has already taken control of my feet and melted them in place (Shaver, Rachel, "Growing Wings").

1. An author reveals **character** by appearance, environment, actions, speech, what others say, and inner thoughts and feelings. Choose four of the above methods and quote how the author has revealed **fear in the mother**:

A. Method:_____Quote:_____

_____

B. Method:_____Quote:_____

_____

C. Method:_____Quote:_____

_____

D.   Method:_____Quote:_____

_____

2.   What can you **infer** the author means by the following phrase: "She knows nothing can float without air so she exhales slowly..."?

_____

3.   A.   In what **tense** is the excerpt written?_____

      B.   Quote three **verbs** to prove this:_____,_____,_____

      C.   **Why** do you think the author chose this tense?_____

_____

4.   A.   Quote a **simile:**_____

      B.   Quote a **metaphor**:_____

      C.   Quote a **personification**:_____

5.   What can you **infer** about the author's reason for listing the contents of the trash can?

_____

6.   Write at least a 100-word passage narrative about when you knew **"something was wrong."**

_____

_____

_____

_____

_____

_____

_____

♡World War II had just ended, and there I was, a fourteen-year-old girl singing in the trendiest spot in town, the Blue Night Lounge. Man, let me tell you, that joint was really jumpin' when everyone found out that the boys were coming home, which meant I had to work overtime, but that wasn't a problem for me because I love what I do. Maybe what I really love, though, is getting more dead presidents put into my black satin handbag. You see, if you're a woman living in the big city and you want to make it big, then there are three things you need: good friends, a good man, and tons of moola (Lindon, Mallory, "Scattered Pictures").

1. What is the rule for the **hyphens** in the first sentence?_____

2. A.   Quote the **appositive**:_____

_____

B.   What is the rule for **punctuating an appositive**?_____

3. What is the reason for the **colon** in the last sentence?_____

_____

4. What do the "dead presidents" **symbolize** for the narrator?_____

_____

5. What is the **setting** of the passage?_____

6. The narrator really loves her job. Write at least a 50-word piece, imagining yourself in a **different environment with a job you love:**

_____

_____

_____

_____

_____

♡Most guys try to impress the girls by wearing the flashy clothes, getting muscles that can lift anything but their "D-" in all eight periods, and telling them how beautiful they are when really they're so ugly their looks could break bullet-proof glass. Me, on the other hand, I don't want any girlfriend. It's too complicated to take them to the movies, give them a gift for their birthday, and talk to them about anything because they're too busy talking about how their hair is all messed up or or they've broken a fingernail or some other ridiculous concept that's only important to girls.

The day I got the note from Meg, the girl I had never seen in my life, I was shocked. "Oh great," I thought to myself as I read the note that said, "I like you."

Then I freaked. What if she's one of those cheerleaders that likes some football player that can punch my lights out all the way to Pluto? I guess they don't sell body armor at the Country Store. Of course, I almost didn't notice the fine print in the purple gel ink that said, "Come to tonight's basketball game. I'm number 25."

"Okay, stay calm. It's just some girl that wants you to come to a basketball game and talk to her," I said to myself as the bell sounded to end eighth period. What could possibly go wrong?" (Roeschen, Michael, "My Secret Valentine").

1.   A.   What is the **tone** of the piece?_____

       B.   Quote two **examples** to prove this:

    1._____

    2._____

2.   Quote two examples of different **comma rules** and **state the rules:**

    A.   Rule:_____Example:_____

_____

    B.   Rule:_____Example:_____

_____

3.   Quote an example of **internal and external conflicts:**

    A.   Internal:_____

    B.   External:_____

4.   Quote a **specific detail for effect** regarding the note:_____

_____

5.   Quote a **magic three**:_____,_____

_____

6.   Write a **humorous passage** that illustrates **how you are unlike "most guys" or "most girls" in some way.**

_____

_____

_____

_____

_____

_____

_____

♡Somehow I missed my chance to be a kid. I never ran around, built forts, or played softball with the kids down the street. I was too busy growing up. My life passed me by, and I was trying to make up for lost opportunities. I mean, I wasn't deprived or anything; spoiled is really the word. The best things in life are free, but all of my happiness had been bought. Nothing was made from the soul. So here I am wasting the quote/unquote "best years of my life," trying to make up for those lost opportunities.

After you've grown up, you kind of lose touch with your imagination. So it's not that easy to pretend. You have to do a little soul searching to find out who you really are.

I never played Peter Pan and flew to Never-Never Land. I was never Cinderella getting ready for the Ball to dance the night away with Prince Charming. I was never Jane waiting for Tarzan in our tree hut. Barbies never overflowed my room. But now my chance had come for me to be a kid again, and I wasn't going to pass it up (Smith, Catherine, "Port Jackson").

    1.   A.   What is the **tone** of the passage?_____

            B.   Quote **proof:**_____

    2.   A.   Quote three **allusions** the author uses:_____,

_____,_____

            B.   Why does the author **choose** these allusions?

_____

3.   A.   What **adage** does the author cite?_____

    B.   How does she **disprove this theory** in her own life?_____

_____

4.   Quote the **magic three** in the first paragraph that the author uses to prove that she's never had a "chance to be a kid."

_____,_____,_____

5.   What is the **universal theme** of the excerpt?_____

6.   The next line in the narrative is "As I crept through Old Man Jackson's backyard...." Write at least 100 words that could follow this story starter.

_____

_____

_____

_____

_____

♡The four of us were chatting about things that happened at school, soaking up some sun rays and watching birds zoom by like jets. I looked up at the perfectly round sun and saw a cloud of feathers. We knew who it was so we prepared for a fight. It was the Wilson brothers.

The oldest one said furiously, "Hey, idiots, where is my bird?"

"First of all, it isn't your bird because it is on our property, and second we are not idiots, idiot!"

"Shut up, Steven," I whispered.

Steven is my little brother and fights with anyone even if they are Shaq's size.

"This is our side of the ditch!" Steven declared with his fist closed.

"We'll just see about that!" was the response we got.

I momentarily thought about getting mad at my brother, but he's only nine, so what was the use. My other two friends, Pat and Jared, are both chubby, but Jared looks like an overgrown orange that can talk.

We woke up early in the morning. The sun was peeking into the darkness, the grass was dewy, and the I-want-to-suck-your-blood mosquitoes were trying to kill us by inhaling as much blood as they could fit into their size-of-periods-on-a-piece-of-paper stomachs.

We saw them coming, crawling through the brush like lions ready to attack their prey. We all knew this was going to be a painful fight (Rios, Isaac, "Our Side of the Ditch").

1. Why would it be **incorrect** to write "watching birds zoom by like **a** jet" and "We saw them coming...like **a** lion"?

_____

2. State two reasons the author **begins new paragraphs** in this selection:

A._____ B._____

3. One method of **combining sentences** is to use a **present participial phrase**, which is an "-ing" word group that works as an adjective (e.g., I looked down, folding my hands as if in prayer).

A.   Quote a **participial phrase** the author has used:_____

_____

B.   To prove the effectiveness of this method of combining, **rewrite the sentence** in a less sophisticated manner:

_____

4.   Why would it be **incorrect to place a comma before the "and"** in the sentence that begins, "STEVEN IS MY LITTLE BROTHER..."?

_____

5.   A.   Quote a **hyphenated modifier**:_____

       B.   Rewrite the sentence, using a **one-word adjective** instead:

_____

6.   Write a **dialogue about you and your friends protecting something akin to your** "SIDE OF THE DITCH." Include a PARTICIPIAL PHRASE, A HYPHENATED MODIFIER, AND FIGURATIVE LANGUAGE. REMEMBER THE RULES FOR DIALOGUE.

_____

_____

_____

_____

_____

Answer Key

*Accept other answers if supported.
*Answers to writing questions will vary.

"Growing Wings"

1. A. Actions–"My mom sinks. She knows nothing can float without air so she exhales slowly...."
    B. Appearance–"layer of tension and worry evidenced through the circles under her eyes"
    C. Speech–" 'Daddy's in there,' she whispers in some strange new noise."
    D. Appearance–"veins popping out of her arms like rivers penetrating throughout her skin"
2. It's as if the mother is barely afloat in fear and "sinking" fast, needing air to "keep her head above water."
3. A. Present tense
    B. *"sinks," "knows," "exhales"
    C. Present tense makes the action more immediate.
4. A. "like trying to bruise concrete"
    B. *"suffocating layer of tension"
    C. "Sound waves hesitate for a moment"
5. We can infer that the author wants the scene to be real to us, that the contents of the narrator's trash can will probably reflect that of our own, thus drawing us even closer to the action by such a simple detail.
6. Answers will vary.

"Scattered Pictures"

1. Hyphenated modifier
2. A. "the trendiest spot in town, the Blue Night Lounge"
    B. Set off appositives in commas.
3. To introduce a list
4. Money
5. a nightclub in a big city just after World War II
6. Answers will vary.

"My Secret Valentine"

1. A. *Humorous, cynical

     B.   "telling them how beautiful they are when really they're so ugly their looks could break bulletproof glass"

2.   A.   Series: "Most guys try to impress the girls by wearing the flashy clothes, getting muscles..., and telling them...."

     B.   Interrupter: "Me, on the other hand,"

3.   A.   "Okay, stay calm."

     B.   "The day I got the note from Meg...I was shocked."

4.   * "Of course, I almost didn't notice the fine print in the purple gel ink...."

5.   * "It's too complicated to take them to the movies, give them a gift for their birthday, and talk to them...."

6.   Answers will vary.

"Port Jackson"

1.   A.   Nostalgic

     B.   "So here I am wasting the quote/unquote 'best years of my life,' trying to make up for those lost opportunities."

2.   A.   "I never played Peter Pan," "I was never Cinderella getting ready for the Ball," and "I was never Jane waiting for Tarzan"

     B.   These allusions represent the fairy tales that kids dream about.

3.   A.   "The best things in life are free"

     B.   The author disproves this theory when she states that "all her happiness had been bought."

4.   "I never ran around, built forts, or played softball with the kids down the street."

5.   "You have to do a little soul searching to find out who you really are."

6.   Answers will vary.

"Our Side of the Ditch"

1.   "Birds" is plural and requires its comparison to be plural, which would be "jets." "Them" is also plural and necessitates the author's using "lions" in agreement.

2.   A.   Dialogue

     B.   * Time change, subject change

3.   A.   * "crawling through the brush like lions ready to attack their prey"

     B.   * "We saw them crawl through the brush...."

4.   It is not a compound sentence; it simply has a compound verb.

5.   A.   * "size-of-periods-on-a-piece-of-paper"; "I-want-to-suck-your-blood"

     B.   Tiny stomachs; hungry mosquitoes

6.   Answers will vary.

Dailies

✳She sits there with her hands on her desk, writing like she's trying to be the first one done. She lets her dark brown hair droop down past her shoulders, brushing it back when it threatens to impair her vision. She has a smile like an angel but a personality like a devil. She's probably worrying whether her paper will be good or not. At this rate, it looks like she'll come in first if speed is any determiner. What's this? She's now writing on her hand--a reminder to call Melissa, homework for old Mrs. B., the name of her true love? I can't make out what it says; her hand has gone back to her hair. She's done, now, with it all. All the motions have stopped. Except for her lips. She's whispering something to the kid in front of her. She should be a ventriloquist. Now silence. Nothing (Molder, Harrison, "The Girl").

1. One way an author can reveal **characterization** is through **actions.** List two of the girl's actions and explain what you can **infer** about her from what she's doing:

A. Action:_____Inference:_____

_____

B. Action:_____Inference:_____

_____

2. Another way to reveal **character** is by **appearance.** Quote two **details** the author uses to give clues to the girl's looks.

A._____ B._____

3. A. Quote a **magic three**:_____,

_____,_____

    B. Explain why you think it is **effective**:_____

4.   A.   One method of **combining sentences** is by using an "-ing" word group called a **participial phrase**. To prove that this is a sophisticated method of combining, **rewrite** the second sentence, not using the "-ing" word group.

_____

       B.   Explain why the author's version is **not a run-on sentence**:

_____

5.   Quote **examples** of the following:

       A.   **Humor**:_____

       B.   **Personification:**_____

       C.   **Fragment for effect**:_____

6.   Write a **magic three** involving three things the girl could have whispered to the kid in front of her. Your magic three must be in one sentence and must contain at least 15 words.

_____

_____

_____

✳Ali, the girl with many friends. Ali, the one who talks too much. Ali, the girl who would make straight "A's" if she'd shut up and start studying. I can't help it if I'm the go-home-and-jump-straight-on-the-phone girl. I think my mom is getting a remote to turn me off, especially when I go on one of my N-Sync rampages. I can't help it. It's like I'm programmed.

My dream boys come on, I stop whatever I'm doing, and I jump, squeal, and scream with my dad in the background yelling, "Ali, wait till the stupid concert! I'll need a hearing aid if you don't shut up! Do you hear me? Shut it up!" Me, shut up? Dream on (Thompson, Ali, "Me").

1. The first three "sentences" are actually **fragments for effect**. Rewrite them into either *one sentence or three.*

    _____

    _____

    _____

2. A. Why is an **apostrophe** used in "*A's*"?_____

    B. Write **another example that would follow this rule besides a letter:**

    _____

    C. Why is "*A's*" enclosed in **quotation marks**?_____

3. Quote a **cause and an effect**:_____

    _____

4. Quote an example of **humor**:_____

5. Quote an example of the following **comma rules:**

    A. **Series**:_____

    B. **Direct address**:_____

    C. **Appositive**:_____

6. Write at least a 50-word **character sketch** about yourself. Include a *hyphenated modifier, humor, and dialogue:*

    _____

    _____

    _____

    _____

    _____

＊He sits in his chair, tapping his pencil to the beat of one of Limp Bizkit's songs, and tries to start conversations or arguments so he doesn't have to work. He can be funny at times, but this must not be one of them. Everyone he's turned to so far has ignored him. I can tell that the main thing on his mind is not writing about some kid. No, I'm sure he's thinking about his Play Station games and every TV show that he's going to watch this weekend. TV has gone beyond a hobby for him; it's this kid's best friend. I know; I've been an unwilling witness. It's like he's in a trance all day, staring and flipping channels, staring and flipping channels, staring....Well, you get the drift. The unique thing about him, though, is that he is now a walking, talking <u>TV Guide</u>. If you want to know what comes on channel 9000, he'll tell you. He's a good friend, but be prepared for his weird personality (Roeschen, Michael, "The Dude").

1. A. Cite two examples of **apostrophes** used to indicate **possession:**

    _____ & _____

    B. Cite two examples of **apostrophes** used for **contractions:**

    _____ & _____

2. A. Explain the **capitalization** rule for capitalizing <u>TV Guide</u>:

    _____

    B. Why is <u>TV Guide</u> **underlined**? _____

3.   Quote an **example** of the following:

    A.   **Personification**:_____

    B.   **Humor**:_____

    C.   **Hyperbole:**_____

4.   What is the **conflict** in this piece?_____

5.   A.   From what **point of view** is this written (I.E., FIRST PERSON, THIRD PERSON, OMNISCIENT)?_____

    B.   Evidence:_____

6.   Write at least a 50-word **character sketch** about a friend of yours. Include ACTIONS and INNER THOUGHTS AND FEELINGS.

_____

_____

_____

_____

✴He is the living, breathing definition of annoying. He thinks he's the teacher's assistant, but even my Aunt Gertie knows that's a lie as big as Dallas. He searches through the teacher's desk like it's a shopping mall. Maybe he'll get lost somewhere in the D-Hall-slip section or the make-up aisle, and he won't turn up for days and days. But I'm dreaming. Let's see, his style is country with his dark denim pants and shiny, black, pointy-toed boots. Right now, this very minute, I can drive into his mind where he keeps the images of deer popping out of the bushes ready to run from him--the almighty hunter--or fish flying from one point all the way across the pond at his beck and call or George Strait singing live in Houston to him only instead of to millions of people. But maybe I'm lying. I stare at the back of his head, trying to open the door to his mind, but somehow I know it's useless. He's too unpredictable (Stoerner, Brianne, "The Annoyance").

1. One way an author can reveal **characterization** is through a character's **inner thoughts and feelings**. Quote the example that the author has used that is also a **magic three:**

_____

_____

_____

2. Quote an example of a **simile** and explain how it is **humorous:**

A. Simile:_____

B. Explanation:_____

3. The author can't really "drive into his mind"; therefore, this phrase would be an example of **figurative language**. What **type** of figurative language is this and why?

A. Type:_____B. Why?_____

4. Quote two sentences the author uses as **transition sentences** to move from one type of description to the next:

_____&_____

5. Explain why there are **hyphens** between "pointy-toed" and "D-Hall-slip sections":

_____

6. Write a **sentence describing someone you know who is annoying**. Do not use his/her name but do employ the method of characterization of **inner thoughts and feelings** or actions.

_____

_____

_____

    *She sits at her desk, sulking about writing. She has that don't-look-at-me-I'm-mad look. Besides the fact that she has to go to the bathroom—I can tell because she keeps crossing and recrossing her legs—she looks miserable. You can tell she'd rather be somewhere else like in a daydream where she is rescued by Prince Charming or racing down the field doing cartwheels and flip-flops and back flips, the crowd going wild or....(Villeareal, Michelle, "She'd Rather Be Somewhere Else").

1.   Rewrite the first sentence, using another **method of combining** besides a **participial phrase** (*i.e., an "-ing" word group used as an adjective*):

_____

_____

2.   A.   To prove that the author's **hyphenated modifier** is effective, write a **one-word modifier** instead:

_____

    B.   **Write your own hyphenated modifier** (*of at least five words*) that could **replace the author's:**

_____

3.   Explain why the author has used the **dashes**:_____

4.   A.   Quote the **unfinished magic three**:_____,

_____,_____

    B.   Explain why there are no **commas in this series**:_____

_____

5.   What is the **contrast** that the author presents?_____

_____

6. **Finish the author's last sentence**, using at least 20 words.

_____

_____

_____

_____

Answer Key

*Accept other answers if supported.
*Answers to writing questions will vary.

"The Girl"

1.   A.   * "She sits there with her hands on her desk, writing like she's trying to be the first one done."--We can infer either that she's a good student and wants to do well or that she doesn't like the assignment and wants to finish as soon as possible.
    B.   * "She's now writing on her hand"--We can infer that she's conscientious and wants to make notes to remind herself of assignments, etc., or she could be writing notes that have nothing to do with school, which would correspond with our second theory about her.
2.   A.   * "She lets her dark brown hair droop down past her shoulders"
    B.   * "She has a smile like an angel"
3.   A.   "a reminder to call Melissa, homework for old Mrs. B., the name of her true love"
    B.   * It's effective in that it creates a poetic rhythm while speculating what the girl could possibly be writing, thus giving us more questions about her.
4.   A.   * She lets her dark brown hair droop down past her shoulders and then brushes it back when it threatens to impair her vision.
    B.   The author's version is not a run-on sentence because the comma is not separating two independent clauses.
5.   A.   "She should be a ventriloquist."
    B.   "when it threatens to impair her vision"
    C.   * "Now silence."
6.   Answers will vary.

"Me"

1.   * I am Ali, the girl with many friends, the girl who talks too much, the girl who would make straight "A's" if she'd shut up and start studying.
2.   A.   An apostrophe is used to make letters plural.
    B.   * Numbers (2's, for example)
    C.   Letters are enclosed in quotation marks just as are words referred to as words.
3.   * "the girl who would make straight 'A's' **[effect]** if she'd shut up and start studying" **[cause]**
4.   "I think my mom is getting a remote to turn me off"
5.   A.   * "I jump, squeal, and scream"

B.   " 'Ali, wait till the stupid concert!'"
C.   * "Ali, the girl with many friends"; "Ali, the one...."
6.   Answers will vary.

"The Dude"

1.   A.   "Limp Bizkit's" & "kid's"
    B.   * "Doesn't" & "I've"
2.   A.   Capitalize the first word and all important words in a title.
    B.   Underline magazine titles or use italics.
3.   A.   * "TV...is this kid's best friend."
    B.   * "He is now a walking, talking <u>TV Guide</u>."
    C.   * "If you want to know what comes on channel 9000, he'll tell you."
4.   * The main character does not want to write and cannot get anyone to talk to him.
5.   A.   * Omniscient
    B.   * "I'm sure he's thinking about his Play Station games"
6.   Answers will vary.

"The Annoyance"

1.   "Right now...where he keeps the images of deer popping out of the bushes...or fish flying...or George Strait singing...."
2.   A.   "He searches through the teacher's desk like it's a shopping mall."
    B.   We can picture this "annoying" kid rifling through the desk as if he were shopping in stores.
3.   A.   Metaphor
    B.   The author is comparing the kid's mind to something that can be driven through.
4.   "But I'm dreaming." & "But maybe I'm lying."
5.   Hyphenated modifiers
6.   Answers will vary.

"She'd Rather Be Somewhere Else"

1.   * She sits at her desk and sulks about writing.
2.   A.   Angry
    B.   Answers will vary.
3.   Parenthetical interruption
4.   A.   "You can tell she'd rather be somewhere else like in a daydream...or racing down the field...or...." (Question 6 asks students to finish the magic three.)
    B.   The items in the series are separated by the word "or."
5.   What is going on in reality versus in the girl's imagination
6.   Answers will vary.

Dailies

❀To this very day I still don't know what part about you caught my eye. Was it your smile, your eyes, your voice? Whatever it was, the instant you looked at me, I forgot my play make-up and little blonde pigtails and cootie shots. I was only twelve but ready to put those "foolish" things behind me forever. You, age eighteen, to save up for college, had come to work on my pa's farm, a place that if you had had more than a field, hay, and horses, you might possibly have even considered the thought that college could, just maybe, be only an option. You smiled at me, and I felt great. Little did I know that the next years would bring a roller coaster of ups and ups and ups and leave me, a thin sheet in the wind.

Bringing iced tea out to you was a daily getaway. Walking through the wheat fields that looked down on me, I would lose myself in the beauty of the day. The sun's rays rained down in golden blankets, wrapping me in their warmth. The thin wheat stalks swaying beneath the sky whispered in unison, carrying me on a cloud of songs that floated in the air. In a seemingly endless while, I would rush back to my consciousness before rushing past you gleaming in sweat and chopping wheat, your strong arms tensing with every whack.

"Hey, hey, hey! Slow down, cowgirl! Where are you off to in such a hurry?" (Kirch, Amy, "Strawberry Wine").

1. A. Look up the word **"apostrophe"** as it applies to literature and write its definition:

    _____

    B. How are the first two paragraphs of this story an example of a **literary apostrophe?**

    _____

2.   What can you **infer** that the author means when she writes that "if you had had more than a field, hay, and horses...college could, just maybe, be only an option"?

_____

3.   Quote examples of the following **figurative language devices**:

   A.   **Metaphor**:_____

   B.   **Personification**:_____

4.   Quote examples of the following **comma rules**:

   A.   **Series**:_____

   B.   **Introductory phrase or clause**:_____

   C.   **Interrupter**:_____

5.   Why do you think the author has altered the **adage** about roller coasters?

_____

6.   In at least 50 words, write an example of a **literary apostrophe** to someone you know. Include figurative language, an adage that you "alter," and end with dialogue.

_____

_____

_____

_____

_____

_____

_____

❁My mom never listens to me about what I have accomplished. It's always, "Oh, that's great," and then she walks off. Or when I make "95" instead of her saying, "Good job!" it's "You should have made a '100.'"

Oh, but my sister is the princess. With her, it's a different universe, planet, time zone, "Mom, Reagan hit me! Mom, Reagan won't leave me alone! Mom, Reagan took my stuff!" And who gets into trouble? Her? Oh, no, never her.

Why can't Mom listen to me instead of the so-called Princess, who doesn't deserve anything? (Moore, Reagan, "The Princess").

1. What is the **comma rule** for a **direct quotation**?_____

2. Quote an example of the **direct address comma rule**:_____

3. Why would "100" be in **single quotation marks**?_____

4. Explain two possible **conflicts** in the excerpt and whether they are **internal or external**:

A. Conflict:_____ B. Type:_____

B. Conflict:_____ B. Type:_____

5. A. What could be considered a **symbol** in the passage?

_____

    B. Of what could it be **symbolic**?_____

6. This piece is based on a **typical sibling conflict**. Write at least 50 words about a conflict with a sibling, parent, or friend. Use dialogue and observe the rules of punctuation and paragraphing.

_____

_____

_____

_____

_____

_____

❀The sky is cloudy and gray with tears. The long, green forest pines look as though they could reach up and grab the stars for me. A small, snowy barn owl appears, swooping down on its prey as fast as a shooting star. My light-brown khakis are soaked, and my gray shirt becomes semi-transparent. I can feel glass-clear water trickling through strands of my hair, and all of this is happening while a pale wolf on a rock howls into the damp afternoon wind (Partin, Wade, "The Afternoon").

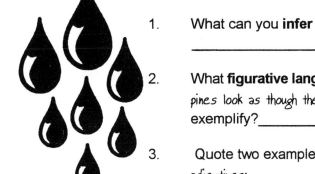

1. What can you **infer** that the "tears" represent?
    _____

2. What **figurative language device** would "the long green forest pines look as though they could reach up and grab the stars for me" exemplify?_____

3. Quote two examples of **commas** used for *coordinate adjectives*:

A._____ B._____

4. Explain the rule for the **hyphen** between "glass" and "clear":_____
    _____

5. A. What are some examples of **sensory imagery**?_____,
    _____,_____

    B. To what **senses** do they appeal?_____,_____,_____

6. This passage describes a **moment in the outdoors**. Write at least 50 words describing a **moment indoors**. Use *sensory imagery and figurative language.*

_____

_____

_____

_____

_____

_____

❀Don't get me wrong.   Nothing like this was supposed to happen. I'm smart enough to figure that out.   I've learned from this that everyone has a flaw to them unique from everyone else's.   But my heart was scared to know that; it ran away when it could taste the impending doom, a taste like candy. I got fat off it.   I'm not going to lie.   I'll make a note of that.   It was wrong, yes, but who's to say it was stupid?   Acting on feeling, on an impulse inside, should never be defined as stupid.   Ignorant and blind maybe, but never stupid.   Just gullible.   Perhaps it was the beauty outside my window that afternoon that kept me dreaming, hoping my reality would someday be as serene, yet at the same time as violently delightful as the ocean, whose waves suggest the minds of young children playfully leaping onto one another, glistening with a tempting iridescence and pleasure.   Somewhere, I believed, pain wasn't an everyday emotion.   In my house, regret was a carousel ride, even before I let him kiss me like that.

My crime started, though, way before that, in the cereal and pasta aisle. One creamy Italian dressing and five oriental Raman noodles packages in my cart later, there I was, looking desperately for cream of mushroom soup, flipping my hair impatiently and sliding my foot in and out of my sandal, in and out, still no mushroom soup.   My hand fumbled with the labels until finally I caught sight of a whole hidden row.   I picked up about ten at a time, looking at my watch.   It was twenty minutes 'till six, and I still had to go by the cleaner's. The biggest problem in my life at that moment was getting the ketchup stain out of my white shorts.   Typically, with the luck I don't have, my whole handful of the cursed cream of mushroom came toppling to the floor all at once, and I bent to pick them up, instantly regretting the pair of blue-jean shorts I decided to wear that morning. Wedged panties. What else did I have to suffer? But what did I care. It's not like I really expected someone important to show up at the grocery store on a Saturday afternoon. Most people had things to do. Most people had a life.

I got up from my crouching position, looking pretty ridiculous trying to juggle ten cans of cream of mushroom soup while maneuvering my legs so that my shorts would be less painful. But coming up, I hit my head hard on someone's chin. The someone ending up being some guy who had been standing right above me this entire time. The cream of mushroom found their places on the tile floor once again as I'm sure I blushed every shade of red there was until my eyes decided the floor--and the soup--might be safer.

"Didn't mean to scare you. I saw you were having trouble so...." He slid his hand behind his head, making his way down to his neck, and I stopped to thank God for large biceps (Shaver, Rachel, "Cream of Mushroom Soup").

1. A. To whom is the author **addressing her introduction** to her short story?

_____

   B. Cite **evidence**:_____

2. **Summarize** what has happened so far in the excerpt:

A. Beginning:_____

B. Middle:_____

C. End:_____

3. Write three **adjectives** that would **characterize the narrator** and quote **evidence**:

A. Adjective:_____Evidence:_____

B. Adjective:_____Evidence:_____

C. Adjective:_____Evidence:_____

4.   What could be considered **ironic** about the first sentence of the second paragraph?

_____

5.   Quote an example of a **Smiley-Face Trick** the author has used and **identify its type**:

A.   Quote:_____

B.   Type:_____

6.   In at least 50 words, add to the author's story.   Use Smiley-Face Tricks.

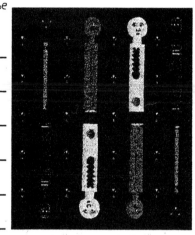

_____

_____

_____

_____

_____

_____

_____

_____

_____

☺ "Do chicken eggs come out of chicken bottoms? How much is a ton? My friend Mike said he had a chicken egg that weighed a ton. Hey, that's cool. I mean don't you think? I do.   Where'd you learn to draw like that? This girl in my class draws, and everybody likes her and her drawing, but she got in trouble for kissing a boy and then she moved into a different class and guess what Ryan said? Stupid. And he got into trouble today, but I stayed with my coloring and...."

Of course, this is all said at the speed of light. No pause. No nothing. Only my brother thinking I am following his every move.

"Matt! Knock it off!"

Thank God it's only 4:00. He only has five more hours to kill me. I hate my brother. I only love him cause I have to. He's as annoying as--come to think of it--he's the most annoying thing in the world. How about this? He's more annoying than that guy Beans on "Even Stevens" plus everything else annoying in the world. Here I am, thinking about how aggravating my brother is when I see his humongous gut coming towards me at 160 miles per hour. Now trust me, that's the scariest thing you'll ever see.

"Matt! I can't wrestle right now," I say to no avail.

Bam! Slosh! Boing! Houston, we have contact!

At 6 p.m.--two hours later--I open my eyes, and everyone is staring at me. Matt gives me a whuz-up look, as Mom walks in.

"I was only giving her a tackle hug, Mom. I didn't mean to hurt her. I wasn't trying to hurt Lauren. She just kind of fell over. I dunno why. I mean I...."

"What's a tackle hug, Matt?" Mom asks innocently.

"Oh, I run as fast as I can and jump on her and give her a hug. And then she usually just falls asleep or something. I mean the first time I thought I had killed her. 'Lauren? Lauren?' I said. I mean I was worried and all since she's my sister, so after the first time when she was all splayed out on the floor and all, I always ask her something to make sure she's alive like 'Hey, could you show me that drawing you've been working on? Or maybe you could show me how to do that math problem. Or it was real funny when you fell to the floor and wouldn't get up, huh?' You know, that sort of stuff to make sure she was paying attention."

"Room! Now! March!" Mom saves the day again. Well, almost.... (Rosenbaum, Lauren, "The Worst Brother, the Best Friend").

1.   **Summarize** what is happening in this narrative excerpt:

A.   Beginning:_____

B.   Middle:_____

C.   End:_____

2.   Quote two **details** that support Lauren's claim that her brother is annoying:

A._____

B._____

3.   A.   In what **tense** is the story written?_____

      B.   Cite five verbs to prove this:_____,_____,'

_____,_____,_____

4.   Cite two examples of how the author uses **humor** to make her story more effective.

A._____

B._____

5.   Explain two things you know about **dialogue** as exemplified in this excerpt.

A._____

B._____

6.   This excerpt is based on a **humorous conflict** between a brother and sister. Write
       at least 100 words of conflict, using dialogue and humor.

_____

_____

_____

_____

_____

_____

_____

_____

Answer Key

*Accept other answers if supported.
*Answers to writing questions will vary.

"Strawberry Wine"

1. A.   Addressing someone not present
   B.   The object of the narrator's affection is not present but is being addressed as if he were.
2. We can infer that if the farm had held more appeal and perhaps if the narrator had been older, maybe the boy would have forgotten about college.
3. A.   * "leave me, a thin sheet in the wind"
   B.   * "Walking through the wheat fields that looked down on me"
4. A.   * "more than a field, hay, and horses"
   B.   * "In a seemingly endless while,"
   C.   * "You, age eighteen,"
5. "A roller coaster of ups and ups" implies good times, not the usual good and bad.
6. Answers will vary.

"The Princess"

1. Separate the quoted material from the speaker tag (e.g., said Mary).
2. * "'Mom, Reagan hit me!'"
3. Since grades such as "A" and "85" are usually put in quotation marks to highlight them and since--in this case--the grade appears in dialogue, the "100" requires single quotation marks.
4. A.   * Mother doesn't listen to narrator's accomplishments--external
   B.   * Narrator versus sister--external
5. A.   Princess
   B.   the positive attention that the narrator would like
6. Answers will vary.

"The Afternoon"

1. We can infer that the "tears" are rain.
2. Personification
3. A.   "The long, green forest pines"
   B.   "A small, snowy barn owl"
4. Hyphenated modifier
5. A.   * "The sky is cloudy and gray with tears," "my light-brown khakis are soaked," "my gray shirt becomes semi-transparent"
   B.   Sight, touch

6.   Answers will vary.

"Cream of Mushroom Soup"

1.   A.   The readers
      B.   "Don't get me wrong."
2.   A.   * The narrator tells the reader that what she has done was "wrong" but not "stupid." We know that somehow her story involves a boy and a kiss.
      B.   * The narrator is in the grocery store, looking for cream of mushroom soup, but, once it is found, she drops all the cans.
      C.   * Righting herself, she comes face to face with a guy.
3.   A.   * Smart—"I've learned from this that everyone has a flaw to them unique from everyone else's."
      B.   * Dreamy, poetic—"Perhaps it was the beauty outside my window that afternoon that kept me dreaming, hoping my reality would someday be as serene...."
      C.   * Adventurous--"yet at the same time as violently delightful as the ocean"
4.   It's ironic that a "crime" of passion would start in the "cereal and pasta aisle."
5.   A.   "Wedged panties. What else did I have to suffer?"
      B.   Humor
6.   Answers will vary.

"The Worst Brother, the Best Friend"

1.   A.   Lauren's brother is asking questions and explaining incidents that happened in his day.
      B.   Lauren illustrates for the reader why her brother is annoying.
      C.   Their mother walks in during Matt's "tackle hug" and sends him to his room.
2.   A.   * "I see this humongous gut coming towards me at 160 miles per hour."
      B.   * "'I mean the first time I thought I had killed her.'"
3.   A.   Present tense
      B.   * Is said, has, hate, love, is
4.   A.   * "He's more annoying than that guy Beans...."
      B.   * "Houston, we have contact."
5.   A.   Begin a new paragraph for each new speaker.
      B.   There must be a punctuation mark separating speaker tags from dialogue.
6.   Answers will vary.

Dailies

☞Dustin yelled at the top of his lungs, "Monkey bars!"

See, that meant that every boy was to go to the only safe haven from the girls, the jungle gym.

"Ben's been touched by a girl and has caught the deadly cootie disease," Dustin informed us all. "We must stay away from girls--and Ben. If you do have to touch them, cross your fingers. We must stop this evil!"

It didn't stop, though, for we saw the girls closing in on a pair of boys playing tetherball on the far side of the field. We knew what was coming, but we were powerless to stop it. As we had feared, our comrades were touched and, of course, immediately cootiefied. There were no words to describe our shock. It was the first time we had actually witnessed an attack. Dustin just turned his back, shaking his head.

"They're coming over here!" someone shouted.

We had no recourse except to run. Seth wasn't fast enough and soon was engulfed in a wave of girls and cootiefied on touch. I turned to save him, but Dustin grabbed me, letting me know it was too late. The girls spread out in a line, their leader stepping forward. Laura Crockett--the girl with enough hair to make Cher look bald, the girl with more money than Bill Gates, the girls with more brains than Einstein--threw a piece of paper at Dustin:

This is girl country

No boys allowed

Any boy found here

Will be cootiefied

Be warned

This is war!

The next thing we knew coach was blowing his whistle, and the girls were stampeding in. We boys, however, stayed back, preparing for tomorrow. We had a plan (Morgan, Jerrod, "School War").

1.   **Summarize** what is happening in this piece:

A.   Beginning:_____

B.   Middle:_____

C.   End:_____

2.   A.   What is the **conflict**?_____

        B.   **Internal or external**?_____

3.   A.   What can you **infer** about the age of the narrator?_____

_____

        B.   Quote **evidence**:_____

4.   Quote an **appositive**:_____

5.   A.   What word acts as a **context clue** to the meaning of "haven"?_____

        B.   What can you **infer** that "haven" means?_____

6.   Write at least 100 words about a **childhood "war" you experienced**. Use
        dialogue (remember to follow the rules for paragraphing) and **humor**.

_____

_____

_____

_____

_____

_____

_____

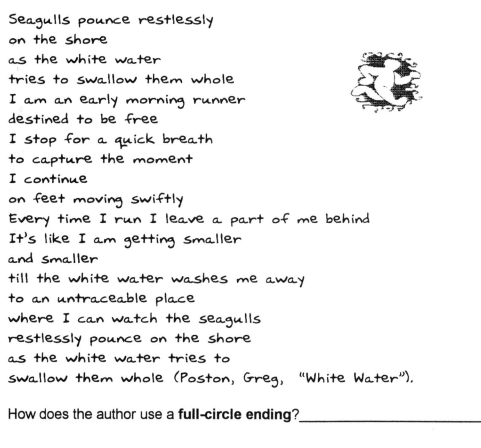

Seagulls pounce restlessly
on the shore
as the white water
tries to swallow them whole
I am an early morning runner
destined to be free
I stop for a quick breath
to capture the moment
I continue
on feet moving swiftly
Every time I run I leave a part of me behind
It's like I am getting smaller
and smaller
till the white water washes me away
to an untraceable place
where I can watch the seagulls
restlessly pounce on the shore
as the white water tries to
swallow them whole (Poston, Greg, "White Water").

1. How does the author use a **full-circle ending**?_____

_____

2. Explain how the author could feel that he is getting **"smaller and smaller."**

_____

3. A. Cite two **vivid verbs**:_____ &_____

    B. Write **less effective synonyms** for each:_____ &_____

4. The author chose not to use **punctuation**. How can you tell where a new sentence or thought starts?

_____

5. A. What is the **theme** of the poem?_____

B.   Give **support** for your answer:_____

_____

6.   The narrator states that he is **"an early morning runner."** Write a poem of at least 50 words based on the line "I am a_____."

☞It all started on a Saturday. Wetness, leaves, mud. The perfect combination to make a life miserable, especially for those who have to rake the leaves tomorrow. Like me. As I picked up my third glazed doughnut at the breakfast table, my mom told me, "Save some for your sister."
"When I'm full."
"Now."
"Fine."
"Okay."
"How can you eat those? They're so fattening," my mom asked.
My mom is very conscious about what she eats, but is often wrong. Glazed doughnuts have sugar, so they're fattening. Apple Fritters have sugar and apples, so they have no fat. It all works. It's all good.
Again I started another day of avoiding. Avoiding what? The freak across the street. Maple Street. Jarod. Jarod, the Saturfreak. Ruining kids' Saturdays for six years straight. He only comes out on Saturdays. After a week of planning, he goes to his chosen victim's house and stays there. All day. The victim can't deny his company. The funny thing is that Jarod is known around the town as "the best, most polite, most well-mannered kid." By the adults, that is. But kids know the real freak (Burnside, Ben, "Maple Freaks").

1. Look up the definition of **"portmanteau word."** To what word from this passage could the definition "loosely" apply?_____

2. A.   Quote three **fragments for effect** that the author uses:

    1._____

    2._____

    3._____

    B.   **Why** do you think the author uses these fragments as opposed to **combining them into sentences?**

    _____

3. How can readers **identify** with this excerpt?_____

    _____

4. Explain the reason for the **apostrophe** being **before** the "s" in "victim" and **after** the "s" in "kids."

    _____

5. Why is "mom" not **capitalized** in the phrase "my mom"?

    _____

6. Write a vignette beginning "It all started on a Saturday." Include **dialogue** and **specific details for effect** with which readers can identify.

    _____

    _____

    _____

    _____

    _____

    _____

    _____

Dailies

☞The ringing returns, loud as a bell/And the headache comes back, a hammer hitting my head/ I cannot find the source, like it's invisible/ The terrible thing that is turning my head inside out again and again/ Then, wait!/There it is! / If I could just reach it/ But no/ It has control/ It won't go away/ It's attached/ The pain, like a fire/ I will fight this/ This cold/ Till the end of time/ And back again/I'll stand my ground/ A soldier in a battlefield (Couch, Cory, "The Cold").

1. What do the **slashes** represent in this

   poem?_____

2. A. What is the **conflict**?

   _____

   B. **Internal or external**?_____

3. A. Quote two **metaphors:**_____

   _____

   B. **Implicit or explicit?**_____

4. Quote a **simile:**_____

5. Quote a **hyperbole:**_____

6. Write a poem about your **conflict** with something similar. Include **figurative language devices.**

A six-year-old girl
Frilly pink swimming suit on
Walks along the beach with her father
Picking up
Little white seashells
Sun beating down on their skin
Waves slapping at their feet
A thirteen-year-old girl
Orange swimming suit on
Sits on a beach towel
Under an umbrella
Without her father
Wishing she could again be the little girl
Whose father has not yet
Gone away   (Lewis, Angie, "Father").

1.   What is the **contrast** illustrated in the poem?_____

2.   What is the **theme**?_____

3.   Quote two lines that are examples of **vivid imagery**:

_____ & _____

4.   A.   In what **tense** is the poem written?_____

      B.   Quote three **verbs** to prove this:_____,_____,_____

5.   Look up the word **"pathos."** How could this poem be an example of pathos?

_____

_____

6.   Write a poem of **exactly 15 lines** involving a **contrast** with which readers could identify. Use the back of this paper.

Answer Key

*Accept other answers if supported.
*Answers to writing questions will vary.

"School War"

1. A. The boys must escape to the money bars as their only "safe haven" from the girls.
    B. The girls have touched the boys, thus "cootiefying" them.
    C. The girls declare war while the boys decide their strategy.
2. A. Girls versus boys
    B. External
3. A. We can infer that the narrator is probably elementary age.
    B. "'Monkey bars!'" & "cootiefied"
4. "Laura Crockett—the girl with enough hair to make Cher look bald...--threw a piece of paper at Dustin."
5. A. Safe
    B. A place that is safe
6. Answers will vary.

"White Water"

1. In the beginning of the poem, the author uses the phrase "swallow them whole," and in the end he repeats the phrase, thus coming full-circle.
2. The author believes that whenever he runs he "leaves a part of (himself) behind."
3. A. "pounce" & "capture"
    B. land & take in
4. The author uses capital letters to indicate the beginnings of new sentences.
5. A. While some of us are "destined to be free," we still must struggle with the elements as well with ourselves.
    B. "till the white water washes me away / to an untraceable place"
6. Answers will vary.

"Maple Freaks"

1. Saturfreaks
2. A. "Wetness, leaves, mud."
    B. "The perfect combination to make a life miserable, especially for those who have to rake the leaves tomorrow."
    C. "Like me."
3. Readers can identify with unwanted chores, disagreements with parents, and "freaks" who live across the street.

4. "Victim's" is singular possessive, as it represents one victim's house. "Kids'" is plural possessive since it refers to many kids' Saturdays.
5. Mom's name cannot be substituted.
6. Answers will vary.

"The Cold"

1. The breaks in the lines of the poem
2. A. The narrator versus a cold
   B. External
3. A. "the headache comes back, a hammer hitting my head" & "I'll stand my ground / A soldier in a battlefield"
   B. Implicit
4. "The ringing returns, loud as a bell"
5. "Till the end of time"
6. Answers will vary.

"Father"

1. The young girl who received the father's attention versus the older girl who does not
2. Sometimes relationships change.
3. * "Picking up / Little white seashells / Sun beating down on their skin / Waves slapping at their feet" & "Orange swimming suit on / Sits on a beach towel / Under an umbrella"
4. A. Present tense
   B. "Walks," "picking, "sits"
5. We feel pity or compassion for the "thirteen-year-old girl" whose father has "gone away," in that she feels he is no longer close to her.
6. Answers will vary.

Dailies

Empty Stomach

Mom sits around all day
holding a book
Sometimes the pages never turn
for her eyes find it impossible to read
Since Dad left two weeks ago
they have been replaced
by cold, gray stones
no sparkle
no life
I told my little brother she's sick
But how can you diagnose someone for sadness?
Despite everything
her anguish hangs in the stale air,
misery in every dirty dish,
silent cries for help in the velvet elevator music
she uses as a futile attempt
to erase the melancholy in all our lives,
which has so obviously coated our thoughts and words,
so that we are deprived of hope,
the hope that left as Dad shut the door on us
One night
on my way to the kitchen to fetch my midnight snack
I caught a glimpse of
Mom
doubled over the toilet,
gagging up her pain,
agony and despair colored in the lines on her face
She looked my way
but saw right through me

I realized then in her eyes
I was transparent
just a body trying desperately
to fill a void in her life
that continues to be scooped out
with every breath inhaled
into her empty stomach
For now
at night I just go hungry
(Shaver, Rachel, "Empty Stomach").

1. Look up the word **"poignant."** Quote **three poignant images** from the poem:

A. _____ B._____ C._____

2. **Summarize** what is happening in the poem:

A. Beginning:_____

B. Middle:_____

C. End:_____

3. A. Quote a **metaphor** having to do with the mother's eyes:

_____

B. Is it **implicit or explicit?**_____

C. **How** do you know?_____

4. The title of the poem is "Empty Stomach." Explain two possible **meanings:**

A._____

B._____

5. Quote **a cause and an effect**:_____

_____

6.   **Write a poem of at least 15 lines** explaining about a mother, father, and/or son/daughter relationship.

✔"Fine," he said.

"Then it's a deal," I said.

That was the first time I ever lost control of life, and I should have known better when I saw him looking at me with those sly, sky-blue eyes and an I'm-about-to-do-something-bad   smirk on his face. It wouldn't have happened if she hadn't come to our school that day.

It started out like any other day as my father dropped me off in our brand-new black Lexus. I got out, walked up the concrete sidewalk into the chattering school. All kinds of conversations were going on: the geeks were talking about who they beat in chess, what happened to Captain Kirk last night, new sites on the Internet; the jocks were having a serious discussion about whose football pads were better, how many shots they had made, who ran the fastest yesterday; everyone else was just a clamor of noise that I decided couldn't be that important. I spotted two of my friends: Lisa Lytle, who had golden blonde hair and sapphire-green eyes, and Dexter Labor, a small person compared to me, but the smartest person to ever step foot in this school. He had black hair that always seemed perfect. They were looking at a group of sixth graders who were about to get into a fight.

"Hey, guys," I said announcing my presence.

"Hey," they said in unison, but not really noticing me as one sixth grader threw punches and jabs and hooks. The rest of the crowd oohed and aahed as the other sixth grader was pummeled into the hard tile floor of the school. As he fell, my attention rose to the fact that there had been a fight that I hadn't instigated and that I had been at school for ten minutes without getting anyone into trouble. There was nothing I could do about the first problem, but I could fix the second problem and told Mrs. Keastly, a.k.a. Mrs. Beastie, that some sixth graders weren't in the cafeteria.

She was there in five seconds flat, and the two warriors, who were fighting like two cats over a mouse who was asking to be eaten, were separated and in the office before you could spell "Mississippi," and—believe me—I tried.

Then, I saw the strangest thing ever—an eighth grader riding the bus. I didn't realize that she was an eighth grader until she came out into the commons because she was new. It's been seven years since that has happened at Marvin Singleton's School for the Gifted and Talented.

But just last week Lisa had spray painted over all the vowels and jumbled up the consonants on our school sign, when Ernie, the janitor, quit and the new janitor was too lazy to fix it (Morgan, Jerrod, "Monopoly Money").

1.   Quote three **Smiley-Face Tricks** the author used:

A._____

B._____

C._____

2.   A.   Quote two **appositives:**

      1._____

      2._____

      B.   What is the rule for **punctuating appositives?**

      _____

3.   An author can reveal **characterization** through environment, inner thoughts and feelings, appearance, what others say, actions, and speech. **Choose one group**, the geeks or the jocks, **quote two phrases** that reveal their character and explain which type they are.

Dailies   5

A.   Quote:_____

      Type:_____

B.   Quote:_____

      Type:_____

4.   A.   What is the central **conflict**?_____

      B.   Is it **internal or external**?_____

5.   Quote a **fact and an opinion** from the passage:

      A.   Fact:_____

      B.   Opinion:_____

6.   Begin your own **vignette with the same dialogue:**
      "Fine," he said.
      "Then it's a deal," I said.

      _____

      _____

      _____

      _____

      _____

      _____

✔ It had been two weeks since my father had made a criticizing comment about me in front of the family. And it had been two weeks since I hadn't spoken to him or to any other person in the house. It was only anger that dwelled deep inside me, and somewhere in there an empty void of love was longing to be filled. However, after Wednesday's Bible Study, an adult friend came up to me.

"What seems to be the problem?" she asked, leaning over and throwing all of her weight on one leg.

"I haven't been the same," I said, shrugging her away coldly with my shoulders. "I don't feel loved any more. I can't stand my family. They're all nothing like me."

"Well, Gregg, I've watched you lately. It seems more than that," she said, pulling back her neatly trimmed hair that rose just above her shoulders. "It seems as if you're not understanding yourself."

"But, I...."

My father and the rest of the family were already in the car, backing out of the lot.

"Can I have your number?" I asked solemnly, glancing into the car at my father, who stared at me with red anger in his eyes.

"Okay," she said.

Quickly, Tavarri took the pen from behind her ear, tore out a piece of the map in her Bible, and scribbled her number on the back. "Call anytime," she whispered.

✂

When I entered my room, I immediately jumped into my bed and stacked the pillows on my head. My father walked in.

"You want something to eat, boy?"

"No, sir," I said, lifting my head from the pillows.

After he left, I cut the light off. And in that loneliness of a room, in that dark, starry night, a misunderstood, unloved child cried himself to sleep (Pelt, Gregg, "Typical Conversations").

1. A. What **context clue** does the author give to express the meaning of "void"?

    _____

    B. What can you **infer** that the word "void" means?

    _____

2. Quote two **participial phrases** ("-ing" word groups used as adjectives) that the author uses to help **characterize** Tavarri.

A._____

B._____

3. Quote two examples of **direct address** and explain the **rule for punctuating** this sort of phrase:

A._____B._____

C. Rule:_____

4. Quote an example of a comma used for a **coordinate adjective:**

_____

5. In your own words, explain the **central cause and effect** of the passage:

A. Cause:_____

B. Effect:_____

6. Write at least 100 words about a **conflict you have with your family**. Use dialogue and various methods of characterization.

_____

_____

_____

_____

_____

_____

✔"Looking good, Mrs. Dead, I mean Deed," I said, thinking the exact opposite because her diet consisted of running thirty minutes and then eating thirty Milky Ways. Of course, she eats the diet kind. Like it helps. My friend and I call her Mrs. Dead because I know at least five different people who want to knock her upside the head. This is because every day it's time to play twenty questions about what you have been doing and it's the same thing every day. By the way, did I mention she was old, really old?
Man, I hope I don't get the quality that most old people have of

always caring--and I mean really caring--about other people and what they do. You know, "And how are you doing?" Or maybe even, "Where were you yesterday at 4:00?" No, wait, that's a lawyer question. And what about the stories that old grandfathers tell? Like "Back in my day we didn't have Dixie paper plates. We stayed in the kitchen till 5:00 in the morning, washing the china until it squeaked and sparkled, or Grandma wouldn't give us dessert." Or "Back in my day we didn't have paper and pencils. All we had was a chisel and a boulder. And we had to carry them around in a stone backpack that weighed at least two tons." Another one commonly heard was, "Back in my day we didn't have TV or the VCR. All we had to do was smash ants with our fingers, even though they would sting us. And also we didn't have shoes. We walked two miles to school each day--barefooted--through ten inches of snow, and that's the way we liked it too."

"Yes, Grandpa, sure Grandpa, I believe you," I would always reply (Burnside, Ben, "Old Grandpas and Mrs. Deed").

1.   What is **ironic** about Mrs. Deed's "dieting"?

_____

2.   A.   Quote a **hyperbole** that Grandpa tells about the "good old days."

_____

      B.   How can **readers identify**?

_____

3.   A.   What is the author's **tone**?_____

      B.   Quote two passages of **proof**:_____ &

_____

4.   A.   What could be a **symbol** in this excerpt?_____

      B.   Of what could it be **symbolic**?_____

5.   Cite three different rules of **capitalization and state the rules**:

A._____Rule:_____

B._____Rule:_____

C._____Rule:_____

6.   This passage is based on the **"good old days."** Write at least 100 words about **you and someone you know who always speaks about the past.**

_____

_____

_____

_____

_____

✔ "I'm getting that football back come hell or high water," as I swear on my word. If he wants a war, he's got it.

See, there are some woods where I plan to make my insertion point. I've already checked with the guys, and they're gonna help me whoop some bootie.

After discussing our plan, we go home to suit up for the war of a lifetime. Maybe this will knock some sense into him. We decide to meet at 6:00 PM because it will be dark by then.

I walk up to my house and twist the knob.

"Dang, it's jammed," I say as I beat on the door like the police would. The knob turns, and my mom answers.

"What?" she yelps.

"Well, it was jammed," I snap at her. I open up the big bag marked "hunting clothes," which is closed with a piece of tape. I rip it and take out a set of my genuine pair of camouflaged pants and one of my long-sleeved shirts. I start to put my clothes on when I hear a knock on the door. I glance down at my watch as I walk to the door. It reads 6:00.

"Dang," I say to myself as I grasp the handle and pull the door open. They answer with a brief "hi" and walk in (Student writer, "The War").

1. How is the opening line an **attention-getter**?_____

    _____

2. A. Quote a phrase from the excerpt that could be considered **dialect:**

        _____

    B. **Rewrite the phrase in formal, standard English:**

        _____

    C. **Why** would the author choose the dialectic version?

        _____

3. A. In what **verb tense** is the story written?_____

    B. Cite three **verbs to prove** this:_____,_____,_____

4. A. What could be considered a **symbol** in the story?_____

    B. Of what could it be **symbolic**?_____

5. A. Quote an example of **figurative language**:_____

    B. Of what **type of figurative language device** is this an example?

        _____

6. Write the **beginning of a short story** (at least 50 words), using the following line: "I'm getting that _____ back....." Use **dialogue and various Smiley-Face Tricks.**

    _____

    _____

    _____

    _____

Answer Key

*Accept other answers if supported.
*Answers to writing questions will vary.

"Empty Stomach"

1. A. "Sometimes the pages never turn"
   B. "Silent cries for help in the velvet elevator music/she uses as a futile attempt/ to erase the melancholy in all our lives"
   C. "Her misery in every dirty dish"
2. A. The mother is extremely distraught because the dad left two weeks ago.
   B. All hope has left with the father, as the mother vomits and does not notice the daughter.
   C. The daughter feels as empty as the mother.
3. A. "they have been replaced / by cold, gray stones"
   B. Implicit
   C. There is no "be" verb.
4. A. The mother is "doubled over the toilet.../with every breath inhaled/into her empty stomach."
   B. The daughter is just as "empty": "For now / at night I just go hungry."
5. "Since Dad left two weeks ago" is the cause, and "Mom sits around all day" is the effect.
6. Answers will vary.

"Monopoly Money"

1. A. "I'm-about-to-do-something-bad smirk"--hyphenated modifier
   B. "the geeks were talking about who they beat in chess, what happened to Captain Kirk last night, new sites on the Internet"--magic three
   C. "who were fighting like two cats over a mouse who was asking to be eaten"-- figurative language
2. A. "I spotted two of my friends: Lisa Lytle..." and "Dexter Labor, a small person"
   B. Appositives are set off by commas. In this case, the appositives are introduced by a colon since the words in apposition are followed by modifiers.
3. A. "the jocks were having a serious discussion about whose football pads were better"--speech

B. "how many shots they had made"--speech/actions
4. A. Narrator versus life ("That was the first time I ever lost control of life")
   B. Both
5. A. "my father dropped me off in our brand-new black Lexus"
   B. "were having a serious discussion"
6. Answers will vary.

"Typical Conversations"

1. A. Empty; longing to be filled
   B. Empty, useless, vacant
2. A. "leaning over me"
   B. "throwing all of her weight on one leg"
3. A. "'Well, Gregg,'"
   B. "'No, `sir,'"
   C. Use commas to set off words of direct address.
4. "dark, starry night"
5. A. The narrator is at odds with himself.
   B. He has trouble communicating with his family.
6. Answers will vary.

"Old Grandpas and Mrs. Deed"

1. It seems contradictory to run to lose weight and then to consume "thirty Milky Ways." If a person is dieting, the Milky Ways would negate the running.
2. A. *"We stayed in the kitchen till 5:00 in the morning, washing the china until it squeaked and sparkled"
   B. Readers can identify because we have all heard stories about "the good old days."
3. A. Humorous/cynical
   B. "'Back in my day we didn't have paper and pencils. All we had was a chisel and a boulder'" & "'All we had to do was smash ants with our fingers'"
4. A. Mrs. Deed, the narrator calls "Mrs. Dead"
   B. An old person who is the antithesis of the way the narrator wants to be, and whose behaviors represent someone who is "dead" or not alive.
5. A. Mrs. Deed--proper noun
   B. Dixie paper plates--brand name
   C. "Where were you yesterday...?"--first word of direct quote
6. Answers will vary.

"The War"

1. The conflict is stated in the opening line.
2. A. "whoop some bootie"
   B. beat the opponent
   C. The dialect is more real; it represents the way people talk.
3. A. Present tense
   B. Am getting, swear, wants
4. A. Football
   B. A possession that is worth a fight
5. A. "war of a lifetime"
   B. Hyperbole
6. Answers will vary.

Dailies

♡ I love the fun, excitement, and exhilaration of fishing. And I usually beat almost everyone, even the kids in my division at the local fishing tournament down at the Galley. I always fished at the end of the dock as far to the right as I could go, which was practically hanging over the wooden railing. If I tried to go out there now, let's just say let's hope there is a lifeguard on duty. Now the dock is falling apart, many of the pickets are missing, and the water has probably been inherited by hundreds and millions and gazillions of piranhas (Fitzwater, Megan, "Fishing").

1. Quote **a magic three:**_____

_____

2. Quote a **hyperbole:**_____

3. What is the **tone** of the passage? Give **support:**

    A. **Tone:**_____

    B. **Support:**:_____

4. Why is there an **apostrophe** in **"let's"**?_____

5. What is the **comma rule** for the sentence that **begins with "If"?**

_____

6. Why is **"Galley" capitalized?**_____

♡"Last night me and the homeboys were chillin', shooting hoops at the Y" (Deming, Adam, "Me and the Homeboys).

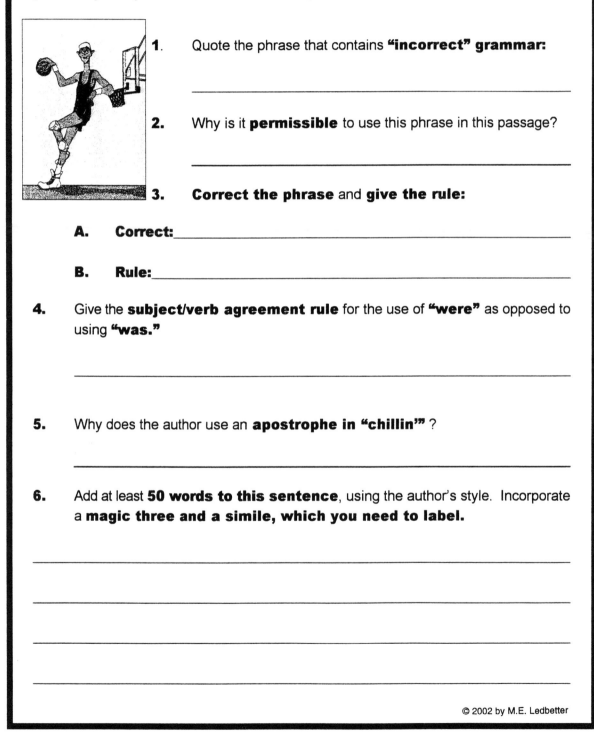

1. Quote the phrase that contains **"incorrect" grammar:**

_____

2. Why is it **permissible** to use this phrase in this passage?

_____

3. **Correct the phrase** and **give the rule:**

A. **Correct:**_____

B. **Rule:**_____

4. Give the **subject/verb agreement rule** for the use of **"were"** as opposed to using **"was."**

_____

5. Why does the author use an **apostrophe in "chillin'"** ?

_____

6. Add at least **50 words to this sentence**, using the author's style. Incorporate a **magic three and a simile, which you need to label.**

_____

_____

_____

_____

♡We carefully step our way over mountainous ant beds, around a ravine of a hole some extremely bored kid must have spent an eternity digging, and slip noiselessly past a huge clump of bush and trees someone had said once housed a crazy, old half-human, half-wombat lady that speared stray animals--cats, dogs, even kids--on sticks and ate them for afternoon brunch, fully-haired, fully-clothed, or hairless; she wasn't picky. Whether that was true or not, we don't want to know so we take the last yards running (Challenger, Jennifer, "Coke Charades").

1. What are some of the **words used to exaggerate** simple things?

    _____

2. Which words tell you that **the old lady wasn't picky?**

    _____

3. Why does the author use **dashes**?_____

4. Why is there a **comma after "crazy"?**_____

5. In what **verb tense** is this paragraph written? Prove it by **quoting five verbs:**

    A. **Tense:**_____

    B. **Five verbs:**_____

6. **Rewrite the passage in the simplest terms**, explaining what is going on.

    _____

    _____

♡I hate how the sun bathes away into the cocoa night. I hate how time lathers nervousness on you, the eagerness for the dollar bill that spoils little kids for more and more (Brown, Rachel, "What I Hate").

1.   Quote **three figurative language devices** and tell their **types:**

   A. Quote:_____Type:_____

   B. Quote:_____ Type:_____

   C. Quote:_____Type:_____

2.   How is **repetition for effect** used?

   _____

3.   Explain what the author means about the **"eagerness for the dollar bill that spoils little kids for more and more."**

   _____

   _____

4.   **Write a passage of at least 50 words** explaining **what you hate**. You must use **at least three figurative language devices**, which you will label.

   _____

   _____

   _____

   _____

5.   In the phrase **"eagerness for the dollar bill that spoils little kids,"** with **what noun does the verb "spoils" agree**? Remember that verbs do not agree with the objects of prepositional phrases._____

♡But our relationship was more than the typical teen's. It wasn't the kind where all you talk about is what that boy in second period, third row, second seat, said to the teacher. Or what that girl during lunch, sitting three tables down, fifth chair to the right, did with her chocolate milk. Not that kind of companionship we see every day (Holmes, Rebecca, "Hand 'n Hand").

1. Explain how a **reader could identify** with this situation.

_____

2. Quote an **alliteration** and explain its **effectiveness.**

   A.   Quote_____

   B.   Effectiveness:_____

3. What is the **primary stylistic device** the author uses? **Quote** an example.

   A.   Device:_____

   B.   Quote:_____

4. Quote a **fragment and rewrite** it, making it a complete sentence.

   A.   Quote:_____

   B.   Rewrite:_____

5. Cite a sentence with a **comma and explain the rule.**

   A.   Quote:_____

   B.   Rule:_____

6. The author says that **"our relationship was more than the typical teen's."** **Write a passage of at least 50 words** explaining what kind of relationship it could have been. Use **at least one figurative language device** and label it.

_____

_____

_____

_____

_____

_____

7. Why is there an **apostrophe** in **"teen's"?**_____

_____

8. **Write a sentence of your own that exemplifies the rule in question #7.**

_____

_____

Answer Key

*Accept other answers if supported.
*Answers for writing questions will vary.

"Fishing"

1. "Now the dock is falling apart, many of the pickets are missing, and the water has probably been inherited...."
2. "water has probably been inherited by hundreds and millions and gazillions of piranhas"
3. A.   Fun, excitement
    B.   "And I usually beat almost everyone, even the kids in my division...."
4. The apostrophe represents the letter "u," which has been omitted. "Let's" is a contraction for "let us."
5. Introductory adverb clause modifying "say" and "hope"
6. Proper noun--specific place

"Me and the Homeboys"

1. "me and the homeboys"
2. The author is using dialect in an effort to make the passage sound authentic.
3. A.   "The homeboys and I"
    B.   Courtesy rule--put yourself last.
4. The sentence contains a plural subject, "me and the homeboys"; therefore, a plural verb is required. "Were" is plural, whereas "was" is singular.
5. The apostrophe stands for the letter "g" that is omitted.
6. Answers will vary.

"Coke Charades"

1. "mountainous," "ravine," "eternity"
2. The passage not only states that "she wasn't picky" but that she "ate them...fully-haired, fully-clothed, or hairless."
3. The dashes set off a parenthetical phrase; in this case, the dashes had to be used instead of commas since the sentence already had a lot of commas.
4. Coordinate adjective
5. Present tense--step, slip, don't, want, take
6. Answers will vary.

"What I Hate"

1.   A.   "bathes away into the cocoa night" (personification)
     B.   "cocoa night" (metaphor)
     C.   "time lathers nervousness on you" (personification)
2.   The author repeats the phrase "I hate how," which adds a poetic quality to the piece.
3.   It's like the adage "Give them an inch and they take a mile." The author's point is that once kids have money, they want more and more.
4.   Answers will vary.
5.   Eagerness

"Hand 'n Hand"

1.   Readers, also, want to believe that their relationships are "more than the typical."
2.   A.   "typical teen's"
     B.   The phrase is "catchy," as opposed to "normal teen's."
3.   A.   Specific details for effect
     B.   * "that boy in second period, third row, second seat"
4.   A.   "Not that kind of companionship we see every day."
     B.   It wasn't that kind of companionship we see every day.
5.   A.   "Or what that girl during lunch, sitting three tables down,"
     B.   Participial phrase or interrupter
6.   Answers will vary.
7.   The apostrophe represents ownership in that the "teen" owns the "relationship."
8.   Answers will vary.

Dailies

✎"It's Stephanie!" Mother yelled. "Hey, I thought you didn't have any friends," my own mother retorted.

Oh, that hurts. But why would Stephanie, the one girl I ever had the courage to ask out, the I-would-rather-go-out-with-a-frog-than-go-out-with-you girl call me?

Maybe she reconsidered. Maybe she wants to go out with me. Maybe I am the man of her dreams. My heart was pounding as fast as the band in a 260/1 tempo. So naturally I ran to the phone. The last person who called me was three years ago, and that was my grandfather to wish me happy birthday.

I picked up the phone and nervously managed to croak, "Hello."

"Uh, is this like Brian or something?" she cooed in her sweet, blonde, valley-girl voice.

I figured this had to be a dream. She knows my name and my phone number. I punched myself in the stomach as hard as I could.

"Yep," I managed to squeak, the breath knocked out of me like I was just hit by a 200-pound linebacker after I had insulted his mom. She must really like me--me, the most picked-on kid in the school. She, the most popular, most beautiful girl in the school.

This is the day I have been dreaming about for my whole life, the day a girl talks to me, and it's not an insult. Me, Brian Burnham. Call the presses, the television studios, the newspapers!

"This is like Brian Johnson? Oh, my gosh, I've been waiting to talk to you like forever. So like do you like Betty cause like I heard you like liked me. But if that's not...."

I laid the phone down, looked up, and said a little prayer. One day a girl will talk to me, and know it's me. It's coming. I can feel it (Burnham, Brian, "The Frog Man").

1. What is the **tone** of the excerpt?_____**Support** your answer by quoting

two passages:

A._____

B._____

2. Quote three **figurative language devices** and identify them by **type** (e.g., simile, metaphor, personification, etc.).

A._____Type:_____

B._____Type:_____

C._____Type:_____

3. List three **rules for dialogue** exemplified in this excerpt:

A._____

B._____

C._____

4. Quote a **fragment for effect** that the author uses and explain the effect:

A.
Fragment:_____

B.   Effect:_____

5. Choose a **literary device** (e.g., conflict, prediction, irony, etc.) and **explain** how the author uses it.

A.   Device:_____

B.   Effect:_____

6. Write at least a **100-word dialogue** with the **same tone as the author's.** Be sure to follow the rules for writing conversation.

_____

_____

_____

_____

_____

_____

_____

✏First of all, I want you to know that I'm not so stupid. I mean, I know things. Seriously. Like how to never clash black with navy and never to button the top two buttons or wear white shoes after Labor Day, or horrors of horrors, leggings with big, gaudy T-shirts over them. And I know to always check for food stuck in my teeth before I talk to someone and to look bored at parties and not to laugh hysterically if a person says something when no one else even thinks it's the least bit funny. See, I'm not so stupid (Shaver, Rachel, "Used Kleenex").

1. How does the author assure that most **readers will identify** with her piece? Quote two examples to prove your point.

   A. Explanation:_____

   B. Quote:_____

   C. Quote:_____

2. Quote the passage that exemplifies the **coordinate adjective comma rule:**

   _____

3. Quote a **fragment and revise** it by making it a sentence:

   _____

   _____

4. What can you **infer** about the narrator?_____

5. Make a **prediction** about the ending of the vignette based on its title:

_____

6. Write at least a **50-word piece** in which you use your own examples to **convince** readers that you are not "_so stupid._"

_____

_____

_____

_____

✏It wouldn't have happened if he had shut up as we walked by. It wouldn't have happened if he had gone back inside. It wouldn't have happened if he had minded his own business, but no, that day he had to say something. That day he had to stand outside. That day he had to get nosy. It started when there had been an outbreak of robberies in our city, Preston, a small country town that you can just barely call a town. Old women hired Boy Scouts for bodyguards, banks locked each and every dollar in its own separate bulletproof-waterproof-fireproof-and-every-other-proof safe, and old man Hutcherson was sitting in his rocking chair that he had chained to his door, not that anyone would steal that rickety thing, and was holding his double-barrel shotgun that he had named Little Ricky (Morgan, Jerrod, "Bakery Bad Boys").

1. Quote two examples of different **repetition for effects** and **explain** the effect:

A. Quote:_____

_____

B. Quote:_____

_____

C. Effect:_____

2.   Explain how the author **"hooks" the reader** at the beginning of his story.

_____

_____

3.   Quote an **appositive:**_____

4.   What is the **setting** of the story? (Remember that setting is time and place.)

_____

5.   Quote a **hyperbole:**_____

6.   Write a beginning to a short story in which you use **repetition for effect as the hook.**

_____

_____

_____

_____

_____

The wind was howling like the coyotes in the mountains. I could hear the Song of the Night singing softly to the creatures living in the woods. I felt the dirt under my feet digging into the soil, trying not to make a sound to wake the bears in the caves, the rabbits resting in their burrows, and the birds nestled in their nests. I was walking barefooted down the path that separated the trees and the river. The hoot of the Great Owl made my body shiver from all directions. Choo. Choo.

Startled, I turned around to see what the sound was that made the world chatter. I felt the eyes of the night animals staring at me, watching my every move. I ran through the woods, downstream where the family of beavers built their dam, across the bare, naked field, and then suddenly out

Dailies

from behind the bushes stretched train tracks. The grass ended with piles of rocks, beyond which lay rusty tracks. I followed their path until my eyes fell upon a wooden tunnel (Stoerner, Brianne, "Oklahoma Runaway").

1.   Quote a **magic three**:

_____,_____,_____

2.   Quote an **example of onomatopoeia**:_____

3.   Quote   a   **hyperbole:**_____

4.   Why are the **ellipses** used, and why does the last set consist of **four periods** instead of the usual three?

_____

_____

5.   List a **vivid verb** regarding the train tracks:_____

What would be a **more common, less effective verb** that the author could have used?_____

6.   Using **sensory imagery**, write at least a 50-word passage **set outdoors**.

_____

_____

_____

_____

_____

✐ Sometimes there are things that you wish you could change. Then there are others you would give your life for. There are people who live happily ever after, but that only occurs in distant lands, in unseen castles, in a child's sleepiest dreams. As a bird caresses the dusky evening sky with its wings, my wishes and goals, dreams and longings soar with it, away into oblivion, never to be seen, heard, or touched. And somewhere a star falls into an ocean, brewing with uncertainty, and is lost. So my journey through life in this tiny, untrustworthy town continues, and I dart through dark streets, dusted with contempt and prejudice (Romans, Mary, "How It Is").

1.   Quote a **magic three**:_____,_____

_____,_____

2.   Quote a **metaphor**:_____

3.   What is the **tone** of the piece?_____Quote an **example**

from the passage as evidence:_____

_____

4.   What is the **conflict** exemplified in the excerpt?_____

_____

Is it **internal or external**?_____

5.   Quote a **personification**:_____

6.   Using at least **three examples of figurative language**, write at least a 50-word passage that exemplifies **conflict. Continue writing your passage on the back of this sheet.**

_____

_____

Answer Key

*Accept other answers if supported.
*Answers will vary.

"The Frog Man"

1. Humor
   A. "I-would-rather-go-out-with-a-frog-than-go-out-with-you girl"
   B. "'This is Brian Johnson? Oh, my gosh, I've been waiting to talk to you like forever. So like do you like Betty cause like I heard you like liked me.'"
2. A. "My heart was pounding as fast as the band in a 260/1 tempo." (simile)
   B. "the breath knocked out of me like I was just hit by a 200-pound linebacker" (simile)
   C. "me, the most picked-on kid in school" (hyperbole)
3. A. Begin a new paragraph for each new speaker.
   B. Use quotation marks to enclose what each speaker says.
   C. Dialogue must be separated from "speaker tags" with the appropriate form of punctuation.
4. A. "She, the most popular, most beautiful girl in the school."
   B. The fragment emphasizes the girl herself, not anything that she does. She simply "is." Her beauty and popularity stand on their own.
5. A. Conflict
   B. At the end of the excerpt the author "laid the phone down, looked up, and said a little prayer. One day a girl will talk to me and know it's me." The narrator has an internal conflict regarding his relationship with girls. He likes the caller, who thinks he's someone else.
6. Answers will vary.

"Used Kleenex"

1. A. The author uses humor to assure that readers will identify with her piece.
   B. "I know to check for food stuck in my teeth"
   C. "not to laugh hysterically if a person says something when no one else even thinks it's the least bit funny"
2. Coordinate adjective
3. Fragment: Seriously
   Sentence: I mean, I know things, seriously.
4. The fact that the narrator repeats that she "is not so stupid" could mean that she is trying to convince her audience (and herself) that she is more sophisticated than she really is.
5. Since the title is "Used Kleenex," the author probably will be hurt by someone or some event that will cause her to cry.
6. Answers will vary.

"Bakery Bad Boys"

1.   A.   "That day he had to say something."
       B.   "That day he had to stand outside."
       C.   The repetition makes the reader wonder what happened "that day."
2.   The repetition of "it wouldn't have happened" is an attention-getter in that the reader wants to know what "happened."
3.   "Preston, a small country town that you can just barely call a town"
4.   Time: the time of the outbreak of robberies   Place: Preston
5.   "Banks locked each and every dollar"
6.   Answers will vary.

"Oklahoma Runaway"

1.   "the bears in the caves, the rabbits resting in their burrows, and the birds nestled in their nests"
2.   "Choo. . . choo"
3.   "what the sound was that made the world chatter"
4.   The three periods represent an omission; the fourth period represents the end of the sentence.
5.   Vivid verb: stretched   Less effective verb: lay
6.   Answers will vary.

"How It Is"

1.   "in distant lands, in unseen castles, in a child's sleepiest dreams"
2.   "my wishes and goals, dreams and longings soar with it"
3.   Unhappy, unsatisfied: "There are people who live happily every after, but that only occurs in distant lands"
4.   The narrator must make the "journey through life in this tiny, untrustworthy town" while darting "through dark streets, dusted with contempt and prejudice." It is both an external conflict (narrator versus town) and an internal one (narrator's dreams longing to be fulfilled).
5.   "a bird caresses the dusky evening sky"
6.   Answers will vary.

Dailies

First kiss
First crush
Your voice gets breathy
His starts cracking
Algebra with a cutie
Science with Charles Munks also known as "The Geek"
A slinky tube dress for the eighth-grade dance
Howard Sminsky, president of the Chess Club, your date
You get taller
Number thirty-three gets shorter
First time you're able to wear make-up
First pimple the size of Mount Everest
You're old enough to stay out late
Old enough to play bingo with Grandma and "The Girls"
You start earning your own money
You had to babysit the McAllen twins
You're old enough to finally be treated like a woman
Start by washing the dishes
Mature enough to watch a PG-13 movie
Your sports-fanatic older brother picked it out
Sometimes you want to never grow up
Sometimes you want to enter the futuristic time machine
But we all have to go through it
There's no way to escape it
It's the predator at night searching for young, innocent blood
To take as it prey
The hungry black widow waiting to take you into her overpowering web
The addictive drug that can make you sick if you let it
The fearless soldier attacking everyone who crosses his path
The rusty nail waiting to occupy the heel of a blameless individual
The virus in the computer destroying every megabyte one by one
The universal plague infecting every teen
If it hasn't happened yet, it will
Be afraid
(Student writer, "Adolescence").

1. A. Explain how the **first half** of the poem is **constructed**:

   _____

   B. At what point does the author **break from that structure?**

   _____

   C. What is the "**pattern**" **or the construction** from then on?

   _____

2. Quote examples of the following:

   A. **Hyperbole**:_____

   B. **Humor**:_____

   C. **Metaphor**:_____

   D. **Personification**:_____

3. A. What is the **theme** of the poem?_____

   B. **Quote proof:**_____

4. Would "science" and "algebra" normally be **capitalized**? Explain.

   _____

5. A. What is the **tone** of the poem?_____

   B. **Quote proof:**_____

6. Write at least a 10-line poem **constructed in the same manner as the first half** of this poem. Use humor and figurative language. Write your poem on the back of this paper.

✏️ I don't want one of those bossy-couch-potato-where's-my-tie husbands or those rule-breaking-snotty-nose kids. I want a mansion all to myself, the one inherited from a dead-far-down-the-family-tree relative. I want it to have a table that seats twenty for all my gentlemen friends.

I'll cook my supper in my pink satin robe and use all the wrong utensils. I'll carry it up to my bedroom by way of my spiral staircase, trickling sauce on each step, leaving a trail behind me as I reach my bedroom door.

There I will sit on my bed atop my white silk duvet. After I have completed my meal, I won't even bother to take my china and silverware down to the kitchen. Instead, I will use my two index fingers to push them over to the side. Then without even putting on pajamas, I will collapse on my bed and fall fast asleep (Student writer, "The Wonder Years").

1. **Replace** all three **hyphenated modifiers** with equally effective ones of your own that would fit the passage:

A._____

B._____

C._____

2. One especially vivid detail for effect is the line "I will use my two index fingers to push them over to the side." **Rewrite the line**, using more general, less effective wording:

_____

3. A. What can you **infer** about the narrator?_____

B. Quote **proof:**_____

4. What do the phrases "seats twenty for all my gentlemen friends" and "use all the wrong utensils" **add to the excerpt?**

_____

5.   Using **context clues**, what do you think the meaning of "duvet" is?

_____

6.   This excerpt is based on what the narrator wants in her **"perfect" future**. Write at least 50 words based on a **dream future that you would like**. Like the narrator, you could begin with what you don't want. Be sure to use **specific details**.

_____

_____

_____

_____

_____

_____

_____

 ✏I HAD TO ADMIT THAT MY HEART DID SKIP A BEAT WHEN I FIRST MET HIM. BUT NOW I DON'T LIKE HIM, NOT IN THE LEAST FOR WHAT HE DID. IT WASN'T BECAUSE HE WAS THE MOST POPULAR BOY IN SCHOOL, PRESIDENT OF THE STUDENT COUNCIL, "A+" STUDENT, AND CAPTAIN OF THE BASKETBALL TEAM. IT WASN'T BECAUSE HE HAD THIS HOT SMILE THAT WOULD MELT ME LIKE A POPSICLE. IT WASN'T BECAUSE HE WAS OH SO CUTE OR BECAUSE HE LOOKED LIKE ONE OF THOSE BODY BUILDERS ON TV. IT WAS BECAUSE OF HIS COMPASSIONATE WAYS AND THOSE ADORABLE HAZEL EYES THAT I DREAMILY LOOKED INTO BEFORE IT HAPPENED.

THAT DAY STILL BITES MY EVERY NERVE LIKE ONE OF THOSE PIECES OF MEAT THAT YOU KEEP CHEWING AND CHEWING, BUT IT JUST DOESN'T SEEM TO GET CHEWY ENOUGH TO SWALLOW. IT ALL STARTED WHEN MY SEVENTH-GRADE LANGUAGE ARTS TEACHER, MRS. HILTON, ANNOUNCED THAT WE WERE EXPECTING A NEW STUDENT.

"CALM DOWN, CLASS," SHE SAID IN HER SOFT VOICE. SHE WAS

REALLY A QUIET PERSON AND A VERY KIND ONE TO ME AND EVERYONE WHO LISTENED TO HER, BUT WHENEVER MRS. HILTON GOT MAD, IT WAS LIKE SHE HAD BEEN BEATEN WITH AN UGLY STICK. HER EYES WOULD POP OUT LIKE BIG GUMBALLS, AND SHE WAS THE GUMBALL MACHINE. HER HAIR WOULD FRIZZ UP AS HER SMALL, TIMID VOICE TURNED INTO AN OBNOXIOUS YELL.

SHE CAME AND STOOD IN FRONT OF THE CLASS. SHE WAS KIND OF CHUBBY, SO IT DID TAKE SOME TIME. "LISTEN, EVERYONE, THIS IS MICHAEL JAMES."

SHE PULLED SOMEONE OUT FROM BEHIND THE CLASSROOM DOOR. I GAZED IN TOTAL ASTONISHMENT. MY MOUTH WAS THE GRAND CANYON, WIDE OPEN.

A FAIRLY TALL, HANDSOME BOY STOOD IN FRONT OF THE CLASS. HE HAD THIS RICH-BOY-PROPER LOOK. I COULD TELL HE WAS SHY WHEN HE PUT HIS HANDS IN THE POCKETS OF HIS NICELY FASHIONED OLD NAVY BIG POCKET JEANS AND BEGAN SWINGING HIS FEET IN FRONT OF HIM SO FAST THAT HE KNOCKED THE TEACHER RIGHT IN HER SHIN (MITCHELL, SARAH, "HEARTBROKEN").

1. How does the first paragraph **entice the reader** to want to read the rest of the story?

_____

2. Quote the **details** that make the narrator **infer** that MICHAEL IS SHY:

_____

3. An author can **reveal character** through APPEARANCE, ENVIRONMENT, INNER THOUGHTS AND FEELINGS, WHAT OTHERS SAY, ACTIONS, AND SPEECH. Choose three ways that the author reveals the character of Mrs. Hilton and give quoted proof:

A. Method:_____Proof:_____

B. Method:_____Proof:_____

C. Method:_____Proof:_____

4. Quote examples of the following **comma rules:**

A. **Appositive**:_____

B. **Series:**_____

C. **Compound sentence**:_____

5. What is the rule for **capitalizing dialogue**?_____

6. In at least 50 words, **write the next part of the story.** Use the AUTHOR'S TONE.

_____

_____

_____

_____

_____

_____

Now before I start, I need to make something clear to you. My grandfather was not an average, everyday grandpa. As far as I'm concerned, he was at the top of the class. James Vincent Dowling. He lived ninety-two years, through two world wars and the Great Depression. He saw the first Model-T Ford in 1908 and witnessed the launching of space shuttles. He had a lot of years of wisdom and love in that gray head of his.

My grandma died when I was eighteen months old so I don't remember her, but I do know that my grandpa's life changed dramatically. Have you ever heard of "Angels in the Outfield"? Well, let me tell you, there are "angels in the kitchen" when a ninety-two-year-old man is cooking breakfast! He never once burned anything but the bacon, but, boy, was it burned! Every morning we had to check on him, and we could smell burned bacon miles away! The kitchen never burned down so we were happy.

He had some stories that could make your heart skip a beat, and some were just plain silly. Many of them were about his school days in Hallettsville. He remembered his first-grade class and his teacher, Mrs. Crabtree, who gave him a paddling that stung like a hundred bees on a mission. If only he hadn't put that frog down Suzie Anderson's back! His whole school was made up of about nine rooms in the shape of a horseshoe. The bathrooms were outhouses, and for lunch he brought an old pail with a piece of fruit and whatever leftovers his mom had from supper the night before. Grandpa was poor and one of nine children so no wonder he got the nickname "Slim." His dad was a struggling cantaloupe farmer, and that didn't bring in much money for food.

I asked him once what his favorite part of school was, and he said it was recess. He was always the first pick of baseball, and because of his height, he was the Michael Jordan of the Halletsville High School basketball team.

✂

It's been three years since he died, but I know heaven is a little sweeter since he's there. God has a new first baseman, and the bacon's never burnt. You know, my grandpa never won a medal in the Olympics or pitched in the World Series, but he won top honors in my heart (Evans, Kristen, "Heaven's New First Baseman").

1. How does it add to the story that the author has chosen to **address the reader**?

_____

2. List three **facts** from the excerpt that could be **looked up in reference sources** and discussed in more specific details had the author chosen to do so (e.g., first Model-T Ford in 1908).

A._____B._____C._____

3. Choose three **methods of characterization** that the author uses to reveal information about the grandfather. Quote proof for each:

A. Method:_____Proof:_____

B. Method:_____Proof:_____

Dailies

C. Method:_____Proof:_____

4. How does the ending come **full circle**?_____

_____

5. List two **details of contrast** between Grandfather's school and schools of today:

_____&_____

6. Begin a paragraph with the line: "He/she had some stories that could make your heart skip a beat." **Tell at least two stories about someone you know**. Be sure to use **specific details and humor** if possible.

_____

_____

_____

_____

_____

_____

School stinks
I've never liked it
I've always hated it
I've never had school spirit
I've always been against it
I've had an assortment of bad history teachers
Mr. Dave, a bald-headed, bad-breath guy
Who cares way too much about Texas
Mrs. Moore, an overweight, flip-flop wearing woman
Who doesn't care enough and assigns maps and castles
I've dug in owl puke
I've had my things vandalized
My food and answers stolen

I've been taken advantage of
People have pretended to be my friend
For answers to the Africa test
My friend total went from zero in sixth period
Two in seventh, and a whopping three in eighth
I've had this long list of people who've insulted me:
Rufus, Chester, W.J., Drew, Pat, Devin,
Ryan, Dan, Al, Shawn, Jerry, and Mike
I've been poked out, poked at, and made fun of
I've been forced to take classes I didn't want to
I've read a long list of stupid books
I've looked at Mustangs and stars
For three years and they only get more meaningless
School stinks

(Burnside, Ben, "School Stinks").

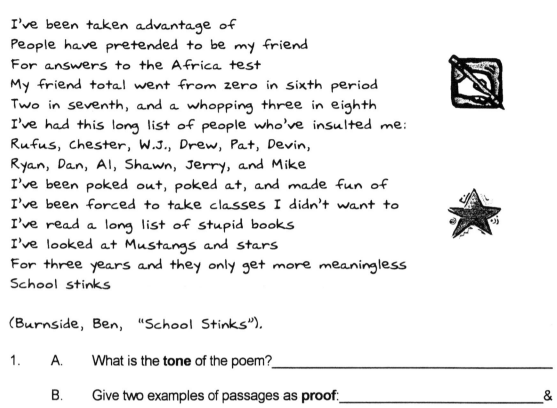

1. A. What is the **tone** of the poem?_____

    B. Give two examples of passages as **proof**:_____&

    _____

2. How does the author make the part about his friend "count" **humorous**?

    _____

3. How does the author **contrast** the two history teachers?_____

    _____

4. What can you **infer** that "Mustangs" and "stars" are?_____

5. Normally, beginning so many lines with "I've..." would be **repetitive** and not effective. How, though, does the author use this to his **advantage**?

    _____

6. Write at least a 10-line poem using a chronicling **of things you don't like.** Use **humor, specific details for effect**, etc. Write your poem on the back of this sheet.

Answer Key

*Accept other answers if supported.
*Answers to writing questions will vary.

"Adolescence"

1. A. Contrasts--good things versus bad related to adolescence
   B. "Sometimes you want to never grow up"
   C. The second half talks to the reader, describing growing up in pejorative terms and cautioning the reader to "be afraid."
2. A. "Sometimes you want to enter the futuristic time machine"
   B. "His starts cracking"
   C. "It's... / the addictive drug"
   D. "It's.../ the fearless soldier"
3. A. Growing up--with its good points and its bad ones--is something we all go through.
   B. "There's no way to escape it"
4. School subjects are capitalized if they are languages (e.g., Russian, English, etc.) or have numbers after them (e.g., Algebra IV).
5. A. Humorous yet ominous
   B. "First kiss" yet "the rusty nail waiting to occupy the heel of a blameless individual"
6. Answers will vary.

"The Wonder Years"

1. *A, B, C.   Answers will vary.
2. *I will push them to the side. (Answers will vary.)
3. A. We can infer that the narrator wants to be rich, yet independent.
   B. "I don't want one of those bossy-couch-potato-where's-my-tie husbands," "I'll carry it up to my bedroom," and "I want a mansion all to myself"
4. The phrases add a sense of humor to the piece.
5. "Duvet" is a bed cover; "There I will sit on my bed atop my white silk duvet."
6. Answers will vary.

"Heartbroken"

1. We want to know what has happened to cause the narrator to proclaim that "now I don't like him, not in the least for what he did." We also are intrigued by the positive description of him.

2.   "She pulled someone out from behind the classroom door" & "I could tell he was shy when he put his hands in his pockets...and began swinging his feet in front of him ...."

3.   A.   " 'Calm down, class,' she said in her soft voice."--speech

          B.   "She was really a quiet person and a very kind one to me and everyone who listened to her, but whenever Mrs. Hilton got mad, it was like she had been beaten with an ugly stick."--what others say, actions, appearance

          C.   "Her eyes would pop out like big gumballs, and she was the gumball machine. Her hair would frizz up as her small, timid voice turned into an obnoxious yell."--appearance & speech

4.   A.   "language arts teacher, Mrs. Hilton,"

          B.   "It wasn't because he was the most popular boy in school, president of the student council, 'A+' student, and captain of the basketball team."

          C.   "Her eyes would pop out like big gumballs, and she was the gumball machine."

5.   Capitalize the first word of a direct quotation.

6.   Answers will vary.

"Heaven's New First Baseman"

1.   We become more involved; it's as if we, too, knew this man.

2.   A.   Two world wars

          B.   Great Depression

          C.   Launching of space shuttles

3.   A.   Environment: "through two world wars and the Great Depression. He saw the first Model-T Ford in 1908 and witnessed the launching of space shuttles."

          B.   Actions: "He never once burned anything but the bacon, but, boy, was it burned!"

          C.   Actions: "If only he hadn't put that frog down Suzie Anderson's back!"

4.   In the second paragraph, the author mentions "Angels in the Outfield" and "angels in the kitchen"; her final paragraph comes full circle with the phrase "heaven is a little sweeter since he's there." She also pulls "threads" from other parts of her work, tying the story up in a sophisticated manner.

5.   "The bathrooms were outhouses" & "for lunch he brought an old pail with a piece of fruit and whatever leftovers his mom had from supper the night before."

6.   Answers will vary.

"School Stinks"

1.   A.   Humorous

          B.   "Mr. Dave, a bald-headed, bad-breath guy" & "Mrs. Moore, an overweight, flip-flop wearing woman"

2. As the day goes on, the narrator's "friend" count escalates according to how many people need answers "to the Africa test." It's even funnier that the narrator starts his count at "zero" and ends with a "whopping three."

3. One "cares way too much about Texas" while the other "doesn't care enough."

4. Since "Mustangs" is capitalized, we can infer it is the school mascot. "Stars" could be decorations or some other emblem associated with the school.

5. The author is making a list of what school has done to him and uses "I've never," "I've always," and "I've been" to emphasize his feelings about what has happened to him.

6. Answers will vary.

Dailies

☺"Hey, Matthew," I would call out every time I wanted to sail the ocean blue, be a spy for the army, or go ride my dirt bike on an imaginary mudding trail.

The boat and adventure, the radar and the slyness, and the dirt bikes and the fun--whether it was a bunk bed drawer, military field, or "drug bust"--we always had fun. It was as if our imagination transported us to another world.

Growing up, I was always imaginative in my own room, on the cul-de-sac, and in my house.

✂

Imaginative, that's what I was growing up. I remember walking into my room seeing my bunk bed and saying, "Hey, Matthew, do you want to play the Boat Game?" That's what we called it back then; every game we played was the "something" game. I still remember pulling out the boat-size drawer from under the bottom bunk. We would throw sheets, bedspreads, and blankets all over the room. We knew we weren't supposed to, we remembered we would have to fold every sheet, like Mom did, but all we hoped was that we wouldn't get caught. After it was all cleared, the worn brown carpet was our newly built deck, the drawer our new houseboat, and the loose sheets were the ropes tying our boat off. After being two mischievous boys playing around on a boat, we would get knocked out into sea, and that was how our journey would begin. My brother and I could almost smell the salt water, the fish, and the smell of a new boat that was about to be wrecked or damaged. We could hear the waves slamming their powerful hands into the boat, the seagulls flying overhead, making their squalling sound. But that was a while ago, the bunk beds have since been taken apart to make two, the brown carpet is gone, and a totally new home stands in place of the old one. The good old days have slowly evaporated like a puddle of water lying in the sun (Vidal, Danie, "Hey, Matthew!").

1. Generally, how can a reader **identify** with the introduction and first body?

   _____

2. A. What is the author's **dominant impression** (the main adjective that his essay supports that he was as a child)?

   _____

   B. Quote the author's **thesis statement**, complete with the three aspects (in this case, three places):

   _____

3. The first sentence of the first body is a **sophisticated structure** in that the adjective comes first. **For comparison purposes, rewrite the sentence so that the adjective comes elsewhere.**

   _____

4. Quote sentences that are examples of the following **comma rules:**

   A. **Direct address:**_____

   B. **Direct quotation:**_____

   C. **Series:**_____

   D. **Introductory phrase or clause:**_____

5. Quote **two details** to prove that the narrator had imagination as a child:

   A._____

   B._____

6. Write at least a **100-word body for a narrative/descriptive essay**, where you, too, prove that you were an imaginative or adventurous child. Remember to include at least three details and supports as well as Smiley-Face Tricks.

_____

_____

_____

_____

_____

_____

_____

_____

"Mirror, mirror on the wall,
Who loves me though I fall?"
I say
I pause a second
Tap a finger
And shift my weight to
My other foot
My reflection stares blankly
With no reply, still no
Answer to my lingering
Question
She just stands there, mimicking
My every move, blinking when
I blink. Her chest moving up and
Down to the rhythm of my
Breathing
But still no reply

Trapped behind a transparent world
She stares back at me, her eyes
Bright with adventure and strength
But dulled by an unknown

Dailies

Fear of what she can't
See within her imprisonment

Her eyes tell a story that
Hasn't been read
They cry out words that
Haven't been heard
This reflection, you see,
Speaks no words
Weeps no tears
But yet I hear her
And I watch her cry
I hope she doesn't notice
My own tears so I quickly
Rub them away
And she does the same

Placing my hands upon
The glass barrier, I
Begin to wonder if I'm
Trapped or is she
Am I trying to get out
Or is she
Trying to get in?

None of my questions are ever
Answered, I notice, but yet she
Tries the first one
She looks at me and recites,
"Mirror, mirror on the wall,
Who loves me though I fall?"
She pauses a second
Taps a finger
And shifts her weight to
The other foot

I stare back with no reply
We shrug our shoulders
And simultaneously
We walk away   (Davis, A'Ryann, "Reflection").

1.   On what **famous line** is the poem based?_____

_____

2.   Quote three lines the author uses to make the poem come **full circle in its ending:**

A._____B._____

C._____

3.   **Summarize** what happens in this narrative poem:

A.   Beginning:_____

B.   Middle:_____

C.   End:_____

4.   Quote a **cause and an effect**:_____

5.   A.   Quote a **paradox**:_____

        B.   **Resolve** the paradox:_____

6.   **Write at least a 15-line poem based on a famous line** that you have **altered** in some way.

☹I don't dislike many things. If I do really dislike something, I guess you could say that I hate it. My aunt calls me a "black and white" guy. She tells me that there are no "gray" areas in my life. I like my family, food, and certain people. I hate crowds, school, and certain people. The certain people that I hate really boils down to a person that I hate. Since he is part of the family, I guess you could say I am stuck with him.

Tom, Tom, Tom, how do I hate thee? Let me count the ways. I hate the way you whine, I hate the way you always get your way, and I hate the way you get better gifts at Christmas. My grandmother thinks I'm making this up and should be nicer to Tom.

It all started when we were born. In my family, Tom and I are considered "twin" cousins. I hate that. Everywhere our family went, everybody thought that Tom and I were brothers. I hate that. That meant we were stuck in the same rides at Six Flags. We were put in the same tent when we went camping. Did I mention he wet the bed? I hate that.

In high school Tom and I were in the same gym class. People there assumed we were brothers. I thought I was going to die when I saw his GI Joe boxer shorts. Tom, Tom, Tom, how do I hate thee? Of course, since we looked a lot alike and had the same last name, the GI Joe story was pinned on me as well. I lived my high school years under a dark cloud. The story appeared in the yearbook. It was ugly. I hated that   (Roeschen, Michael, "GI Joe Boxer Shorts").

1.   This excerpt uses several techniques to invoke **humor.** Quote the instances involved in the following devices:

A.   **Alteration of a famous line:**_____

B.   **Repetition for effect** (Almost a refrain):_____

C.   Specific instances with which the **reader can identify:**_____

_____

2.   A.   Why would "GI Joe" be **capitalized** but not "boxer shorts"?_____

_____

    B.   Why is "Six Flags" **capitalized**?_____

3.   What two possible **comma rules** could explain the commas after "Tom"?

_____ & _____

4.   A.   Of what is "Tom" a **symbol** to the narrator?_____

    B.   **Quote proof:**_____

5.   What can you **infer** about the narrator from the statement that his aunt calls him a "black and white" guy with no "gray areas" in his life?

_____

6.   Write at least a **100-word humorous vignette** about something/someone you dislike. Try to use some of the author's tricks, including a refrain.

_____

_____

_____

_____

_____

_____

_____

☹ "This is all your fault!"

"My fault! I'm not the one maxing out ten credit cards a day."

"That's absurd. I'm only trying to make this dump you bought look like a home."

Another night's rest disturbed. That was all it was.

Sunday they argued about Mom buying a new table for the living room. Saturday they argued about Dad working until midnight. Friday they argued about Mom buying a new china set. Thursday they argued about Dad staying out with his friends or the "bad influences" as Mom called them until two in the morning. And tonight they're arguing about Mom buying herself a pair of diamond earrings.

When my sister was born, you couldn't catch them saying a mean word to each other. It wasn't until my sister was two that they started arguing. The ironic thing is that I used to think they didn't talk enough. By the time she turned five, they were arguing every night. I had no idea how my sister could sleep through their noise. Every morning she would wake up like she had never heard a sound. Unlike my sister, I heard the arguing constantly.

It was after dinner one night while I was in bed that once again I heard the arguing. They argued plenty, but this was the first time I had ever heard that horrible word in our home. A home where I thought we were protected from the elements of the world, this word came whisking through the halls like a tornado. Somehow it sneaked past the security system, crept by the dog, and just waltzed into our home. It came right out of my dad's mouth, "I want a divorce!" (Morgan, Jerrod, "That Word").

1. Explain three reasons for the **author's paragraphing**:

A._____ B._____

C._____

2. Sometimes authors choose the "real" over the "grammatically correct." Explain the reason it is "proper" to write the following: "Mom's buying," "Dad's working," "Dad's staying"—as opposed to **"Mom buying,"** etc. In other words, why is it correct to use the **possessive form of the noun**?

_____

3. Explain what the author means when he says that "the ironic thing is that I used to think they didn't talk enough." (How is this **ironic**?)

_____

4. Quote a **magic three** that is a **personification:**_____,

_____,_____

5. Explain two **contrasting ideas** in the passage:

A._____ B._____

6. Write a vignette about an **argument** beginning with the line: "It's all your fault!" Be sure to use figurative language, dialogue, etc.

_____

_____

_____

_____

_____

WHEELS TURNING

HAIR FLYING

FEET PEDALING

HEART RACING

HOUSE BY HOUSE

PASSING IN SECONDS

PEOPLE STARING

CARS HONKING

ME LAUGHING

ZIPPING THROUGH THE NEIGHBORHOOD

JOURNEY ENDING

DOING IT ALL AGAIN

WHEELS STILL TURNING

HAIR STILL FLYING

FEET STILL PEDALING

HEART STILL RACING

ME STILL LAUGHING

(SHANNON, JESSICA, "MY JOURNEY")

1. How has the author **structured** the poem?_____

2. A. What is the **tone** of the poem?_____

    B. Quoted **proof:**_____

3. **Summarize** what is happening in the poem:

A. Beginning:_____

B. Middle:_____

C. End:_____

4. What **adverb** signals the repeat of the journey?_____

5. The author has the beginning of a **noun absolute** poem (*I.E., NOUNS FOLLOWED BY "-ING" OR "-ED" VERBS*). If the author had written **"My wheels turning, I raced around the neighborhood,"** she would have used a sophisticated sentence beginning with a noun absolute before the independent clause. **Rewrite two of the author's phrases, making them into sentences with noun absolutes,** *WHICH MAY COME AT THE BEGINNING, MIDDLE, OR END OF A SENTENCE.*

A._____

B._____

6. Exchange a list of **ten nouns and ten "-ing" verbs** with a neighbor. Choose five of each and write a **poem modeled on the structure of the author's.** Write the poem on the back of this sheet.

Answer Key

*Accept other answers if supported.
*Answers to writing questions will vary.

"Hey, Matthew"

1.   We can identify because we, too, were probably imaginative as children.
2.   A.   Imaginative
        B.   "Growing up, I was always imaginative in my own room, on the cul-de-sac, and in my house."
3.   *I was imaginative when I was growing up.
4.   A.   "'Hey, Matthew'"
        B.   "'Hey, Matthew,' I would call...."
        C.   "sail the ocean blue, be a spy for the army, or go ride ...."
        D.   "Growing up,"
5.   A.   "After it was all cleared, the worn brown carpet was our newly built deck, the drawer our new houseboat, and the loose sheets were the ropes tying our boat off."
        B.   "My brother and I could almost smell the salt water...."
6.   Answers will vary.

"Reflection"

1.   "Mirror, mirror on the wall"
2.   A.   "pauses a second"
        B.   "taps a finger"
        C.   "shifts her weight"
3.   A.   The narrator asks the mirror, "Who loves me though I fall?"
        B.   The narrator identifies with the reflection's pain.
        C.   The narrator wonders who the "trapped" one really is, but she receives no answers.
4.   "Trapped behind a transparent world **[cause]** / She stares back at me **[effect]**"
5.   A.   "Her eyes tell a story that / Hasn't been read/ They cry out words that/ Haven't been heard"
        B.   Even though the "reflection's" story and words have not been heard, the narrator knows them, as they are her own.
6.   Answers will vary.

"GI Joe Boxer Shorts"

1. A. "How do I love thee? Let me count the ways." (Famous line)
   B. "I hate that."
   C. "Since he is part of the family, I guess you could say I am stuck with him."
2. A. Proper adjective but not product
   B. Specific place, an amusement park
3. Direct address & series
4. A. Another thing that he hates
   B. "Tom, Tom, Tom, how do I hate thee?"
5. We can infer that the narrator has distinctive likes and dislikes--with nothing falling in between.
6. Answers will vary.

"That Word"

1. A. Dialogue
   B. Time change
   C. Emphasis--"Another night's rest disturbed. That was all it was."
2. The rule is to use the possessive form before a gerund.
3. It is ironic in that the narrator's parents talk too much now--in the form of arguing.
4. "Somehow it sneaked past the security system, crept by the dog, and just waltzed into our home."
5. A. "When my sister was born, you couldn't catch them saying a mean word to each other."
   B. "Unlike my sister, I heard the arguing constantly."
6. Answers will vary.

"My Journey"

1. The author has structured the poem by first giving us images of her "zipping through the neighborhood," then "doing it all again" during the second half of the poem.
2. A. Carefree
   B. "Me still laughing"
3. A. The narrator is riding her bike through the neighborhood.
   B. Her journey ends.
   C. She does it all over again.
4. "Again"
5. *A. My wheels turning, I zipped through the neighborhood.
   *B. I zipped through the neighborhood, my hair flying.
6. Answers will vary.

Dailies

⊖Not only was I mischievous in the yard, but the bathroom was also a terrific trouble-starter for me. The bathroom was the place where the fun started, and trouble was the enormous string attached. After a hard, grueling day at kindergarten, I would go straight to the bathroom, my little hideaway. I would arm myself with some new toy I had gotten, perhaps a Power Ranger or Ninja Turtle sword for thwarting off attacks of evil demons and ghost warriors that would threaten my survival if I did not stab aimlessly into thin air.

For every fun, imaginative game, though, there was an accident. With my swinging, there would be a sound of the sword hitting and cracking the sliding glass, shatter-resistant, opaque door of the bathtub. Unfortunately, there were no hills to run to in my house so I would inevitably be cornered and punished until I had learned yet another lesson.

Then on weekends when my relatives came over, we would have water balloon fights. My mother always said, "Don't fill water balloons in the house," but, constantly thinking how to be mischievous, I would fill them up in the bathroom so that I could sneak up and blast somebody a good one. Yet again I would suffer the consequences for dropping the dreaded water balloon on the carpet.

Maybe I was a little on the bad side, but that's what growing up is all about. Soon I found that the bathroom was not the only place for being "playful." There were better places for getting into trouble, and a whole world of dumb ideas to try. Now that I think back, maybe I should have just stayed in the bathroom (Couch, Cory, "Mischievous").

1. This is the **second body** in an essay containing two other bodies, an introduction (not shown) and a conclusion.

    A. What is the **topic** (in this instance a place) of the author's **first body**?

    _____

    B. What **transition words** does the author use to connect the opening paragraph to the body?_____

    C. What is the **topic** (the place) of **this body**?_____

2. A well-written body must have at least **three supports or examples**. List three examples that prove the author was indeed mischievous:

A._____ B._____ C._____

3. **Dialogue** is one **method of elaboration**. What dialogue has the author included to support his point?

    _____

4. Quote examples of the following **comma rules:**

    A. **Appositive:**_____

    B. **Coordinate adjective:**_____

    C. **Compound sentence:**_____

5. What is the author's **theme**?_____

6. An introduction must include an attention-getter and a thesis statement, complete with the three aspects to be covered. **Write an introduction for this essay.** The author's thesis is the fact that he was mischievous in his yard, the bathroom, and the kitchen. Put the thesis in brackets and put check marks on the three places.

    _____

    _____

    _____

_____

_____

_____

⊙I was always alone, especially in my room, where solitude was inscribed on the walls.   My only escape from the cold, hard reality that I was the only person seemingly within miles was slumber. In my room days would go by with the blink of the eye or the flipping of a calendar, for every time I would blink I would see time go by like water running through my fingers. My room was the place where I was sent for months at a time if I got into trouble. I can remember one time I went to a friend's house while my parents were gone, and, when I came back, I was sentenced to three months. In the room. No friends, no TV, no escape. So there I sat in the room, watching the ceiling fan slowly rotate counterclockwise as if taunting me that time wasn't moving forward but backward. I could feel the warmth on certain parts of my body where the tree branches hadn't managed to block me. This warmth was like hope, very little but paradoxically so much. Then when that hope was just a flicker, I would realize I had just one more day to serve, and excitement would fill me. The problem was that I would get into trouble all over again. Isolation was my destiny (Nored, Brandon, "Isolation").

1.   In the topic sentence, what **dominant impression** (main idea) does the author give the reader and where is the **place that will support this**?_____

A.   **Dominant Impression:**_____

B.   **Place:**_____

2.   What does the author mean that "days would go by with the blink of the eye or the flipping of a calendar"?

_____

3. A. Look up **"paradox"** in the dictionary and write its **definition:**

_____

B. Explain the author's **paradox**:_____

_____

4. A. What can you **infer** that the "warmth" is?_____

B. **Clues:**_____

5. Quote two **fragments for effect** and explain why the author chose not to make these sentences:

A. **Fragment**:_____

B. **Fragment**:_____

C. **Explanation**:_____

6. Write a poem or a paragraph about a **time you felt isolated**. Use specific details for effect (e.g., watching the ceiling fan) and figurative language.

⊙As a kid, I had a blast playing outside. It was really like one of those Disney stories. I had a big, round, fat tree in my front yard. I'd climb up, crawl around, sit, and hang. But the big, round, fat tree would change. It never stayed just "a tree." I could transform it into just about anything, like a boat surrounded by alligators. I could never crawl lower than the second branch from the bottom, or the alligators might get me. Yes, living on a boat in the middle of a sea of alligators was challenging. Tossing a rope to the dry land (the driveway) was a safe escape. Mother could only throw snacks to me from the front porch, as I was saving her from sure death in the jaws of those ferocious green beasts.

The green grass was actually monstrous blue waves. No one dared to jump in. Eventually boredom or a spider were the only things that could stop my personal "Survivor" series.   Yes, if I'd see a spider, I would run as fast as I could to the front door-- waves or no waves.

My back yard was just as much fun. The trampoline was always base. My sisters and my neighbors would play hide-and-go- seek. I'd feel a hand on my back, pushing me, then my next-door neighbor would yell, "Ha ha, you're it!"

Drat! But now I was in the game. I would count, "One, ten, twenty-five, fifty, ready or not, here I come!" I would sprint for the boogie monster tree that my sister always hid behind, and I would tag her. "Ha ha, you're it," I would say.

Her reaction would always be, "Y'all, this game is getting boring." Everyone would dash inside, leaving me just standing there with my nature friends, but that was okay with me (Heinrich, Michael, "My Imagination").

1.   What two **allusions** has the author used?_____&_____

2.   Why would the author **repeat** "big, round, fat tree" instead of finding **synonyms** for the adjectives?

_____

3.   Why does the author change **paragraphs** in telling about the hide-and-seek game?

_____

4.   Give two **specific details** the author uses and then **write a general, less specific version** for each:

A.   **Detail**:_____

      General:_____

B.   **Detail**:_____

      General:_____

5.   Explain the following **grammar rules**:

      A.   **Y'all** (Why the apostrophe and what does the word stand for?)

      _____

      B.   The **hyphen** in "twenty-five":_____

      C.   **Quotation marks** around "Survivor":_____

      D.   **Apostrophe** in "you're":_____

6.   Write a **body paragraph** whose **topic sentence involves your having fun outside when you were a kid**. Use at least three supports. Remember to include specific details and figurative language. You might want to try inserting some dialogue as a method of elaboration.

_____

_____

_____

_____

_____

_____

_____

_____

_____

☀Adventurous, that was what I felt at my maw-maw's pool. I'll always remember the sight of the diving board longing for a little girl like me to jump on it. I watched in awe as my older brother would perform daredevilish tricks off it and into the deep, unknown waters. Before that summer was over, I would jump off that thing, the monster board. Suddenly, though, my daydreams would be interrupted by the aroma of the hot cheese pizza that my maw-maw had just taken out of the oven. I would look up to see her waiting with a warm, fluffy towel and a big glass of iced tea. That hot, freshly baked pizza would be welcoming me from the picnic table. I would climb out of that cool water and into the warm air.

There they went again down that slide looming into the clouds. The time had come. I would try. I would succeed. I would conquer. I went up the ladder step-by-step; there was no turning back. This was it. "One, two, three, go!" I yelled.

Now I was the one doing the daredevilish tricks, trying to outdo my brother, and my cousin was the one turning green. I gave them one last warning--"Cannonball!"--as I drowned them in a tsunami of a splash (Martin, Courtney, "Trying To Touch the Clouds").

1.   The author uses **imagery** to appeal to the reader's **senses**. Quote images that appeal to the following:

A.   **Sight**:_____

B.   **Sound**:_____

C.   **Taste**:_____

D.   **Smell:**_____

E.   **Touch**:_____

2.   Quote a **metaphor**:_____

3. A. Use a **context clue** to **infer** what "tsunami" means._____

    B. **Clue**:_____

4. Quote examples of the following **comma rules**:

    A. **Appositive**:_____

    B. **Coordinate adjective**:_____

5. A. When the author writes "I went up the ladder step-by-step; there was no turning back," why does she use a **semicolon**?_____

    B. Rewrite the sentence using a different **method of combining**:

    _____

6. Write **five sentences**, each of which is an example of a **different sensory image**. You could write about the classroom, and even if one sense is absent (e.g., smell, taste, etc.), you could write that you can "almost smell." Remember to use **specific details**.

    A. **Sight**:_____

    _____

    B. **Sound**:_____

    _____

    C. **Taste**:_____

    _____

D. **Smell**:_____

_____

E. **Touch**:_____

_____

①THE FOREMOST PLACE I FELT ADVENTUROUS WAS IN MY NEIGHBORHOOD. EVERY DAY WAS ANOTHER BIG ADVENTURE. THE NEIGHBORHOOD KIDS AND I WOULD RIDE AROUND, TRYING TO FIND THE BIGGEST, WIDEST, DEEPEST DITCH SO THAT WE COULD FLY AT FULL SPEED, LIKE DOGS ON FIRE, JUST TO SEE JUST HOW FAR OVER THE DITCH WE COULD GET. I WAS A PRO STUNT WOMAN DRIVING MY MOTORCYCLE OVER A WIDE CANYON. A FEW TIMES WE ACTUALLY MADE IT. AS I FLEW INTO THE DITCHES, I COULD TASTE THE MUDDY, YUCKY WATER. I COULD FEEL IT IN MY EARS. I COULD SMELL IT ON MY SKIN.

AFTER ABOUT WHAT SEEMED LIKE ONE MILLION TIMES IN THAT DITCH, WE WOULD HEAD TO OUR LITTLE SPOT WE CALLED J&J HURST. IT WAS WHERE THERE WERE TREES AS TALL AS SKYSCRAPERS, PATHS AS BUMPY AS GOING UP A ROLLER COASTER, AND HILLS AS STEEP AS CLIFFS. BEING THE BIGGEST DAREDEVIL IN THE WORLD, I WOULD BE THE FIRST TO GO UP THE TREES AND SEE HOW FAR I COULD GET WITHOUT FALLING OFF. I WOULD GO THROUGH THE PATHS TO SEE HOW MANY KILLER BUMPS I COULD GO OVER WITHOUT FALLING ON MY FACE. OR I WOULD GO DOWN THE HILLS TO SEE HOW FAR DOWN I COULD GET WITHOUT FLIPPING.

BUT NOW IT IS SO DIFFERENT. IT'S NOW ONLY MY BEST FRIEND AND I, NOT THE NEIGHBORHOOD KIDS, JUST US WALKING AROUND AND EXERCISING. BUT EVERY ONCE IN A WHILE, I WILL GO BACK THERE TO THE TREES, TO THE DITCHES, TO THE HILLS AND PATHS JUST TO SEE HOW MUCH THEY HAVE CHANGED, AND THEY HAVE. THE TREES AREN'T THAT TALL. THE HILLS AREN'T THAT STEEP. THE PATHS AREN'T THAT BUMPY. AND THE DITCHES AREN'T THAT BIG. MAYBE THEY'VE CHANGED. OR MAYBE I HAVE (TODD, JO ANN, "AN EVERYDAY LIFE WITH ADVENTURES").

1.   Quote an example of the following **figurative language devices**:

A.   **Hyperbole:**_____

B.   **Metaphor:**_____

C.   **Simile:**_____

2. Quote a **magic three**:_____,

_____,_____

3. What **contrast** does the author present?_____

_____

4. Quote examples of the following **imagery**:

   A. **Smell:**_____

   B. **Touch:**_____

5. A. What **symbol**(s) could the passage contain?_____

   B. Of what could it (they) be **symbolic**?_____

6. Write a **concluding paragraph** for an essay whose dominant impression is ADVENTUROUS and whose three places are the NEIGHBORHOOD, GRANDMA'S HOUSE, AND the TRESTLES. Remember that a conclusion needs an **attention-getter** and a **restatement of the thesis**, complete with the dominant impression and three aspects to be covered (i.e., places).

_____

_____

_____

_____

_____

_____

_____

_____

_____

Answer Key

*Accept other answers if supported.
*Answers to writing questions will vary.

"Mischievous"

1. A.   The yard
    B.   "Not only was I mischievous in the yard,"
    C.   The bathroom
2. A.   "I would arm myself with some new toy I had gotten...if I did not stab aimlessly into thin air."
    B.   "With my swinging, there would be a sound of the sword hitting and cracking...."
    C.   "we would have water balloon fights"
3. "My mother always said, 'Don't fill water balloons in the house.'"
4. A.   "the bathroom, my little hideaway"
    B.   "hard, grueling day"
    C.   "The bathroom was the place where fun started, and trouble was the enormous string attached."
5. Growing up usually involves a little mischief.
6. Answers will vary.

"Isolation"

1. A.   Isolation, being alone
    B.   Room
2. The author perhaps means that some days seem to pass instantly ("with the blink of an eye"), whereas others move slowly (with "the flipping of a calendar"--as if the author must wait to turn the page or as if the duration were so long).
3. A.   A statement seemingly self-contradictory or absurd but in reality expressing a possible truth
    B.   The warmth of the sun seems like such a small thing to provide hope, but that is the only hope the narrator has, making it far more important.
4. A.   The sun's rays
    B.   "where the tree branches hadn't managed to block me"
5. A.   "In the room."
    B.   "No friends, no TV, no escape."
    C.   The fragments highlight the solitude.
6. Answers will vary.

"My Imagination"

1. Disney stories & "Survivor" series
2. Perhaps the author wants to emphasize what the tree was before its transformation.
3. The author has changed places--to her back yard.
4. A. * "I could never crawl lower than the second branch from the bottom"-- I could never crawl lower.
   B. * "The green grass was actually monstrous blue waves."-- The grass was waves.
5. A. The apostrophe is used for the contraction, meaning "you all."
   B. Compound numbers require hyphens.
   C. TV shows are enclosed in quotation marks.
   D. The apostrophe is needed in contractions (i.e., you're = you are).
6. Answers will vary.

"Trying To Touch the Clouds"

1. A. "I watched in awe as my older brother would perform daredevilish tricks off it and into the deep, unknown waters."
   B. "tsunami of a splash"
   C. "The hot, freshly baked pizza would be welcoming me from the picnic table."
   D. "the aroma of the hot cheese pizza"
   E. "I would climb out of that cool water into the warm air."
2. "tsunami of a splash"
3. A. a large wave
   B. "drowned them"
4. A. "I would jump off that thing, the monster board"
   B. "warm, fluffy towel"
5. A. The semicolon separates the two sentences.
   B. * As I went up the ladder, I realized there was no turning back.

6. Answers will vary.

"An Everyday Life with Adventures"

1.   A.   "After about what seemed like a million times"
         B.   "I was a pro stunt woman"
         C.   "like dogs on fire"
2.   "It was where there were trees as tall as skyscrapers, paths as bumpy as going up a roller coaster, and hills as steep as cliffs."
3.   The contrast is what the author did as a child (adventurous, imaginative activities) to what the author does now (normal, teenage "walking around and exercising").
4.   A.   "I could smell it [the water] on my skin."
         B.   "I could feel it in my ears."
5.   A.   the trees, ditches, hills, and paths
         B.   the adventure of childhood
6.   Answers will vary.

Dailies

✏️"You want what, young lady?" Daddy said, his ears red, his face muscles tight, the veins in his neck bulging.

"All I said was that I want a black bikini. No bigee. Get it? No bigee!"

Daddy wasn't amused. In fact, he looked like he was about to blow a gasket.

"See," I continued my argument, "all my friends are getting them. They're the 'in' thing. One pieces are for old ladies." I was proud of myself. The old-lady trick might work since Daddy always called me his pretty baby. Surely he wouldn't want his "pretty baby" to resemble in any shape or form an old lady.

"Bethany Finnagin and Ellen Bower had one pieces on at your pool party," Daddy cut in with a you're-not-winning-this-argument-little-girl tone.

"My point exactly, Daddy. Bethany wears goggle glasses that make her look like she's underwater all the time. Last week she single-handedly pinned Wallace Taylor up against her locker just for looking at her funny, and she wears a beehive for heaven's sake. And Ellen, Daddy, come on! Ellen's body looks like it hasn't seen the light of day since the doctor whacked her on her tiny white-as-a-snowdrift butt when she was born. She'd wear a scuba diving outfit if she could just to cover up her scaly white skin. Come on, Daddy. It's 1965. Let your hair down!"

"I'm bald, or haven't you noticed!" Daddy said, rubbing the place on his head where hair used to sprout in abundance.

"Well, see, you're exposing skin; I just want the same opportunity."

"I fail to see how my losing my hair and your losing your mind are remotely connected."

"Look, Daddy, is it the color? 'Cause if it is, keep in mind that color is just a state of mind. Think of black as a neutral."

Daddy began to relax. His ears were almost back to their

original color, his face muscles were only twitching now and then, and his neck had deluged somehow and had become more like his regular I-need-a-hug neck.

"Black is not the issue, <u>kitzel</u>. The issue is that you're twelve years old and you want a bikini. I think you actually said a 'string bikini.' In black. First of all, a daughter of mine will be a lady at all times or know the reason why."

"But, Daddy...."

"And that's the other thing. Your 'rear end' won't be covered in black. Black's for funerals, black's for hit men, black's for that mystery dish your mother made last night"
(Teacher Example, "The Bikini").

1. Why is a **quote within a quote** used on several occasions (e.g., 'in' thing)?

_____

2. Quote sentences that are examples of the following **comma rules**:

   A. **Direct address**:_____

   B. **Introductory phrase**:_____

   C. **Interrupter**:_____

3. Why is the word "kitzel" **underlined**? (Note: It could have been put in **italics**; instead except the font prohibited it.)

_____

4. A. Quote a **figurative language device** that you particularly like:

_____

   B. Of what **type** of figurative language device is it an example?

_____

5. A. What is the **conflict** of the piece?_____

   B. Is it **internal or external**?_____

C.   Quote **proof**:_____

6.   Write at least a 100-word vignette about a **conflict you have had with your parents**. Use **dialogue** (and remember the rules for paragraphing and punctuating), **figurative language, and humor**.

_____

_____

_____

_____

_____

_____

_____

_____

    I hated sitting on the roads for hours. It made me enjoy school more. At least there we roamed from hall to hall. I looked outside at the many houses lit with Christmas lights, and the frost of the air from my open window made me cover myself with my black leather jacket. Dad sipped coffee as he drove, and my mother rested her head on the back of the seat. My brothers and sisters were already into a deep sleep.

    It was two days before Christmas Eve, and I still didn't know if I had a present. Daddy must have figured a vacation would do for us, but Daddy had the wrong idea. I slumped on the seat and lay my head back.

    I thought of the Christmases the years before. In 1992 I had gotten a tuxedo set. I was five years old. I hated it because when Daddy handed it to me, he tripped over my copy of <u>The Little Engine That Could</u>-- that I had received the Christmas before that--and spilled black coffee all over the only thing that kept me going. Who cared about a silly tuxedo if your confidence is stained?

    In 1989, when I was two, I can't recall what I got. In 1988, my second Christmas, I probably got to see Santa at the mall. In 1987, the year I was born, just being able to see was a present.

I also have never believed in any of that mumbo-jumbo mess about Santa climbing inside chimneys, stealing cookies, or even existing for that matter. He was as fake as...well, I don't know what, maybe my very own father, but I do know that Santa wasn't real. I was five when I first really saw him and paid any attention. I never told anyone but, when he yawned, I saw a string attached to his nose, which made up his wanna-be beard.
(Pelt, Gregg, "A Mishap on Christmas Vacation").

1.   A.   What can you **infer** about the **setting** of this piece?

_____

B.   Give **quoted proof**:_____

2.   In the first paragraph, quote two examples of a **compound sentence**:

A._____

B._____

3.   A.   Why is <u>The Little Engine That Could</u> **underlined**?

_____

B.   What is the rule for which words should be **capitalized in titles**?

_____

4.   Quote an example of **humor** in the piece:_____

_____

5.   A.   What can you **infer** about the narrator's personality?

_____

B.   Quote **proof**:_____

_____

    C.   What can you **infer** about the father's personality?

_____

    D.   Quote **proof**:_____

6.   This piece is based on a "mishap on Christmas vacation." **Write at least 50 words that could serve as the beginning of a narrative about a "mishap" you have had.**

_____

_____

_____

_____

_____

I don't know this man
He calls me early in the morning
to tell me to get up
to say "I love you"
yet
he is never home
Work runs his life
Wake up
get ready
go to work
and so on
Always gone
all day
all week
all weekends

I ♥ Dad

But
when he is there
he is like my pot of gold
at the end of the rainbow
my comforter
my helper
my healer
And when I see him
this stranger
sitting on the top row of the bleachers
(Haberman, Heather, "The Stranger at My House")

1.   Explain the **contrast** in the poem:_____

_____

2.   Quote a **magic three**:_____,_____,_____

3.   Explain the significance of the **capitalization**:_____

_____

4.   What is the **cliche** that is used, and how has the author altered it to make it effective?

A._____

B._____

5.   What **word** does the author use in the poem to confirm that at times she "does not know this man"?

_____

6.   Using at least 30 words, finish the poem.

He left
without a trace
no tiptoeing
      s
        t
          e
            p
              s
on the creaky hardwood floor
He left
as though
carried by the wind
leaving behind
      no note
      no footprints
      no memories
He left
in the middle of the month
with the leaves falling on the softened ground
He left
taking with him his frets
dealing with mortality and immortality
He left
leaving our sorrowed, solitary hearts
behind
He left
taking with him doubts
and burden-bound loads of shame
He left
with no joy on his fumbled face
He left
with no child-like dreams
no halo of hope
He left
not bothering to realize
what he had left behind
(Duvall, Beth, "He Left").

1.   What **refrain** does the author use to tie the poem together?_____

_____

2. A. Look up **"pathos"** in the dictionary and give its definition:

    _____

    B. How would the **ending be an example of pathos**?

    _____

3. Explain why you think the author has chosen to write **"steps"** in such a manner:

    _____

4. A. What can you **infer** about the **setting** of the poem?

    _____

    B. Quote **evidence**:_____

    _____

5. A. What can you **infer** about the **personality** of the subject of the poem?

    _____

    B. Quote **evidence**:_____

    _____

6. Write at least a ten-line poem entitled "_____Left." Try experimenting with **line form, figurative language,** etc.

✎Our relationship was more. He was my knight in shining armor, my Greek god, my faithful companion. When I even mentioned his name to friends, they all--laughingly, yet with that serious, far-away look in their eyes--asked if he has a brother. I would laugh, too, but I knew what they were after. They, too, envisioned flowers on special occasions, and hours of phone conversations about what life meant to us, and the kind of hand holding that said, "I am here for you and always will be." You see, our relationship was more. (Teacher Sample, "Our Relationship").

1. Quote a **magic three**:_____,_____,

_____

2. Explain the reason for the **dashes**:_____

_____

3. A. Explain the rule for **capitalizing** "Greek" (but not "god"):

_____

B. Give **three more instances of this rule** followed by **lower case nouns**:

_____,_____,_____

4. Give three **details** (besides the magic three you've already quoted) that prove their "relationship was more":

A._____B._____

C._____

5. What can you **infer** about the friends' "far-away look in their eyes"?

_____

6. Write a **parody** of the "our-relationship-was-more" piece by **describing your relationship with an inanimate object** (e.g., a car, your computer, money, etc.).

_____

_____

_____

_____

_____

_____

_____

_____

Answer Key

*Accept other answers if supported.
*Answers to writing questions will vary.

"The Bikini"

1. Quotation marks are already used for dialogue; therefore, quotes within quotes must be used for emphasis.
2. A. "'You want what, young lady?'"
    B. " 'See,' I continued....' "
    C. "Daddy said, his ears red, "
3. Foreign words are italicized or underlined. *Kitzel* is the German word for "kitten."
4. A. "white-as-a-snowdrift butt"
    B. Simile
5. A. Daughter's wanting bikini versus Father's refusal
    B. External
6. Answers will vary.

"A Mishap on Christmas Vacation"

1. A. Christmas time / on the road in a car during the winter
    B. "I looked outside at the many houses lit with Christmas lights," "It was two days before Christmas Eve," "I hated sitting on the road for hours," and "Dad sipped coffee as he drove."
2. A. "I looked outside at the many houses lit with Christmas lights, and the frost of the air...."
    B. "Dad sipped coffee as he drove, and my mother...."
3. A. Titles of books are underlined or in italics.
    B. First word, last word, and all important words
4. "Who cared about a silly tuxedo if your confidence is stained?"
5. A. We can infer that the narrator is a realist.
    B. "I was five when I first really saw him and paid any attention. I never told anyone but, when he yawned, I saw a string attached to his nose, which made up his wanna-be beard."
    C. We can infer that the father doesn't really "know" his family.
    D. "Daddy must have figured a vacation would do for us, but Daddy had the wrong idea."
6. Answers will vary.

"The Stranger at My House"

1. Father gone versus. Father at home
2. "my comforter / my helper / my healer"
3. Capitals signify sentence beginnings.
4. A. "A pot of gold at the end of the rainbow"
   B. The author has personalized it--"my" pot of gold
5. Stranger
6. Answers will vary.

"He Left"

1. "He left"
2. A. "Evoking a feeling of pity or compassion"
   B. The fact that the subject leaves and does not "realize / what he had left behind" evokes a feeling of pity in the reader.
3. The author's writing of "steps" mimics the meaning of the word.
4. A. We can infer that it's fall.
   B. "He left / in the middle of the month / with the leaves falling on the softened ground"
5. A. * We can infer that the subject is ashamed and confused.
   B. "He left / taking with him doubts / and burden-bound loads of shame"
6. Answers will vary.

"Our Relationship"

1. "He was my knight in shining armor, my Greek god, my faithful companion."
2. Parenthetical information
3. A. Proper adjective; "god" is not used as a proper noun in this instance
   B. *1. Mexican food
      2. Chinese laundry
      3. Russian language
4. A. "envisioned flowers on special occasions"
   B. "hours of phone conversations about what life meant to us"
   C. "the kind of hand holding ...."
5. We can infer that the friends are envisioning this sort of relationship for themselves.
6. Answers will vary.

Dailies

The sun setting, the clouds covering the sky
sheltering Earth from the outside world
The sound of the wind roaring, the leaves on the
oak trees
transforming into hues of red and yellow and orange
and brown
then falling to the ground, not making a sudden move,
not a sound to be heard
The sharp edges of the rocks as I walk barefoot
down the path of the train track
to my destiny, my home
the sweat dripping from the tips of my long, loose hair
As I walk through the tunnel, the entrance that
leads back to my home
to Oklahoma
the darkness swallows me whole, forbidding me never
to turn my back again
I feel the darkness inside my body fading, its mouth opening
so I can finish my journey home
The vibration from the train coming to transport me
to the place
where I will say the "hello's"
and the "I miss you's"
and the "I love you's"
to my family that I left long ago

I'm coming home, Mama, back to my sea-green room
where I left the picture of little Jimmy boy sleeping
on a branch up in Forest Lake
I'm coming home, Papa, back for the horse rides up in Canyon Valley,
back home to help you feed the animals we both love so well
I'm coming home, Brother Billy,
so you will have company for your morning trips to our fishing hole
back to make believing that the cloud up above is a choo-choo train
on its way to the big city

How far do I have to go?
Over the hilltops, through the west woods, across the river
and from then on through Barstow
where I'll hear the familiar church bells
where I'll catch the aroma of fresh baked pies from Miss Carol's
My destiny is waiting for me
My family is waiting
My home
Barstow, Oklahoma
I'm coming home to you
Oklahoma

(Stoerner, Brianne, "My Journey Home to Oklahoma")

1. Quote examples of **imagery**:

A. **Sight:**_____

B. **Sound:**_____

C. **Touch (Feeling):**_____

D. **Smell:**_____

2. A. Why would the author write **"the hello's"** as opposed to "hello"?

_____

B. Why is the **apostrophe** necessary?_____

3. A. To whom is the **first stanza** directed?_____

B. Who is the intended "audience" for the **second stanza**?_____

C. To whom is the narrator speaking in the **third stanza**?_____

4. A. What is the **conflict**?_____

B. **Internal or external**?_____

5. Cite two **commas** and explain their **rules**:

A. Quote:_____Rule:_____

B. Quote:_____Rule:_____

6. The poem is based on the **narrator's journey home**. **Write at least a 20-line poem about your journey home**. Remember that a journey does not have to be a physical one--but possibly a spiritual, mental, emotional one, a returning to one's roots. Use imagery and figurative language.

✈We stop the car, do a full 360, and race back to get what she whined about all the way until we stopped. And what was the reason for all this? Simple. She wanted...her hat.

Her hat. Because of her hat, we were now late. Late to my interview, my only really good chance to get into the university. I'm late because of a hat. I'm late because of a fact I've faced long ago, but one she has yet to acknowlege apparently.

"Know what? I am going to throw your beloved Laker's hat out of the top of this convertible once again, run it over six times, and then set it on fire. That's if we find it!"

"Hey!"

"Then I'll drown it!"

"Hey!"

"What? What I'd like to know is what's the big deal with the hat? You don't have hair? Obviously you do 'cause I'm looking at it when I'm not looking for that stupid hat like some kind of road kill somewhere on the last 800 miles of pavement! We're like a search party for some $2.50 piece of...."

"It was $5.50. And the thing with my hair is..well, it's just a little bit frizzier than usual or something today."

"It's always like this, Honey." I still don't get why our parents named her that.

"Maybe it's the humidity."

"Let me make this a little bit clearer for you. Have you ever noticed that the women in our family have bad hair. Ugly hair. Hair that is the 'before' shots on shampoo commercials. Get the picture."

"Oh."

Were our parents fully aware of what was in store for them when she was conceived? Is she just naturally stupid? "Well, see, when we're young--and I mean like still in the crib--we have fabulous blonde hair. You've seen the pictures--you, me, smooth as silk curls. But now look at us. And it'll get worse. It'll get frizzy and white as goose down by the time we're forty."

"Oh."

"And while we're at it, maybe you've noticed the nose thing."

"What nose thing?"

"I swear I'm going to stop this car and beat you to a pulp, so you won't have to worry about the hat or the hair or the nose thing."

"No, really, what nose thing?"

"Dad's nose thing. I don't know about you, but I've already noticed some of those Grand-Canyon-like pores and those unsightly black hairs creeping out like Shirley Temple's tendrils or something."

"Oh, yeah, I see one in your left nostril now."

"Shut up! As I was saying, I have this picture. I'm finally at that expensive French restaurant with that extremely good looking mail boy at my office, the one who could be on the cover of those tacky romance novels, the one that has never had a pimple in his life-- well, as we're sipping our wine, he says, 'You have a piece of fuzz--or something--in your nose,' and he proceeds to try to brush it off (being the romantic that he is), but it's attached, so he keeps pulling and pulling...oh it's a nightmare."

"Oh."

(Ponder, Danielle, "Beautiful").

1. A. What is the **tone** of the piece?_____

   B. Quote **evidence**:_____

2. The author has used an **expanded moment (a Smiley-Face Trick)** in the next to the last paragraph. To emphasize the effect of details used to expand the moment, **in one sentence explain what is happening**:

   _____

3. A. What can you **infer** about the way the narrator feels about the person to whom she is talking?

   _____**Evidence:**_____

   B. What can you **infer** about the **identity of the person** to whom the narrator is speaking?

   _____**Evidence:**_____

4. A. What **allusion** to a famous person does the author make?_____

   B. Explain the **effect** of the allusion:_____

5. Quote an **example** of the following:

   A. **Magic three**:_____,_____,_____

B.   **Metaphor:**_____

C.   **Hyperbole:**_____

6.   This piece is based on the **real or imagined faults someone finds about herself**. Its effectiveness is based on its **exaggeration.** Write at least 50 words about things you **hate or like about yourself**. Use the author's trick of exaggerating and using humor. You might want to speak to someone--as she has done--to provide a ready audience for the "griping" or "bragging."

_____

_____

_____

_____

_____

_____

✈I'm John B. Done. I'm very unusual. Lazy people call me crazy, and some people take their index fingers and do a circle around their heads while looking at me cross-eyed. I ask what it means, but they just laugh like loco hyenas. When I first saw someone do it, I thought that it meant that I was a stupid computer freak, but it didn't seem like a decent insult for the connoisseur jokesters to be calling me. Yet it seems like a logical conclusion based on the fact that I seem to know as much as a computer engineer. Also, I act on my odd name, John B. Done. That's right, I do every chore, project, or anything that has to do with work right away. I don't lie either. All I've said so far is true. Now if you listen to the rest of my story that I'm dying to tell you about, you may not believe me, but it's all true, seriously--odd stuff like the first commercial computer, the "super intelligent life form," and even the secret room.

It all started on a cool, crisp, cloudy morning in November, when the wind was singing, the trees looked like they were taking Tae-Bo, and those poor turkeys were about to go near extinction once again. As for me, I was taking a snooze with my window open and the wind singing me asleep, leaving me with nothing to do but count turkeys leaping over a fence. Moments later, my internal alarm clock went off, providing me no choice but to arise.

As I got up, I focused on my collection of Astros beanies from several years of being a die-hard Astros fan and numerous years of selling said beanies for big bucks. I was wearing my navy Astros shirt signed by Craig Biggio, and on my dresser was a home-run ball that I had caught and later had signed by Jeff Bagwell.

I finished getting dressed, walked out of my room, and went into my upstairs hallway and down my stairs, which seemed to be my family's version of the Swiss Alps, and finally headed into my spacious kitchen. (Kinda makes my house sound big, huh?) I grabbed my usual breakfast, a soda, and hoisted my bags over my shoulder, and was off to a day of making people jealous and correcting the teachers.

I walked to school (because it's great exercise) and waved bye to my immense house. What I didn't know then was the surprise that would be waiting for me when I returned (Partin, Wade, "The Secret Room").

1. List two **adjectives** that you think would best **describe the narrator** so far and give **evidence** from the excerpt:

A. Adjective:_____Evidence:_____

B. Adjective:_____Evidence:_____

2. A. What does the author mean when he writes "those poor turkeys were about to go near extinction again"?_____

     B.   What would have been a **less humorous way of stating this**?

_____

     C.   What information does the quotation in "question A" emphasize about the **setting**?

_____

3.   Quote a **magic three** that involves **two personifications**:

_____,_____,_____

4.   How has the author played on the **narrator's name**?_____

_____

5.   List three **tricks** the author uses to **entice the reader** to read the rest of the story:

A._____

B._____

C._____

6.   **Predict** what the **secret room will be**. Write at least 100 words about what could be waiting in surprise for the narrator in the form of a secret room. Use the **narrator's style**, which includes talking to the reader and providing specific details for effect:

_____

_____

_____

_____

_____

_____

_____

✈School. The word that strikes fear in every kid's heart. The word that somehow detects that part of the brain, that infinitesimal part that knows the meaning of freedom, and totally obliterates it. The one word, besides "spinach," that sounds exactly like ten-inch nails on a wet blackboard. The word that can easily be destroyed by the two ordinary words that, when put together, are the whole reason why we even go to school. Summer vacation. And just when you think it'll never come, it arrives on a wave of Kool-Aid and happiness. So that's where I was in the last week of May, caught between a refuge and the depths of the underworld.

As I sat there in math class, silently begging the bell to ring, I looked around and around the classroom, wondering why--year after year--I stay in the same uncomfortable, boring place for nine out of twelve months. Why wasn't I somewhere else?

Five minutes left. I could tell summer vacation wasn't far away. It was like by some cryptic force that everything in the classroom was telling me to go. The chalkboard was somehow writing mysterious good-bye messages on itself. The clock, waving its arms around, was urging me to go away, to get out of this school forever, and the door joined in its you're-not-welcome-anymore ritual. Couldn't any of the teachers see this like I did?

I glanced at the clock festooned with numbers. Four minutes to go. Why couldn't I be at home on the lumpy potato-couch with the TV on, a gallon of ice cream and bucket of hot wings in my arms, and a remote by my side? I could be watching Jenny Jones or Ricki Lake right then, yelling at the top of my lungs that he ain't good enough for her, once a dog, always a dog! (Challenger, Jennifer, "The Evils of the Clock").

1. A. The author has used several **fragments for effect**. Choose three and **rewrite them into sentences:**

_____

_____

_____

    B.   What do you think the **effect of the fragments** is?_____

    C.   Why would question #1 B not be written as follows: What do you think the effect of the fragments **are**?_____

2.   What can you **infer** the "refuge" and the "depths of the underworld" are?

_____

3.   Look up "infinitesimal," "cryptic," "festooned," and "obliterated." Write **less effective synonyms** for each:

_____,_____,_____,_____

4.   Quote **examples** of the following:

A.   **Personification:**_____

B.   **Hyperbole:**_____

C.   **Metaphor:**_____

D.   **Simile:**_____

E.   **Humor:**_____

5.   The author has used **sophisticated sentence structure**. Quote examples of the following:

A.   **Participial phrase:**_____

B.   **Magic three:**_____,_____,_____

C.   **Introductory adverb clause:**_____

6.   This excerpt is an excellent example of an **expanded moment**. The narrator watches the clock, and--as readers--we know her thoughts, what is happening in

the room, etc., minute by minute. **Write at least 50 words of an expanded moment**, letting the reader in on your thoughts, actions, etc., minute by minute.

_____

_____

_____

_____

_____

_____

_____

_____

I'm a four-wheeler revved to the max
A machine that never quits
I rephrase the phrase "Army of One"
I am the only army
I am fire searching for more to burn
My trademark is flames
I am the unexpected rolling hill
With a deadly drop off at the end
I'm a rock in the middle of a prairie of grass
I am fingernails on a chalk board
No one knows the real me

(Breazeale, Casey, "Myself").

1.   List two **adjectives** that would best describe the narrator and **quote proof**:

A.   Adjective:_____Proof:_____

B.   Adjective:_____Proof:_____

2.   A.   What could one **symbol** of the poem be?_____

      B.   Of what could it be **symbolic**?_____

3. A. Which **figurative language device** is most frequently used in the poem?

_____

B. Quote three **examples**:_____,

_____,_____

4. A. What is the **theme** of the poem?_____

B. **Support:**_____

5. **Using the author's words and some of your own,** write sentences that are examples of the following (and punctuate them correctly):

A. **Appositive:**_____

_____

B. **Compound Sentence:**_____

_____

C. **Introductory Phrase or Clause:**_____

_____

6. In at least 10 lines, **write a poem that describes you.** Base your poem on primarily one type of figurative language device.

Answer Key

*Accept other answers if supported.
*Answers to writing questions will vary.

"My Journey Home to Oklahoma"

1. A. "back to my sea-green room / where I left the picture of little Jimmy boy sleeping / on a branch in Forest Lake"
   B. "the wind roaring"
   C. "I feel the darkness inside my body fading, its mouth opening"
   D. "the aroma of fresh baked pies from Miss Carol's"
2. A. The narrator will be greeting several people. "Hello" implies singular.
   B. An apostrophe is used to form the plural of words referred to as words.
3. A. The reader
   B. The narrator's family
   C. Oklahoma
4. A. Narrator's journey home
   B. Both: external ("the sweat dripping from the tips of my long, loose hair")
         internal ("I can feel the darkness inside my body")
5. A. "ground, not making a sudden move,"--interrupter
   B. "my destiny, my home"--appositive
6. Answers will vary.

"Beautiful"

1. A. Humorous
   B. * "Obviously you do 'cause I'm looking at it when I'm not looking for that stupid hat like some kind of road kill"
2. *I'll be at a restaurant with a boy, who will pull something in my nose which will turn out to be a nose hair.
3. A. We can infer that the narrator thinks the person to whom she is talking is stupid. ("Were our parents fully aware of what was in store for them when she was conceived? Is she just naturally stupid?")
   B. We can infer that the person to whom the narrator is speaking is her sister. (See above quote.)
4. A. Shirley Temple
   B. The allusion makes the nose hairs sound worse--longer and curlier, like Shirley Temple's hair.
5. A. "We stop the car, do a full 360, and race back...."
   B. "It's a nightmare."
   C. "I swear I'm going to stop this car and beat you to a pulp"
6. Answers will vary.

"The Secret Room"

1.   A.   Hard-working–"I do every chore, project, or anything that has to do with work right away."
     B.   Knowledgeable--"I seem to know as much as a computer engineer."
2.   A.   The turkeys were going to be killed.
     B.   (See above.)
     C.   It's around Thanksgiving time.
3. "the wind was singing, the trees looked like they were taking Tae-Bo, and those poor turkeys were about to go near extinction once again"
4. The narrator, John, wants to "be done" with all his work right away; therefore, the author has named him "John B. Done" as a type of pun.
5.   A.   "I'm John B. Done. I'm very unusual."
     B.   "Now if you listen to the rest of my story that I'm dying to tell you about, you may not believe me...."
     C.   "What I didn't know then was the surprise that would be waiting for me when I returned."
6. Answers will vary.

"The Evils of the Clock"

1.   A.   1.   School is the word that strikes fear in every kid's heart.
             2.   It is the word that somehow detects that part of the brain....
             3.   It is the one word, besides "spinach,"....
     B.   The effect is that the fragments emphasize the word "school," the one "word" that has the described effects on kids.
     C.   The singular verb "is" must agree with the singular noun "effect."
2. We can infer that the "refuge" is summer vacation while the "depths of the underworld" is school.
3. small, mysterious, decorated, destroys
4.   A.   "The chalkboard was somehow writing mysterious good-bye messages on itself."
     B.   "The word that strikes fear in every kid's heart."
     C.   "on the lumpy potato-couch"
     D.   "It was like by some cryptic force that everything in the classroom was telling me to go."
     E.   "yelling at the top of my lungs that he ain't good enough for her, once a dog, always a dog!"

5.   A.   "silently begging the bell to ring"
      B.   "with the TV on, a gallon of ice cream and a bucket of hot wings in my arms, and a remote by my side"
      C.   "As I sat there in math class"
6.   Answers will vary.

"Myself"

1.   A.   *Adventurous--"I'm a four-wheeler revved to the max"
      B.   *Fearless--"I am the only army"
2.   A.   Hill
      B.   Something "unexpected," exciting
3.   A.   Metaphor
      B.   "A machine that never quits," "I am fire," "I am fingernails"
4.   A.   The narrator is complex; he is many things and, therefore, unknown to most people.
      B.   He states that "no one knows the real me."
5.   A.   *I'm something that never quits, a machine.
      B.   *My trademark is flames, and I am always searching for more to burn.

      C.   *Since I am so many things, no one knows the real me.
6.   Answers will vary.

Dailies

★

Suenos
Dreams

Scuffle
Scurry
Bump
Our shoes scamper across the Sunday morning floor
Waking indolently in sleepy yellow sun
To church we go
And when we get home the shoes will come off
And our feet will pad across the dewy midmorning grass
In tree patches behind our yard
Thick with loamy scents and moths
We'll cartwheel across the brilliant canvas of
Green
Violet
Pink
Blue
Converse with the hushed babbling of a spring stream
Rustling among the silent *suenos*
Dreams
Woven by a million dozing creatures
Until from a distant land
Momma shouts dinner is getting cold
And we tumble out from our imaginations
But for now we scurry to the car
In our sleepy Sunday shoes

(Romans, Mary Katharine,   *Suenos*).

1.   **Summarize** what happens in the **beginning, middle, and end** of this poem:

A._____

   B._____

   C._____

2.   A.   Quote three **vivid verbs:**_____,_____,_____

   B.   Write **less effective** verbs for each:_____,_____,_____

3.   Quote examples of the following **figurative language devices:**

A.   **Metaphor:**_____

B.   **Personification:**_____

C.   **Hyperbole**:_____

D.   **Alliteration:**_____

4.   A.   What do you think **"indolently"** means?_____

   B.   What word could serve as a **context clue**?_____

5.   Why do you think the author uses **"suenos"**?_____

_____

6.   Write a poem **personifying** an object (e.g.,   sleepy Sunday shoes).   Use
   all of the figurative language devices listed in question 3 as well as
   vivid verbs.   You may finish the poem on the back of this page.

_____

_____

_____

_____

_____

_____

Dailies

★Watching the sky build up with gray ash, I yell up at it, "Go away, clouds! Come back another day!" Looking down at the ground, at my shoes, at the small rain puddles that are forming, I shake my head in disgust and walk up to the porch.

Before I open the door to my house, I turn back around and take one last glance at my world that will soon be engulfed with rain. Walking back inside, slamming the door behind me, I yell down the hall to an empty house, "Why does it always have to rain?" (Green, Kathleen, "Rain").

1.   Why would it be **grammatically incorrect** to say, "Watching the sky build up with gray ash, the clouds..."?

_____

2.   For what is the "gray ash" a **metaphor**?_____

3.   Quote the **prepositional phrases** that the author uses as a **magic three**:

_____,_____,_____

4.   A.   What is the **conflict?**_____

      B.   **Internal or external?**_____

5.   Quote examples of the following **comma rules:**

      A.   **Direct quotation:**_____

      B.   **Introductory phrase/clause:**_____

      C.   **Interrupter:**_____

6.   Write at least 50 words in **praise of rain.** You may choose to do a poem or vignette. Use dialogue and figurative language.

★I FLEW THROUGH THE FOREST LIKE A DEER, JUMPED OVER DEAD TREES, SWAM ACROSS CREEKS. I WAS BEING CHASED BY A BLACK BEAR . I WAS PANTING HARD, RUNNING TO THE LIGHT AT THE END OF THE FOREST, WHEN I RAN INTO A MAN WITH A DOUBLE-BARRELED SHOTGUN.

HE YELLED, "DUCK!" AND I DROPPED TO THE GROUND. HE FIRED TWO SHOTS AS FAST AS A CHEETAH CHASING A GAZELLE ON THE DESERT-DRY GRASS. THEN THE BEAR FLEW BACK LIKE A SPARROW GETTING HIT BY A MISSILE.

WHEN I GOT UP, THE MAN WAS GONE, VANISHED. HE HAD FLED, BUT THE BEAR WAS THERE, BLEEDING.

I STARTED MY JOURNEY OUT OF THE FOREST ONCE AGAIN (MARTINEZ, DANNY, "MY JOURNEY").

1. Quote two **similes**:_____ & _____

2. Quote a **magic three**:_____,

_____,_____

3. A. What does the **prepositional phrase** "ON THE DESERT-DRY GRASS" add to the piece?_____

    B. Why is there a **hyphen** between "DESERT" and "DRY"?_____

_____

    C. Use the word "DESSERT" in a sentence:_____

_____

4. If this were a short story, give **one rising action, the climax, and a falling action**:

A. **Rising action**:_____

B. **Climax**:_____

C. **Falling action**:_____

5.   A.   Of what could the BEAR be a **symbol**?_____

Why?_____

B.   Of what could the MAN be a **symbol**?_____

Why?_____

6.   Write at least a 50-word passage about a **person who appears out of nowhere to "solve" a conflict**. Use FIGURATIVE LANGUAGE AND DIALOGUE.

_____

_____

_____

_____

_____

_____

_____

_____

_____

★The swamp-like trees with their ropes of moss surrounded her. Everywhere she went beaming red eyes glared back as if they were about to devour her. The forest smelled as if it were a dumpster waiting to be dumped. But, oh, the feeling was like no feeling she had ever had before. The humid air fell on her skin, making the hair on her arms stand straight up. The sound of buzzing mosquitoes annoyed her every move. On her tongue was the taste of something she couldn't quite recognize--dew, pool water, fear? She began to realize that the forest was her living nightmare, which she had to escape (Flippo, Lacey, "The Forest").

1.	What **figurative language device** would "ropes of moss" exemplify?

_____

2.	A.	Look up **"subjunctive mood"** in the dictionary and write its definition:

_____

B.	Why would it be **grammatically correct** to write "the forest smelled as if it were a dumpster" as opposed to "as if it was a dumpster"?

_____

3.	The author has used a **participial phrase** ("making the hair on her arms stand straight up") to **combine the sentence** that begins "The humid air fell on her skin." Rewrite the sentence, using a **different method of combining**:

_____

4.	Why does the author use the **dashes** in the next to the last sentence as opposed to commas?_____

5.	Quote a **fact and an opinion** from the passage:

A.	**Fact:**_____

B.	**Opinion:**_____

6.	The author writes about the **forest in a pejorative manner**. Write at least 50 words about the forest, using **honorific terms**.

_____

_____

_____

_____

_____

_____

★I'm not stupid. I knew he wouldn't call, I knew he'd be late, and I knew he would just play games. I mean I am like a princess waiting for my prince to save me, but instead of me, he saves the others. Anyone but me. You see, he's stupid, and I'm not. There he was having love all along in his face, in his own back yard, on his own terms. But he decided to throw it away. I'll move on, but he'll find no one like me. See, he's stupid, not me (Huerta, Crystal, "Who's Stupid Now?").

1. Quote a **simile**:_____

2. A. Quote a **fragment for effect**:_____

    B. What is the **effect**?_____

3. Quote a **magic three**:_____,

    _____,_____

4. What is the **irony** involved in the passage?_____

5. A. What can you **infer** about the object of the narrator's affection?

    _____

    B. **Clues:**_____

6. Begin a vignette with the line "I'll move on, but he'll [she'll] find no one like me." If more room is needed, continue the vignette on the back of this sheet.

    _____

    _____

    _____

    _____

    _____

    _____

Answer Key

*Accept other answers if supported.
*Answers to writing questions will vary.

"Suenos"
Dreams

1.   A.   The narrator and relatives wake up lazily on a Sunday and go to church in "shoes [that] scamper across the Sunday morning floor."
      B.   When they return, they will have fun, barefooted, outside.
      C.   * Momma will announce that dinner is done, and imaginations will be cut off while shoes will be put back on.
2.   A.   * Scurry, scamper, pad `
      B.   Run, run, walk
3.   A.   "Brilliant canvas"
      B.   "Sleepy Sunday shoes"
      C.   "A million dozing creatures"
      D.   * "Scuffle / Scurry"
4.   A.   Lazily
      B.   "Sleepy"
5.   * The author might have chosen to use "*suenos*" to emphasize the dream-like state and the "distant land."
6.   Answers will vary.

"Rain"

1.   It would be a dangling modifier. The "clouds" are not "watching the sky build with gray ash"; the narrator is.
2.   the rain clouds
3.   "at the ground, at my shoes, at the small rain puddles that are forming"
4.   A.   Narrator versus rain
      B.   External
5.   A.   "I yell at it, 'Go away, clouds!'"
      B.   "Before I open the door to my house,"
      C.   "Walking back inside, slamming the door behind me,"
6.   Answers will vary.

"My Journey"

1.   "I flew through the forest like a deer" & "He fired two shots as fast as a cheetah"
2.   "I flew through the forest like a deer, jumped over dead trees, swam across creeks."

3. A. The phrase gives more details, more vivid imagery.
   B. Hyphenated modifier
   C. *I love dessert, but it's so fattening.
4. A. The narrator is being chased by a black bear.
   B. A mysterious man kills the bear.
   C. The narrator resumes his journey through the forest.
5. A. danger--It could prevent the narrator's mission.
   B. hero--He saves the narrator and allows the action to continue.
6. Answers will vary.

"The Forest"

1. Metaphor
2. A. Contrary to fact, "wish" mood
   B. The forest is not a dumpster; therefore, the subjunctive mood should be used, making the phrase "as if it were a dumpster" correct.
3. *When the humid air fell on her skin, the hair on her arms stood straight up.

4. "Dew," " pool water," and "fear" are in apposition to the "taste" that she cannot recognize. Since, the appositives already have commas, a dash to set them off is less confusing for the reader.
5. A. "The sound of buzzing mosquitoes"
   B. "Everywhere she went beaming red eyes glared back as if they were about to devour her."
6. Answers will vary.

"Who's Stupid Now?"

1. "I am like a princess waiting for my prince to save me"
2. A. "Anyone but me."
   B. The fragment emphasizes that everyone will be saved, everyone--that is-- except the narrator.
3. "I knew he wouldn't call, I knew he'd be late, and I knew he would just play games."
4. The narrator's object of her love had love--namely, the narrator--all along, but he couldn't see it.
5. A. We can infer that he is a person who wants things his own way.
   B. "on his own terms"
6. Answers will vary.

Dailies

Introduction

The house was quiet. Mom had just fixed her coffee, and Dad had just left for work. There was little activity in the still, dark morning as the sun made its first appearance, the first rays straining to illuminate the city.

I peeked at Mom from behind the couch. She sat very still, her coffee in one hand, the crossword puzzle from the paper in the other. Her morning ritual. I smiled and walked back toward my bedroom. Then I charged full force into the kitchen.

"Here I come to save the day!" I screamed as I raced toward her. Mom's eyes widened like dinner plates. When it was all over, the coffee had spilled on the half-done crossword, and what was left of the cup lay on the floor. Mom was none too thrilled with my Mighty Mouse impression.

My childhood was great. It was fine and dandy like sour candy, you could say. I was the most adventurous kid on the block. No matter where I went or what I did, I couldn't seem to live in the present. I was always somewhere else, doing something more exciting. Although I'm barely old enough to call my past "My Past," I can still remember the fun, especially in my room, pre-school, and the family pool.

First Body

My earliest adventures took place in my room. Ah, my room...that four-walled shrine to all things exciting. I could make anything much more fun than it should have been. I could look out the window and see the red, harsh climate of Mars, or, when the mood hit me, the steamy trees of the dark, dangerous jungle. In one day I could be a king, a knight, a brave pilot (my bed made a great plane or spaceship), a secret agent going after "Goldfinger" (gotta love James Bond), the British Prime Minister running a country, or the President of the United States of America, or anything else that came to mind. Sometimes

I was a train conductor racing through winding tunnels to escape the bad guy, or a race driver pushing my imaginary car as hard as I could through the final lap, or even the great Zambonie Smith, the cunning lead swami of Southern Trebekistan. I remember when I was about five, I saw a Western on TV. Now, thinking back, I wonder why being a cowboy hadn't occurred to me sooner. What fun! I made a cowboy hat out of some paper, and my tennis shoes made really good "boots." I swaggered around my room, yelling, "Stick me up!" and "Well patner" (sic) (I was just five) to my clown lamp. My old wooden desk became my horse, and as I rode through the desert, seeing the vast countryside of the wild wild West, eating at the old Ranch House, I saved many ladies and shot down the worst of villains. (Hales, Zac, "The Imagination of a Four-Year-Old Genius").

1. The author's **introduction** is longer than a "normal" introduction because the paper is a five-page essay. How does the author **grab the reader's attention**. Cite three specific passages and explain their appeal:

A._____

Appeal:_____

B._____

Appeal:_____

C._____

Appeal:_____

2. Write the **thesis** of the paper. Circle the **dominant impression** (main idea) and put check marks over the **three aspects** to be covered (in this case, the three places).

_____

3. The author's job is to **support his thesis with at least three details**. List three details from the **first body** that support the dominant impression.

A._____

B._____

C._____

4.   A.   Quote examples of the following **comma rules**:

            1.   **Coordinate adjective:**_____

            2.   **Interrupter:**_____

            3.   **Direct quotation:**_____

    B.   Look up **"sic"** in the dictionary and explain why the author uses it next to "*patner*":

_____

5.   Quote **a cause and an effect** from the introduction:

_____

6.   Write a **conclusion** for this essay that comes **full circle.** Refer to the introduction (and to your Smiley-Face Tricks sheet) to use some of the same details in a different way. You will end with a **restatement of the thesis and the three aspects**.

_____

_____

_____

_____

_____

_____

_____

_____

Running
Body contorted
In odd shapes
Pat. Slap. Whomp.
The rhythmic beat of my feet slapping the pavement
Boom! Boom!
My heart exploding in a steady pace
I grip my side
Me, in love with the pleasant pain
Like a burning fire inside my chest
I stop to allow myself to rest
The pain of the earth comes back to me
The realization of it
Smashes me like a hammer
"Run" I tell myself
Get away from it all
And run is what I do
I run, my life depending on it
I can't stop
I won't let myself stop
Stopping is futile
So I run with the
Gentle teasing, taunting breeze in my face
Knowing I can never quit
Never look back
I will run from the East Coast
To West Coast in a desperate plea
To the pain
The hate
The unceasing sins
Life
I run like the wind
With the wind
Running
To survive
I run

(Burnham, Brian, "I Run")

1.   Quote an example of an **onomatopoeia**:_____

2.   A.   How is "my heart exploding in a steady pace" an example of a **paradox**?

_____

       B.   Quote an example of another **paradox**:

_____

3.   Using a **context clue**, what do you think the meaning of "taunting" is?

_____Clue:_____

4.   Why are "East Coast" and "West Coast" **capitalized**?_____

_____

5.   List two **characteristics** that you can **infer** about the narrator and give proof:

       A._____

       Proof:_____

       B._____

       Proof:_____

6.   The narrator runs to "survive." Write at least a 10-line poem **explaining what you do to survive**. Use figurative language.

THE TURTLE
HAS JUST HATCHED
OUT OF ITS
SHELL LIKE GODZILLA
EMERGING FROM THE
VAST OCEAN
CRAWLING RHYTHMICALLY
IN TUNE TO SOME RAP SONG
ONLY HE CAN HEAR
THINKING WHY
DO I HAVE TO
BE
A SLOW
GREEN FREAK
WHY CAN'T
I BE LIKE A SEAGULL FLYING IN THE SKY
PEACEFULLY
OR
LIKE THE BLUE ANGELS SOARING
SERENELY OVER THE OCEAN
OR
A CHEETAH
THE FASTEST ANIMAL
IN THE WORLD
RUNNING LIKE A SPEEDING BULLET
BUT I AM
SLOW
WAITING COMPLACENTLY
TO DESCEND TO THE
VAST BLUE OCEAN
CONTINUING FOREVER LIKE
THE BRIGHT GHOSTLY
MOON
DROPPING INTO THE
SEA
(STUDENT WRITER,
  "THE GREEN FREAK")

Turtle
X-ing

1. A. What is the **conflict** in the poem?_____

    B. **Internal or external**?_____

2. A. What could be considered a **symbol** in the poem BESiDES THE TURTLE?_____

    B. Of what could it be **symbolic**?_____

3. Quote a **hyperbole**:_____

4. From what **point of view** is this poem written (FiRST PERSON, THiRD, OMNiSCiENT)?_____

    Proof:_____

5. List two **adverbs** the author uses to describe HOW THE TURTLE WOULD LiKE HiS ACTiONS TO BE :

    _____&_____

6. **Line divisions, capitalization, and punctuation in poems** are part of the choices an author makes. Rewrite at least ten lines of the poem, experimenting with different line divisions, etc.

Ever since I can remember, my stupid, wanna-be-me little sister has gotten her way. Being nineteen months apart from me, she has always had my mother wrapped around all ten of her chubby little fingers. But why, I ask myself, considering this kid's so stupid. Oh, and if I were to lay a hand on her, like usual her blood-curdling scream would send Mother running to her side, staring at me with her who-do-you-think-you-are-torturing-this-poor-defenseless-little-girl look.

Every day since the moment she came home from the hospital, she's got first pick on where to go, what to do, and all sorts of things that I don't mind sharing, but this time it's gotten out of hand. This time she gets to pick the family vacation. What does she do with all that power? She picks the middle of nowhere-- Grandma's house. What a loser!

So I have a whole one day of freedom until we leave. Actually I can't really call it freedom because the little twerp has been bothering me with the shadow game: you know, the I'll-pop-out-from-behind-the-door-and-scare-the-wonkers-out-of-you routine and the I-get-to-hit-you-but-you-can't-touch-me-or-I'll-scream trick. I'm stunned that we're related.

So to get away without her following my every move, I try shutting her in our room and tying a rope on my door and my mom's door so that the brat can't open it with the other door shut. I creep out of the house only, unfortunately, to hear her and my mom screaming at me to get back inside.

Oh well, at least I got a breath of fresh summer air before my sister got there to inhale all my fun (Cowan, Kristen, "My Annoying Sister").

1. Why would it be **grammatically incorrect** to write the following: "Being nineteen months apart from me, my mother..."? (Opposed to the following: "Being nineteen months apart from me, she...")?

_____

_____

2.   What type of **figurative language** would the following be?

    A.   "inhale all my fun":_____

    B.   "following my every move":_____

3.   **Summarize** what happens in the passage:

A.   Beginning:_____

B.   Middle:_____

C.   End:_____

4.   A.   Why would there be a **hyphen** between "blood" and "curdling"?

_____

    B.   Why is there a **colon** after "game"?_____

5.   To emphasize the effectiveness of the **hyphenated modifiers** describing the game, replace them with one-word, less effective ones:

A._____   B._____

6.   Write at least 50 words **about something someone does that annoys you.** Use hyphenated modifiers and figurative language.

_____

_____

_____

_____

_____

_____

_____

"I am here to help you with your problems."
"I don't have any problems."
"Ben, you failed shop."
"I didn't need a bird house."
"You failed physical education."
"I didn't feel like running."
"You failed band."
"I don't like my instrument. I want to play sax."
"You failed algebra."
"I didn't feel like adding that day."
"You failed science."
"I didn't want to hurt the frog."
"You failed English."
"I don't think the teacher likes me."
"Ben, I told you that I am here to help you with your problems."
"I don't have any problems."
(Student Writer, "Problems")

1.   What is the rule for **capitalizing** school subjects?_____

_____

2.   Why is each line a new **paragraph**?_____

3.   The author has chosen not to use **"speaker tags"** (e.g., he said, as he ran his hand through his hair). **For the first four lines, add speaker tags** that are more than "he said," "he replied," etc.

A._____B._____

C._____D._____

4.   When you add the speaker tags, what changes will you have to make regarding **punctuation**?

_____

5.   A.   What can you **infer** about the **setting** of this vignette?

_____

       B.   **Clues:**_____

6.   This **dialogue** is obviously based on **one person's excuses**. Write a dialogue of at least 50 words with at least **four speaker tags** where one person answers another with excuses. Remember the rules for **paragraphing**.

_____

_____

_____

_____

_____

_____

_____

_____

Answer Key

*Accept other answers if supported.
*Answers to writing questions will vary.

"The Imagination of a Four-Year-Old Genius"

1.   A.   "The house was quiet. Mom had just fixed her coffee...."--The introduction has a narrative scenario beginning. Stories appeal to readers--even "snippets" of stories.
     B.   "There was little activity in the still, dark morning as the sun made its first appearance, the first rays straining to illuminate the city...."--The setting is identified, giving the reader a vivid image of a typical day of "the most adventurous kid on the block."
     C.   "Here I come to save the day!"--We recognize the "Mighty Mouse" allusion, and the bit of dialogue adds punch to the piece, making it more realistic.
2.   "Although I'm barely old enough to call my past `My Past,' I can still remember the fun **[dominant impression]**, especially in my room, pre-school, and the family pool **[three places]**."
3.   A.   "I could look out the window and see the red, harsh climate of Mars"
     B.   "or, when the mood hit me, the steamy trees of the dark, dangerous jungle"
     C.   "In one day I could be a king, a knight, a brave pilot...a secret agent...the British Prime Minister...or the President of the United States of America, or anything else that came to mind."
4.   A.   1.   "red, harsh climate"
           2.   "She sat very still, her coffee in one hand,"
           3.   "I swaggered around my room, yelling, 'Stick me up!'"
     B.   *Sic* is used for an intentional mistake, such as the author's kid-version spelling of "partner."
5.   "I screamed as I raced toward her" (cause); "the coffee had spilled on the half-done crossword" (effect)
6.   Answers will vary.

"I Run"
1.   "Boom!"
2.   A.   An "explosion" does not imply an action that could happen "at a steady pace."
     B.   "Me, in love with the pleasant pain"
3.   To mock, provoke, tease; "gentle teasing"
4.   Proper nouns--specific places
5.   A.   Aware -- "The pain of the earth comes back to me"
     B.   Tenacious--"I can't stop / I won't let myself stop"
6.   Answers will vary.

"The Green Freak"

1. A. Turtle versus himself
   B. Internal
2. A. Seagull
   B. Peace; freedom
3. "Continuing forever"
4. Omniscient—"Thinking why / do I have to / be / a slow / green freak" (knows turtle's thoughts)
5. "Peacefully" & "Serenely"
6. Answers will vary.

"My Annoying Sister"

1. It would be a dangling modifier, as the "mother" is not "nineteen months apart" from the narrator; the narrator's sister is.
2. A. Metaphor
   B. Hyperbole
3. A. The narrator is lamenting the fact that her younger sister gets preferential treatment from their mother.
   B. Now the sister has done the ultimate; she has chosen the family vacation site "in the middle of nowhere--Grandma's house."
   C. The narrator has tried to pull a prank on her sister to get some privacy. While she does manage to "creep out of the house," she is caught up short by her mother "screaming...[at her] to get back inside." The narrator is resigned to her symbolic "breath of fresh summer air" before her sister once again "inhales" all her good times.
4. A. Hyphenated adjective
   B. The colon introduces what the game is; it gives further explanation.
5. A. Scary
   B. Unfair
6. Answers will vary.

"Problems"

1. Capitalize languages and courses with numbers after them.
2. Dialogue requires a new paragraph for each new speaker.
3. Answers will vary.
4. Speaker tags are set off from dialogue with commas.
5. A. School or a place of study (e.g., home)
   B. "'I am here to help you with your problems.'"
6. Answers will vary.

Dailies

Let's get one thing straight. I didn't actually tell her--or at least by my own will. She seemed to just suck it out of my head. She had the irresistible if-you-don't-tell-me-I'll-cry-sick-little-puppy-face thing going on, which made me spit it out, and I mean all out.

It was just a boring old I-wish-I-had-a-pool-or-video-arcade-so-I-would-have-something-to-do day when all of a sudden the telephone rings. It was as if my prayers had been answered, although you will find out it was the opposite as if someone down below had a grudge against me.

When I said, "Hello," I heard the most beautiful sound. It was as peaceful as waves splashing on a beach, as sweet as a bluebird's song in spring, and so smooth my knees could have given at any second. It was Priscilla Patterson, the most gorgeous girl in junior high.

My heart started fluttering like butterflies' wings until all of a sudden--faster than it had risen--my heart fell, making a thud probably somewhere near my ankles, when she asked, "Do you think Billy Bob Joe likes me? I thought you might know because you're his best friend."

Yeah, I knew. I knew Billy Bob hated Priscilla's beautiful guts--although I can't imagine why. But if I told her, she would tell everyone--and I mean everyone--that he was a rude, vicious, slimy, no-good...well, you get the idea. Teenage girls work this way. And Billy Bob would kill me, being a good 100 pounds heavier than me and all. So I said, "No, I don't really know."

When I said this, I could envision her little pout and her sky-blue eyes making that sad little puppy face, and I crumbled like a cookie in an earthquake saying, "Actually, he...he...hates you. He thinks you're Miss Prissy Princess, and he really hates Prissy Princesses. I don't know why, but he does."

After that there was a long pause and a click, and I knew that click was the sound of the last of my heart because I knew only too well that my life would soon be over since I knew Billy Bob so well and all.

I don't know why I told her. Maybe it was her voice as sweet as honey or the picture of that face, that I'm-going-to-be-a-supermodel-someday-but-you're-making-me-sad face which I pictured. Whatever it was, I spilled the whole bucket of beans. She just seemed to suck it out of my head along with every ounce of dignity I had left (Duvall, Greg, "I Don't Know Why I Told Her").

1. How does the author come **full circle** with his vignette?_____

_____

2. A. Quote the **hyphenated modifier** in the second paragraph:

_____

B. **Write a hyphenated modifier** (at least 10 words) that could replace the

author's:_____

C. Why is there **no hyphen** between "do" and "day"?_____

3. Explain three **conflicts** in this piece:_____,

_____,_____

4. Quote a **magic three**:_____,

_____,_____

5. Quote examples of the following **comma rules**:

A. **Compound sentence:**_____

B. **Direct quotation:**_____

C. **Appositive:**_____

6. **Write the beginning of a vignette** (at least 75 words) **about something you regret doing**. Begin with the line "Let's get this straight. I didn't actually...." Include **humor, a hyphenated modifier, and a magic three**.

_____

_____

_____

_____

_____

Anna quietly slipped through the door like a shapeless gust of wind on a dark, gloomy April day. Her clothes were drenched with mud, and her hair was plastered against her mud-covered cheeks. It was Tuesday night, and her mom, a single parent, worked the night shift. Anna raced up the stairs into her room and propped herself up against her closet door as she slipped off her shoes. She was cold, and goose bumps sprang up all over her body (Francis, Marina, "When the Lights Go Out").

1. What is the **setting** (time and place) of the piece?_____

2. How does the story beginning **grab your attention**?_____

_____

3. Quote examples of the following **comma rules**:

A. **Appositive:**_____

B. **Coordinate adjective:**_____

C. **Compound sentence:**_____

D. Why would some students **incorrectly place a comma** after "Anna raced up the

stairs into her room"?_____

4.   Quote an example of **figurative language** and tell the **type**:

A._____B._____

5.   A.   In what **tense** is the story written?_____

      B.   Give **five examples** to prove this:_____,_____,

_____,_____,_____

6.   Write the **beginning of a story** (at least 50 words) **using the setting** as a major
      focus.   Begin with a sentence containing figurative language.

_____

_____

_____

_____

       It began just before dawn. Sunlight filtered through the rows
of pines and began to warm the air. A steady breeze moved through
the trees. Moisture had condensed on the leaves of the plants during
the night. It had collected in frozen droplets and now slowly dripped
onto the soil near a quail feeding in the morning shade of the tree
line.

       As the sun appeared higher in the sky, our side of the world
began to wake up. There I was perched precariously on a boulder,
watching wildlife as it was meant to be. I looked down to see the
cold water trickle into mysterious little pools. It was a record-
breaking low in my book. It was nineteen degrees this morning, and
only God knows how cold it got last night. Since it
was this cold, I was hoping to catch one glimpse of
what I longed to see, a deer. If I played my cards
right, I would get to be up close and personal (Poston,
Greg, "Dawn").

Dailies

1.   A.   What is the setting of the piece (time and place)?

_____&_____

       B.   How does the author use the setting as an **attention-getter**?

_____

2.   A.   Cite two examples of particularly **vivid verbs**:_____&_____

       B.   List **two common, less effective verbs** that the author could have used:

_____&_____

3.   A.   Quote your favorite example of **imagery**:_____

_____

       B.   What has the author done to make this line so **effective**?

_____

4.   Why would there not be a **comma** between "droplets" and "and" on the fourth line?

_____

5.   Quote an example of **personification**:_____

6.   Using at least 50 words, describe **your favorite place outdoors**. Use **vivid verbs** and **specific details for effect** to help the reader visualize your scene.

_____

_____

_____

_____

_____

I was walking down the hall, thinking I was hot. I had on this look-at-me-I'm-fine dress with an in-case-you-haven't-noticed-I've-got-this-cute-as-a-button-split-down-the-back--about four inches long, in case you're wondering.

Talk about wondering. I was doing some wondering myself. Like wondering why people were staring at me, wondering why they were laughing and snickering, why everyone's fingers were pointing to my cute little split down the back.

Then I felt it. It was a cool breeze, the kind you feel on a warm summer night. That's when I knew my Jockey pink-and-white flowered underwear was showing. The cute little split had taken it upon itself to grow (Curette, Margo, "The Worst Day of My Life").

1. The author's first sentence could have originated from two sentences: "I was walking down the hall. I thought I was hot." She chose to combine the sentences, however, using a **participial phrase** (an "-ing" phrase used as an adjective). **Combine the two sentences in two different ways:**

A._____

B._____

2. **Rewrite the second sentence,** describing the dress in a different way but still using **two sets of hyphenated modifiers:**

_____

_____

3. Quote an example of a **personification:**_____

4. Quote a **fact** and an **opinion** stated in the excerpt:

A. **Fact:**_____

B. **Opinion:**_____

5. Quote **a cause and an effect:**_____

_____

6.   Write at least 50 words of the **beginning of the worst day of your life**. Use humor, sentence combining, and at least one personification:

_____

_____

_____

_____

_____

The June heat
the smell of camp in Kerrville
the lake houses
Nobody wanted to leave
especially Cassidy and Jake
They had just met and had fallen in love
They would never forget their
secret meeting place
behind the honeysuckles
and blackberries
and the stream
and the trees
The cool, crisp wind
would always remind them
of the summer they had fallen in love
All they did that summer
was get to know each other
California
and
Maine
were too far apart for them
and Jake wasn't coming back next summer
How could a summer exist
without him

(Larson, Ashlee, "Unconditional Love")

1.   A.   Why do you think the author chose to use "and" to separate her **series** of places instead of **commas**?

_____

B.   Why would the author give **"California"** and **"Maine" separate lines**?

_____

2.   **Summarize** this narrative poem:

A.   Beginning:_____

B.   Middle:_____

C.   End:_____

3.   A.   What is the **conflict** in the poem?_____

B.   **Internal or external**?_____

4.   A.   What is the **comma rule** for the comma that separates **"cool"** and **"crisp"**?

_____

B.   Give the **principal parts of the verb "fall"**:_____,_____,_____

5.   A.   Of what **figurative language device** would the last two lines be an example?

_____

B.   **Why**?_____

6.   In at least ten lines begin a **narrative poem** using imagery and specific details for effect. Base it on a **conflict** that you have known.

Answer Key

*Accept other answers if supported.
*Answers to writing questions will vary.

"I Don't Know Why I Told Her"

1. In the beginning, the author stated that "she seemed to just suck it out of my head," and in the end he repeats the phrase, thus coming full-circle.
2. A. "I-wish-I-had-a-pool-or-a-video-arcade-so-I-would-have-something-to-do day"
   B. Answers will vary.
   C. A hyphen is not used between the last adjective of the series and the word it modifies.
3. A. Narrator versus concept of Priscilla
   B. Narrator versus reality of Priscilla
   C. Narrator versus himself for telling
4. "It was as peaceful as waves splashing on a beach, as sweet as a bluebird's song in spring, and so smooth my knees could have given at any second."
5. A. "He thinks you're Miss Prissy Princess, and he really hates Prissy Princesses."
   B. "When I said, 'Hello,'"
   C. "It was Priscilla Patterson, the most gorgeous girl in junior high."
6. Answers will vary.

"When the Lights Go Out"

1. "dark, gloomy April day," "Tuesday night," "Anna's house"
2. The simile grabs the reader's attention as it is unusual--"like a shapeless gust of wind." It adds to the suspense.
3. A. "her mom, a single parent,"
   B. "dark, gloomy April day"
   C. "Her clothes were drenched with mud, and her hair was plastered...."
   D. The sentence is not compound; it simply has a compound verb.
4. A. "like a shapeless gust of wind"
   B. Simile
5. A. Past tense
   B. "slipped," "were drenched," "was plastered," "was," "raced"
6. Answers will vary.

"Dawn"

1. A. "Just before dawn" & forest
   B. We are told that "it" began "just before dawn"; therefore, we wonder what the "it" is. Besides the mystery of the beginning sentence, the author creates more interest in having his character "perched precariously on a boulder."
2. A. "filtered" & "condensed"
   B. Shone & collected
3. A. "It had collected in frozen droplets and now slowly dripped onto the soil near a quail feeding in the morning shade of the tree line."
   B. The author almost "freezes" the moment so that we, as readers, can picture the scene.
4. The sentence is not a compound sentence but only contains a compound verb, which does not require a comma.
5. "our side of the world began to wake up"
6. Answers will vary.

"The Worst Day of My Life"

1. A. *As I was walking down the hall, I was thinking....
   B. *Walking down the hall, I was thinking....

2. Answers will vary.
3. "The cute little split had taken it upon itself to grow."
4. A. "I was walking down the hall"
   B. "I had on this look-at-me-I'm-fine dress"
5. "That's when I knew my Jockey...underwear was showing" **(cause);** "people were staring at me" **(effect).**
6. Answers will vary.

"Unconditional Love"
1. A. To create a more poetic effect
   B. To emphasize how much they were separated
2. A. Jake and Cassidy had fallen in love in a camp in Kerrville.
   B. They had gotten to know each other that summer.
   C. They lived too far apart so they would probably not see each other again.
3. A. Lovers versus Place
   B. External
4. A. Coordinate adjective
   B. Fall, fell, fallen
5. A. Hyperbole
   B. Exaggeration
6. Answers will vary.